HOW TO
START YOUR OWN
FASHION
LABEL

ALISON LOWE MBE

Orders: For bulk orders, please contact Alison@felicities.co.uk

ISBN: 978-1-9996684-0-2

First published: 2019

Disclaimer
Although the author and publisher have made every effort to ensure that the information in this book was correct at the time of going to press, the author and publisher do not assume and hereby disclaim any liability to any party for any loss, damage, or disruption caused by errors or omissions, whether such errors or omissions result from negligence, accident, or any other cause.

About the Author

Alison Lowe MBE

Alison has built a reputation over the past 16 years as one of the leading supporters of emerging fashion. She is passionate about supporting creative talent and preparing them for the challenges of balancing creativity and commerciality. Renowned for her practical, realistic approach to running a creative business, Alison acts as a consultant to brands across the globe from start-ups to established fashion businesses, supporting fashion brands, retailers, manufacturers and training providers.

Alison started her career in show business, having dropped out of school at 16. She studied drama and music before working as both an actress on numerous primetime TV programmes and as a singer, releasing a record in the charts in the late 80s. However, after working for a few years in the industry with moderate success due to hard work and determination, she realised her passion was entrepreneurial spirit and found a more profitable vocation in the business world.

As a serial entrepreneur, Alison has a natural talent for discovering a gap in the market and creating a business solution to meet the need. This led her to start several businesses including "Chameleon" a creative recruitment agency and "Road Runners" an express courier business. Although she found success in her business endeavors, changes in personal circumstances meant an enforced career break in the early 90s to bring up her two daughters as a single parent.

Looking for ways to fill her time, Alison sought opportunities to engage back in the world outside the home, and started taking some adult education courses. She discovered a passion for learning that she had not had at school. Over a 6-year period whilst her daughters were small, she studied numerous courses with the Open University which resulted in a host of qualifications including BSc(Hons) in Business Management, a Professional Certificate in Management, a Diploma in Applied Social Sciences and several teacher training qualifications. By the time her daughters were in nursery school, Alison was back in the workforce working as a training and development manager in the voluntary sector, before moving over to the public sector to work as a Business Support Consultant with Business Link.

Whilst working at Business Link, Alison realised she loved supporting both start-up and in particular creative businesses. She decided to specialise in this area and began acting as a consultant to creative and design businesses from fine artists to car designers, architects to property developers.

Alison's move into fashion came from a freelance consultancy role with a fashion week platform, which resulted in her discovering that emerging fashion labels lacked support and advice in developing long term, successful businesses. In 2003 she established Felicities, a specialist PR and business incubator for startup and emerging fashion and creative brands. Over the past 16 years, the agency has worked with over 2000 labels, supporting them in developing their brands and providing them with advice and opportunities to build their labels and introduce their businesses into new markets.

The agency had increasing interest from brands around the world who wanted support to build their businesses, however Felicities had limited capacity for the number of brands it could work with. The agencies in-depth approach meant that it needed to restrict the number of brands it could work with each year. Looking at ways to resolve this, Alison identified a new opportunity to offer support options to more brands and launched an on-line platform Start Your Own Fashion Label. This platform offers up-to-date industry information on subjects that brands need, such as how to contact buyers, talk to press, work with manufacturers and how to create a line sheet to name a few. This information is presented in easy to understand, downloadable guides and templates that provide easy ways for startup brands to implement the learning straightaway. Start Your Own Fashion Label also offers mentoring and membership options to both UK and international designers.

Alongside running her two businesses and her consultancy roles with a range of brands in the UK and Internationally, Alison teaches on several business courses at London College of Fashion, where she is also the Start Up Entrepreneur in Residence, to support graduates in preparing to start their own labels. She also delivers an MSc level programme in business creation for the British School of Fashion, and is an industry expert and mentor for international on-line training provider Mastered. Alison is regularly invited to be a guest speaker at international conferences, fashion weeks, events and universities and is a founding member of the Centre for Entrepreneurs and on the judging panel of the Great British Entrepreneurs competition.

Alison has won numerous awards and honours, the highlight of which was being awarded an MBE for Services to the Fashion Industry in HRH The Queen's Birthday Honours 2017. Alison was also nominated and awarded as one of the Maserati100 in 2016. This award was created by the luxury car manufacturer to recognize one hundred game-changing entrepreneurs who are disrupting the business world. The Maserati 100 is dedicated to celebrating the positive impact entrepreneurs have on the economy and society as a whole and Alison was named alongside dynamic entrepreneurs such as Richard Branson, Julie Deane from the Cambridge Satchel company, Sir Charles Dunstone founder of Carphone Warehouse and Pret a Manger founders Sinclair Beecham and Julian Metcalfe.

For more information about Alison and her businesses please see the links below

www.alisonjlowe.com

Instagram - @alijaynelowe

LinkedIn and Facebook - Alison Lowe

www.startyourownfashionlabel.com

Instagram - @startafashionco

Facebook Page and Group – Start Your Own Fashion Label

www.felicities.co.uk

Instagram - @felicitiespr

Facebook Page - Felicities

PREFACE

The common perception of the fashion industry is that it is an incredibly exciting and glamourous place to work. This is true, to some extent. However, for many people the reality is very different.

I am very lucky that my life working in fashion has been great. II have had, and continue to have, the most amazing opportunities every month to meet exciting new designers, view fabulous collections, visit showrooms and attend stunning fashion week events and catwalk shows around the world.

So, you may wonder, why then am I bothering to write this book? Believe me when I say, I have asked myself that same question many times over the year it has taken me to write it, particularly when facing a blank page!

I am writing the book because although I have been lucky in finding a fantastic career working in fashion, it has been very challenging and at times deeply disappointing. I have seen amazing talents fail to achieve their dreams or been crushed by what is at times a heartless industry. I love working in fashion because I get to meet so many incredible people, but I also hate it for the way young designers, or people new to the industry, are often treated.

I came into the fashion industry nearly 20 years ago, when I was invited to work with a fashion agency to market their fashion week platform. I came straight into the very glamourous side of the industry. I couldn't believe my luck, having followed the shows on Vogue since I was a teenager, to be invited to attend fashion week so that I could see how the platform worked.

I had an amazing time at my first fashion week with an all-access wristband pass that meant sitting FROW (Front Row) at the shows, and full access to go back stage to meet the designers and see the collections. At the end of the day, my special wristband gained me access to the best parties in town.

It was every fashionista's dream and what a fantastic time I had! However, after a few days, my inner entrepreneur started to question what I was seeing and what was really happening. Or maybe it was common sense kicking in! The reality was that I was seeing a lot of people having a really great time, lots of partying and lots of narcissistic behaviour, that was all at the expense of the designer! And that was years before the introduction of the 'influencer' and the Instagram selfie.

After the fashion week, I decided to start looking more deeply into the fashion industry and how it worked. Very quickly I noticed that the younger design brands were often totally unprepared for running a business. They were naïve in their view of the industry and therefore often susceptible to being taken advantage of by unscrupulous agencies, celebrities, fashion week organisers and media.

I was intrigued about why the designers were so unprepared and why the industry seemed so careless in its support of new talent. I became really passionate about finding ways to support start-up brands. This led me to launch my agency Felicities in 2003, working with new designers to not only promote their brands, but make sure they were prepared for the market with the right product, at the right price in the right place.

It has been amazing to work with over 2,000 start up brands in the past 16 years from all over the world. I have also been invited to teach and mentor hundreds of fashion students, and the issues remain the same where-ever I go. Fashion schools around the world are excellent at teaching designers to design, but the information and skills needed to start up your own label and run a business are a different matter. I am often shocked how many designers did not seek business advice and support when they start, or worse they are given really bad or out-of-date advice that results in their business failing in the first few years.

The fashion industry is renowned for being totally focused on finding new talent each season, but if in the following year that business fails, then no-one cares because there will be another exciting new label coming next season. Designers have been pushed to grow their businesses too quickly, investing every penny they have into putting on catwalk shows and taking part in trade shows, without any consideration of whether this is the best use of their money or right for their brand.

Designers really struggle to find people to support them in building and growing their businesses. They feel isolated, stressed, financially stretched, unsure of what to do and where to go for help, and fearful of having their ideas and designs stolen.

I have dedicated much of my time and energy over the last 16 years to find ways to make the life of a start-up fashion brand easier.

The fashion industry is exciting, dynamic, diverse, fast paced and glamourous. At the same time the market is saturated, it is more challenging than ever, and the processes and consumer are constantly changing. There are still very few up-to-date resources for start-up fashion businesses and limited places for them to go for advice and guidance. Although many books have been written on the subject of starting and running a fashion label, due to the constantly changing industry, many are now out-of-date and no longer relevant.

I want this book to be a really practical guide, giving you some very realistic steps in starting up and running your own fashion label, helping you to make it a success now and be a sustainable business model for the future.

I will look at what is happening in the fashion industry today and give you totally practical and realistic steps to help you set up, launch and grow your business. From the advice given in this book, you can start to implement steps, or make changes straight away, that will help you start to grow your business in an effective and economical way.

You can read the book from cover to cover, or dip into it to look at a particular element that you are working on at that time, but I highly recommend that you do go through all of the book to make sure you don't leave any crucial element to chance. Setting up your own fashion label is really exciting, but it is important to not rush in and make mistakes in the early stages that could impact your business later.

Remember knowledge is power and success comes from knowing as much as possible about all aspects of running your own label.

I am thrilled to help you on your journey to setting up and growing your own successful fashion label and wish you lots of luck in turning your dream into a reality.

I would love to hear how you get on, so drop me an email at any point on Alison@startyourownfashionlabel.com

Good luck

Ali

Contents

Getting Started

Starting a brand takes talent, connections and more money than you can imagine!

Before you start throwing cash around, make sure you have considered these ten key points!

In your enthusiasm to launch your own label it is very easy to rush ahead, consequently missing some very important areas that will affect your business later on. Many start-up fashion labels fail due to missing out some key steps needed before making your first pieces. Problems also come from not having the vision of all the areas you need to consider for your business. One comment I regularly hear from all start up fashion brands is "we didn't know how much hard work and money it would take to start our label. If only we had known more about the business side of the fashion industry or understood how much the industry has changed, then we could have saved a fortune."

Many designers fail in their first year of trading because they do not really understand how the fashion industry works and are not prepared for the numerous challenges they will face. The majority of designers, by the time they reach out for help, are too far along the process and have already suffered a lot of failures and lost a lot of money,

I want to make sure you don't have this experience too, so this book covers all the areas that designers tell me they need more knowledge, skills and help with.

I will go through all of these points in more detail in the book, but I know that not everyone reads a book from start to finish. This book has been written in a way that makes it possible to dip in and out of the different chapters to pick up information as and when you need it. However, I highly recommend you do take a few minutes to just review these key points, so that you don't miss an area that could affect the future success of your business.

1. **Do your Research**

    Learning more, leads to earning more! It is essential that before you start your label you do as much research as possible. Your success will depend on you really understanding the market, knowing who your competitors and customers are, identifying changing consumer behaviours, finding suppliers who will work with you, and being aware of product prices.

You will not find all the information you need from research in a library, field research is also really important. You need to visit stores, or check them out online to see what brands they carry and the price points of the product. Research and follow your competitors to see what they are producing, who their customers are, what press and marketing they do and follow their social media to understand their brand story. Also talk to potential customers, even if these are initially just friends and family, to ask them why they buy certain products, why they choose to follow some brands on social media and what they want when they are buying fashion. This will really help you understand how customers buy product and/or buy into brand names and lifestyles.

2. Find Your Signature

Fashion schools often tell designers that they need to always be designing something new and different. Contrary to this, is the need for a brand to have a distinctive, repeatable signature if it is going to survive. The signature is the design element that comes through in subtle ways each season that makes your collection stand out and instantly recognisable. Examples include the Burberry check, the four stitches of Maison Margiela and the Louboutin red sole.

If you don't have a signature, then you are just creating product and your chance of success is really limited, as hundreds of brands already create product. You have to stand out and be different. If you don't have a signature yet, then you are not ready to launch your label.

3. Create a Brand Story

If you don't create a brand story then you are just selling product, another commodity in an already full market place. Your brand story makes your label stand out and tells the value, depth, meaning and DNA of the brand. These are all the reasons the customer should buy from you rather than another brand. What usually separates the successful brands from the failures is the story telling. You also need to consider what methods you will use to tell your story. The story creates an emotional connection with the customer, so you need to decide the best methods to create that connection, including using video, social media, imagery, press coverage and fashion film.

4. Understand the Worldwide Customer

We now live in a global market place and we can access fashion from anywhere around the world to be delivered to our own front door. No matter where a brand is based, they all want to stocked in international high fashion stores around the world. Therefore, a designer has to think outside of their current local customer to understand the needs of customers in different countries and cultures.

Customers are not the same all around the world. They all have their own needs, desires and knowledge of what they want from fashion. In different countries customers have access to different, more or less brands, so your competitor base is also different in other countries. To create product for a global market, you need to think about different body sizes and shapes, cultural differences and alternative attitudes and opinions. You also need to review your brand storytelling to ensure it is impactful in different countries.

5. Focus on Sales

Starting and running a fashion business will take more money than you can possibly imagine, therefore you need to start selling as soon as possible. But what is your business model? Wholesale, direct retail or e-commerce?

Many young designers get carried away when they launch their own labels, focussing on having catwalk shows, getting press and designing the new collection. They don't focus enough on sales. Without sales, you are running an expensive hobby. You are only a business once you start selling!

How will you sell your collection? In the past, all new brands focused on just the wholesale market, where they only produced stock to meet orders gathered from stores. But as the industry has changed and fewer wholesale buyers are taking on new brands, more start-up brands are focussing their business model on selling direct to the customer, through e-commerce and direct through social selling, pop up shops and trunk shows. This is having a drastic effect on how the brand operates and on their cash flow, as they have to generate stock for their own sales channels.

Cash flow is the lifeblood of the business and a lack of cash flow is the most likely reason a brand fails. Cash flow needs to planned and managed carefully to ensure you don't run out of money at a key time. You also need to be totally realistic about cash flow and always overestimate the expenses and underestimate the revenue.

6. Images are everything

Images are everything! It is really essential that your brand has high quality, appropriate images in order to succeed. You need great images to get anyone to even look at your brand. Images of the collection are the first thing a buyer or journalist would ask for and if they aren't very good, then that is the end of the conversation. If you are selling through your own website you need images that appeal to your customer if you want to make sales! With Instagram now influencing sales on a global level, the content and images you include on your page are the most important way to tell your brand story to the world.

As images are such a crucial part of your business, make sure you work with professionals who understand what you need and who your customer is. Think carefully about what type of images you need for your business and the story you want to tell through your brand pictures.

7. Build your tribe

No-one can run a business on their own and every young business needs a host of people to help them. These days we talk about building your tribe – your group of people who will support your business, be your network, connect you with others, work with you, supply services to you and of course buy from you!

Your tribe will be a support network, your ambassadors or a group of people who share ideas. These don't have to be identical ideas, but everyone in your tribe will be willing to work towards an end goal together and each bring their own skills and knowledge to the table.

Your tribe will help connect you to new people so that you find partnerships, networks and potentially collaborations that will be beneficial to everyone involved. The type of people in your tribe could include business mentors, creatives, photographers, stores etc. etc.

8. Be Entrepreneurial

In the current market, it isn't enough to be a really talented designer anymore. You have to be an entrepreneur too. Designers have to understand a spreadsheet, and profit and loss, as much as they need to understand pattern cutting and draping. It is a very difficult industry to survive in. Designers making a success in the fashion industry are the ones that are adopting entrepreneurial spirit. They are thinking about new opportunities, finding new ways to showcase, building partnerships with corporate brands, focussing on sales rather than fame, and most of all running their labels as a business!

9. Be Patient

As the saying goes "Fools rush in!" One important part of launching your own label is learning patience. Many young designers get carried away by the glamour of the industry and rush into setting up their own label. They quickly discover that it takes more money, knowledge, information and resources than they thought and start to flounder!

If you have followed all the steps above, then you are more likely to be ready to start your own label, but only if you have done your research and really understand who your customer is.

Once you have set up your label, don't rush into catwalk shows, opening your own store or moving into a fancy showroom or studio.

You will need to carefully manage your cash flow as your label grows, so need to spend carefully in the first few seasons.

10. Don't Give Up

Starting your own fashion label is not going to be easy, as I said before it takes time, patience, knowledge, skill and lots and lots of money. But no matter how much it takes, if you are passionate about what you do, then it is worth it. It is a risk, but if you follow your gut instinct, believe passionately about what you create and are prepared to work really hard, then don't give up. You can make it work!

As I said at the beginning of this section, we cover all these points and others in much more detail in the rest of the book, but these top ten tips might be useful later, so make sure you have covered all the bases.

Many of the sections are also covered on my website www.startyourownfashionlabel.com where you can also buy and download templates that can be easily adapted to your needs.

To access a wealth of additional free information, please subscribe to my newsletter on the Start Your Own Fashion Label.com website. Then each month you will receive my monthly tips, industry updates and offers, as well as access to our private fashion networking groups.

Chapter 1 – The Changing Reality of the Fashion Industry

There is a new reality in the fashion industry, and the fashion rulebook has been ripped apart and thrown away. I wrote this book to share ideas about the new ways that start-up fashion brands can achieve success, as the old business models that brands usually follow, no longer work. While there are lots of elements of the fashion industry that are currently broken, I believe it is 'a new dawn' for start-up brands if they want to do things differently.

I came into fashion in early 2003 and I expected it to be a dynamic, disruptive, brave and avant-garde industry. What I actually found was an industry that was very prescriptive and the fashion brands were very compliant, following the 'perceived' rules. Brands from all around the world all followed the same system in making, showing and selling their collections. This didn't make any sense to me. By following the same calendar, business models and methods, start-up brands were putting themselves at a disadvantage both economically, as well as offering limited differentiation. If the system actually worked then I would have understood why the brands all followed it, however the economy and the consumer were already starting to change. In 2003 I felt it was time for the fashion industry to change, but they seemed unwilling to adapt. Sixteen years later and many in the industry today are still clinging on to the old industry methods.

I have spent my whole career in the fashion industry battling against old systems, out-dated attitudes and archaic business models. I have been passionate about showing start-up brands that they need to be entrepreneurial and shouldn't start their labels following outmoded systems. Throughout this book I will be talking about the changing reality of the fashion industry and the challenges of moving away from the old system.

The fashion industry is renowned for its smoke and mirrors approach. Unfortunately, many start-up brands fail to see the reality behind the engineered image. It suits the industry and brands to only show the glamorous side, as it is the glamour and success that generates consumer interest and sales. However, someone looking to start a fashion label needs to find out what is really happening. For your start-up brand to succeed, you need to create your business with the knowledge and understanding of the new paradigm that is taking shape in the fashion industry. A new brand can't set up their label following old systems, as the old fashion industry rules just don't work anymore.

The fashion industry is broken but that doesn't mean that it is impossible to develop a brand in the current market. Instead I think it is 'a new dawn'.

For many years I have proved that if you understand what is not working in the industry and where changes need to happen, then brands have more chance of succeeding and growing.

Therefore, please don't take the following section as bad news! I am purely giving you the reality so that you can avoid the pitfalls and overcome the challenges.

A broken fashion industry

Before we can look at the new fashion system, we need to review where there are problems with the old model and look at the challenges that a start-up brand needs to consider.

Many fashion brands have not changed the way they run their businesses in decades. Others are still holding onto the concept that fashion is 'art' not business; therefore, they don't need to consider other industry models. Established brands are often inflexible, as they are part of huge corporations that are very difficult to turn to new methods. For others, the old system still works, because they have been able to control the market.

One of the other reasons that many brands continue to follow the old business model is due to learning from out-dated education systems and books. Some fashion courses are predominantly taught by academics who haven't worked in the industry for many years. This may mean that, despite their best efforts, they may not have kept up with the latest business changes.

For a young brand with no established market, recognised name and limited resource, then the only option is to look to the future and avoid the pitfalls of the broken system.

The fashion industry is broken in many areas. Below are some of the problems that have been identified:

Too many designers and brands
There is a lot of talk about the oversaturation of brands and too many fashion design students trying to join an already overflowing market. Our universities and colleges are filled with students training to be designers and in the UK alone over 3,000 + students graduate every year as fashion designers. Then there are the fashion design students who graduate from every other fashion school around the world. There are not enough jobs for this number of students to become designers. Nor are there opportunities for them to all start their own fashion labels, or manufacturers to create their collections. In comparison to the number of students learning design, very few study the practical skills of pattern making and sewing skills.

Factories all over the world tell me that there is a shortage of high quality, technically trained staff to make fashion.

The oversaturation of brands means that many fail due to having no point of difference in a limited market. Many brands fail to specialise in a new area or consider offering the consumer something different in regards to either product or experience.

Seasonal collections
It has been said, "seasons are so last season." So, why then do designers still create seasonal collections?

We now live in a world where climate changes mean we can have hot days in mid February and cold rainy days all summer. We reside and work in properties that are artificially heated or cooled thanks to high tech air conditioning and heating systems. We are all global travellers seeking out different climates, as well purchasing fashion product from international retailers that is then shipped across the world. Consumers also rarely have a separate summer and winter wardrobes, instead layering pieces in different weathers.

It no longer makes sense to create an autumn winter or spring summer collection when the climate and consumer has changed so much. So why are designers creating product for a particular climate at a particular time of year?

The fashion week circus is a major part of the fashion industry problems. The seasonal collections were originally based around the fashion week calendars, where brands showed collections a season ahead. This meant the brand had enough time to show the collection on the runway and then create their commercial lines in response to buyer interest. The Spring/Summer shows take place in September the year before and Autumn/Winter shows take place in February, with six months between the show and product arriving at the store. Brands are forced to show collections months in advance for an alternative season, yet the images are now widely circulated within seconds of the show. This leads to unhappy consumers, who want to buy what they see, but for most brands the product isn't available for six months.

The seasonal model does not appeal to the modern consumer. If they see a product on the catwalk they want it now. They also want to shop for garments for different climates at the time they need them. They no longer think about buying a product now to wear later! If its hot they want a cotton dress now and it is cold they want a woollen top to wear immediately.

Major brick and mortar retailers also add to the seasonal problem by still working on a 1950s business model. This model places seasonal product on the shop floor at a set time, leaving it to sit there for months until the new season arrives. These retailers do not take into consideration the changing climate or consumer behaviours. The customer is frustrated and no longer sees the relevance of shopping on the high street when the stores don't have the product they want at the right time. They also know that if they wait long enough, the store will have no alternative but to heavily discount product at the end of the season to clear it.

The end of wholesale
The fashion retail industry is suffering monumental problems and struggling to adapt to changing consumer behaviours and the diminishing footfall into brick and mortar stores. They have the challenge of buying products in mass quantities, managing their store, promoting the products and trying to sell them to a customer who can now access similar product from a myriad of places. They are also struggling to adapt to changing climates, which often results in them having the wrong products in the store at the wrong time.

This is having an impact on the buying process, with more stores now looking to take less risk and change the process of how they stock their shops. This means they now take many collections on a consignment (sale or return) basis and expect the brand to do more of the work in attracting the customer and promoting the collection. They may also want to place short orders, which means they order the product they need at the last minute and the brand has to deliver in about 3 weeks.

For start-up brands, the result is a very limited wholesale market for them and the wholesale terms are very unfavourable. Many emerging brands are still trying hard to make the wholesale market work, by participating in trade fairs and showrooms but with very little chance of success. This strategy is very risky and not economically viable for most start-ups.

Changing consumer demands
In many ways the fashion industry is disconnected from reality. Many fashion labels have little or no understanding of how the consumer feels about brands promoting wool coats to them whilst they are basking in a heat wave. These same brands then wonder why the customer is longer coming into their stores.

Consumer buying behaviours are changing and evolving, and the customer is now in the driving seat. Today's consumer wants it all and they want it now! The fashion consumer is looking for brands that adapt to new fashion and social trends, as well as offering seamless, easy purchasing options and more in-store experiences. They seek brands that also offer greater authenticity and transparency.

Today's customer has more choice, more information, more access and greater expectations, so fashion brands have to adapt to this. Brands that are still using out-dated methods to sell fashion products are losing market share to brands that are being more disruptive and entrepreneurial in attracting the customer. The customer is looking for a brand that offers a great online shopping experience, quick and easy delivery and returns, as well a brand that connects with them through social media.

The greatest change has been the consumer now looks for experience rather than product. They would rather 'do' something than 'buy' a possession. Or the possession comes after, as they buy something to remind themselves of the great experience they had. The effect of this is that consumers now spend more of their disposable money on experiences, or even buying food or drink, which has resulted in a reduction of foot traffic in fashion retail environments.

Overproduction
The fashion industry has an internationally documented problem with overproduction. Many fashion powerhouses have reportedly disposed of millions of dollars worth of fashion product, by either burning it or sending it to landfill. Overproduction has affected luxury fashion labels as well as fast fashion brands. Some fashion brands at the value level are also dealing with returns that are not worth them reprocessing and putting back out for sale. This leaves them with no alternative than to instantly dispose of the products that are returned.

Overproduction is the result of poor buying decisions, lack of understanding of the brand's customer and poor relationships with factories. Many times, overproduction occurs because the brand is focussed on producing product at a certain price, which means they may have to produce more of the garment in order to reach the price point they desire, as they were unable to negotiate better deals with their factory.

There is a growing outrage, as more of the overproduction scandals become public knowledge and fashion brands are facing mounting pressure from both consumers and the industry to clean up their acts.

Sustainability

Alongside the issues of overproduction and the disposal methods of unsold inventory, there are numerous concerns with sustainability in the fashion industry. There are huge environmental costs of producing clothes and the industry has sustainability problems at its very core.

Fast fashion is perceived to be a fundamental cause of many of the sustainability problems in the industry due to the consumer's constant desire for new and different. However, all fashion brands, fast fashion and luxury product, can cause damage to the environment. It is widely stated that fashion is the second largest polluter in the world after the oil industry. Fashion brands can cause environmental impact from many processes:

o   Water is often polluted in the countries where garments are produced. Toxic substances, such as lead and mercury from the dying process, pollute the water, which is harmful to aquatic and human life.

o   The fashion industry consumes extreme levels of water to produce our clothes. This leads to scarcity of water in some cotton growing regions, which has a huge ecological impact.

o   Our synthetic garments release microfibers every time we wash our clothes, which introduces plastic into our food chain.

o   Heavy chemicals are used in cotton farming as well as during fabric production, dyeing and bleaching. These result in water pollution and soil degradation, as well as being extremely harmful to humans.

o   The fashion industry accounts for a large percentage of global carbon emissions or greenhouse gases, due to the amount of energy used in the production and transporting of clothing.

o   The fashion industry plays a major part in degrading soil by overgrazing land, or due to the massive use of chemicals.

o   Deforestation comes from the use of wood-based fibres like rayon.

28

Although it is being stated that the fashion industry is contributing to the rapid destruction of our planet, many brands are reluctant to talk about sustainability for fear of becoming a target for ethical campaigners. They are also scared that if they talk about sustainability then fail to meet their goals, then they will receive a backlash from the consumers and the industry.

Having identified many ways in which the fashion industry is broken, people will often then ask me if they should avoid launching their own fashion label. I advise them, as I will advise you, that this is actually the perfect time to launch a fashion brand, as it is 'a new dawn' for start-up labels that will do things differently. It you are creating a fashion label that has a vision for the future and are aware of the elements in the industry that are broken, you will then stand every chance of success.

New Dawn

The new dawn of the fashion industry means that start-up fashion labels do not adhere to the rules of the past. Now start-ups should build the brand that they want to build, following a business model that is best for their label, rather than doing the same thing as everyone else.

It is important for a start-up label to research new business concepts and ideas, and understand future developments. You need to be visionary, creating a brand with longevity for the future and not build a brand for today.

The new brands that are succeeding are the ones that are creating their own rules and building labels that are unique. They may find differentiation in the products they create, or the way they sell their collections or promote them. These disruptive brands are looking at all the elements that are broken in the fashion industry and finding new ways to create businesses for the future.

Here are some of the ways to counter a broken fashion industry:

Awesome designs

If you want your brand to succeed in the new fashion industry, then you need to make sure that your designs are awesome. There is no place in the industry now for mediocrity. Your designs need to stand out or there is no point entering the market. The stores are full of product that is all the same, with little point of difference other than price, which is why many brands are struggling or failing. Nor is there a place in the world now for the arrogant designer who thinks that they know it all, or are so awesome that people will automatically buy their designs. Today's designers need to connect with their customers, creating designs that meet the consumer's needs and desires.

Differentiated Brands

In an overpopulated market, you will need to create a brand that stands out and has a point of difference from others. That difference can come from a unique feature, product, story, delivery or process or a combination of all these elements. Without a point of difference, you will struggle to be heard in such a packed market.

The biggest change in the new dawn comes from the need for a start-up fashion label to be a lifestyle brand, one that has a purpose and meaning that is authentic and connects with the consumer. Customers want to buy more than product. They want to buy into the lifestyle that the brand offers them. Therefore, your brand needs to offer more than product; you also need to create a unique brand value, personality and identity. If you successfully develop these elements, then the customer will connect with your brand, which will generate sales and brand loyalty.

Seasonless collections

Due to changing climates and consumer buying behaviours, the new dawn will see more brands moving away from the traditional seasonal collections and adapting their business models to be more responsive to consumer need.

Some brands have adapted to these changes by moving their collections to 'See Now Buy Now." This means that their collection is launched in the stores on the same day as their catwalk show. This model works well for brands with a younger demographic that want things more quickly. It may not work for a brand with more expensive product or an older customer who takes longer to make decisions to purchase, needing to see it in magazines and stores before buying.

Other brands are stopping seasonal collections altogether, as they feel that they conflict with a move to sustainability. A seasonal collection encourages excessiveness in both the production but also promoting that the customer buys more 'stuff.' With customers starting to look at more sustainable purchasing behaviour, it means that they will be looking to brands to provide 'slow' fashion pieces that can be worn, treasured for years and passed on. This new customer will buy more consciously and not be looking for pieces that can only be worn for one short season.

Capsule collections and product drops

Brands that move away from seasonal collections can concentrate on creating small capsule collections that are more niche. They focus on designing a capsule range that allows their signature style or design to be recognised, rather than creating a range with something for everyone.

Many of the start-up brands that I work with, now create core collections of 6 or 8 pieces. They produce small runs of 5-10 of each piece and then drop in one or two new pieces every few months. The benefits of this business model for a start-up brand are plentiful:

- o Less financial investment, as making small production runs enables a brand to manage their cash flow.

- o Creating more interest on the e-commerce shop by dropping new pieces that drive the customer back constantly to see what is new.

- o The range shows a strong brand signature, which isn't diluted by too many products, and this gives the label a point of difference.

- o With smaller production runs, the brand can test the market without incurring financial disaster. The risk is huge if a brand puts a full collection into production and then most of it doesn't sell.

- o Seasonal collections mean seasonal sales, therefore opting out of the season's means a brand doesn't have to discount. A brand can continue to sell core product for much longer and there is no need to have an end of season sale.

I have seen start-up brands that have successfully launched with just one really strong signature piece to test the market and have then gone on to create larger international companies.

Experiential retailing

Fashion retailing has struggled since the global recession and the high street has struggled with diminishing footfall. The new dawn is focussed on how to encourage the customer to return to brick and mortar stores. The consumer now happily shops online for product, but if they visit a physical store, they look for experience over product. Consumers are spending more on dining out, entertainment and travel as well as health and wellness, so fashion brands need to work a lot harder to drive the customer back.

For the fashion industry, experience is important as we mainly buy product on an emotional basis. The customer needs to shop in an environment that excites them, that makes them feel good and appeals to their five senses. This experiential retail environment may be technologically enhanced, or it may offer the consumer an immersive and interactive experience that will create an emotional connection with them. Many brands are trying different kinds of in-store environments to see what connects best with their customer, as one size does not fit all. Others are creating their own flagship, concept stores to raise their customer's aspiration for the label.

Your start-up brand may not have your own flagship store at the beginning, but you do need to set your label up as an experiential brand. You need to offer your customer an experience, whether they are shopping online, on Instagram or in person. The experience needs to be unique to your brand, connecting with your brand storytelling.

Your brand needs to offer the customer an amazing user journey from start to finish. You should invite the customer into your world, to be part of your community and give them a fabulous experience that brings them back time and time again. Your whole focus should be on developing happy customers who love your brand, product, message and values. This customer will then help you attract others.

Direct to consumer sales

With the disappearing wholesale market or unfavourable wholesale terms, more brands are turning their attention to a direct to consumer sales model. Dealing directly with your consumer allows a brand to test the market and also get feedback that can inform future brand developments.

The brands that are adopting the direct to consumer sales channel are embracing it. They can see their brands are growing, sales are coming in and they find greater satisfaction from their connection with the customer. It is not an easy strategy initially. It can take some hard work to change your business model, but the long-term opportunities are worth it. This strategy will help the brand grow through sales with a healthy margin, as selling direct gives you better profit margins.

To generate sales, it might be necessary to start initially with a simpler design that could appeal to a broader customer. Though it may be a simpler piece, it should still have a clear brand signature. It can be frustrating for a designer to create simpler pieces, but there will be an opportunity to develop more creative designs later on when you start generating consistent sales.

To make a success out of the direct to consumer model, brands need to be entrepreneurial, looking for new ways to meet and connect with customers. An online shop may not work on its own initially, so the brand will usually need to take part in events and run marketing campaigns to drive the customer to their site. Successful brands are marketing their labels through pop-up shops, trunk shows, open studio events and selling parties.

Authenticity and Transparency

Authenticity is a hugely important element in growing a new fashion brand. A brand starting today needs to be authentic and have a clear message that cuts through all the noise the other brands are making. Brands can no longer be silent, or hide their approach to sustainability, as the customer and industry expect them to be transparent about how their products are made, the impact on the environment and the brands plan to improve their processes.

As well as being transparent in their business dealings and processes, customers are seeking brands that are authentic in their storytelling. They want to know the people behind the brand and how the products are made, as much as they want to know the price, quality and buying process. People buy from people, so a start-up brand has the benefit of being able to connect through their start-up story. Todays customer is much more astute and they can see through the fashion industry 'smoke and mirrors.' They seek brands that are transparent, showing the reality behind the scenes, as well as the inspirations, passion and beliefs of the label. A brand needs to be open, honest and have values and opinions that connect with the customer. Values matter and as customers start to feel uneasy about the 'fast fashion' market, they are more demanding of brands that give something back in both social and environmental terms.

A new brand has the opportunity to track and record their whole process from the start and offer transparency to their customer. This could include tracking where fabrics and trims have been made and shipped from; where the collection was made; the people who created it and the team behind all the different business processes that takes a garment from concept to consumer. It is impossible for a brand to solve all the challenges of creating a sustainable brand at once. It is all right to start with one or two areas of sustainability and build from this, explaining to the consumer what you are doing to overcome the challenges you are facing. A consumer will form a better connection with a brand that is honest in their approach, than with one who hides their processes or overstates what they are actually doing.

Engagement
The days of a brand just pushing out information through advertising and press releases is over. Today the buzz is all about brands having direct engagement with the consumer. Brand engagement is the process of creating an emotional connection between a consumer and the brand. Engagement can be achieved through various channels and can be something as simple as a mention on social media, a consumer opening your newsletter or a conversation in store. The ultimate purpose of engagement is to connect with the consumer so that they become loyal customers of the brand.

Engagement has become important, as the traditional marketing approaches of the past such as newspaper and magazine features and advertising no longer work. The consumer is bombarded with advertising from all angles and has become immune to its effects. They no longer purchase or consume magazines in the same way and the magazines generate little response or drive to action.

Engagement is at the core of social media and social networking. These channels are about communication on a personal level. It is about making a connection with the consumer, bringing them into the brands lifestyle and influencing their purchasing decisions. Engagement on social media only works if you create and post great content and images that connect with the consumer. A brand needs to create a strategy to manage their social media content and engagement, rather than leave it to chance or sporadic posting. Poor content, limited connection with the consumer and no strategy will result in little, if any engagement, and that will damage the brands chance of sales and success. To engage with consumers, the content has to be appropriate and it is usually the genuine, informal and authentic posts that have more impact than glossy high-fashion style imagery.

If you execute an effective Instagram strategy you will build brand awareness and more importantly push sales and brand loyalty. Instagram offers great opportunities for social proofing, as showing one happy customer can make another feel more confident to make a purchase. This approach is far more effective than advertising in today's market.

A final important element of engagement is to provide high-level customer service, as customers can now quickly share their complaints and opinions as well as positive reviews and compliments. Therefore, a brand needs to publicly show that they care about their customers and respond quickly to enquiries or complaints.

A visionary future

When you start your own fashion label, you need to create a brand for the future, not just for today. Having a vision for the future of your brand isn't just about the money you will make, or the acclaim you will receive. The vision should be about identifying new opportunities, discovering new technologies, understanding the changing market and relating to the future consumer. Without vision your brand could be left behind as your competitors take advantage of future developments.

A visionary brand leader will constantly look at the bigger picture, seeking new ways to push the company forward and identifying new and innovative products that meet the consumer's needs.

There are numerous developments on the horizon that a start-up fashion brand should consider:

Changing political and economic environments
Ahead there may be volatility, uncertainty and shifts in the global economy, as well as geopolitical conflicts. A brand needs agility to respond to changing circumstances. It is necessary to constantly look ahead, to be aware of possible global economic downturns and consider any forces that could destabilise your business. Brands that understand the challenges that may come in the future will create business strategies that enable them to survive any storms.

The End of Ownership
Fashion product has a changing lifespan as new business models evolve, such as more brands developing pre-owned, rental, circular, repair and upcycle models. Brands are tapping into these markets as opportunities to connect with new customers, as there is a new generation of consumers who care less about what they own and more about what they do. The future may result in consumers moving away from permanently owning their clothing.

Increasing awareness
Sometimes called 'getting woke,' younger generations of consumers have an increasing awareness of social and environmental causes. They seek fashion labels that are more purpose-driven, have

stronger opinions and greater social and environmental brand values.

Speed to consumer

The consumer will become more demanding and impatient to immediately purchase and receive the products they discover. Brands will need to increase their speed to market, offering shorter lead times and ensuring any products that are advertised or promoted are immediately available. The speed a brand can respond to consumer demands will be a critical success factor. Creating small batch product drops and achieving just-in-time production can improve the speed to consumer.

Authenticity and transparency

In the future, brands will need to build even greater consumer trust by sharing information and having high level brand transparency around price, quality and production. Brands will need to focus on communicating their authenticity and build more genuine connections with the consumer rather than just promoting products.

Omni-channel

Brands in the future will be available on numerous different channels, but they will need to create a seamless consumer experience between them all. Consumers will switch between in-store and online, from web to mobile, desktop to tablet, store to web. They will need brands to develop the right experience at the right time and the brands need to understand and leverage the omni-channel opportunities. At the most basic level this will include click and collect, buy in-store then home delivery, as well as creating a consistent luxury shopping experience both online and in-store. An effective omni-channel strategy can encourage the customer back to the brick and mortar store and help brands increase efficiencies, increase revenues and reduce costs.

Technology

Visionary brands will keep up-to-date with changing technology and the new opportunities it offers. New technologies could include:

- New social media channels and tools for connecting with consumers and increasing sales.

- Blockchain and RFID (Radio Frequency IDentification) will improve sustainability and offer verification of originality by tracking and recording all elements of the production process of garments.

- o   Smart fabrics will provide more functionality, from monitoring your heart rate, checking your temperature to changing colour according to the environment or sounds around you.

- o   New in-store technology, which will include smart mirrors, self-checkout, digital screens, interactive windows and virtual reality.

- o   Artificial intelligence will help brands use data for predictive forecasting, planning and merchandising, as well as offer the consumer better browsing and personalisation.

- o   Augmented reality will offer an enhanced customer experience and opportunities such as sampling or trying on products without having to go into store.

- o   Contactless shopping through unmanned stores which customers can enter using QR codes or facial recognition, and then shop and checkout through their mobile.

Sustainable focus

Every brand in the future will have a sustainable focus, even if initially they only identify one or two areas where they will make a difference. One brand alone cannot fix the industry's sustainability problems, but the industry could come together to affect change. Brands will start to invest more into sustainable options as they realise the damaging impact on their reputation of ignoring the changing consumer demand, or to offset future regulatory costs. Successful brands of the future will be ones that work genuinely in the commercial, the environmental and the social dimensions.

Know your 'why' for success and happiness

Setting up your own fashion label will be challenging, but it can also be really rewarding. To ensure running your own business fulfils your dreams then you will need to is know your 'why,' Why have you started your own label, why are you running it the way you do, why do you care about your product? Discovering your 'why' will help you stay committed to your dreams if things are tough in the beginning.

In creating your business, you need to think about what you want to achieve and determine how you will measure success. When setting up a business most of us want to make money, but what else do you want? Some people will do it for the fame; others for a sense of personal achievement, and many will do it so they have more control over their lives and how they work. If you don't consider what you will see as success, then you will never know if you have achieved it. The fashion industry can be high pressure and a difficult market to beat. Everyday you can face a rollercoaster of emotions and you will need a strong mental attitude to get you through the challenging times. It can really help you maintain your passion and drive if you celebrate the wins as you go along.

Entrepreneurs are often so goal-focussed that rather than celebrate achieving a goal, they move straight on to the next one. If you don't stop and celebrate the successes, even if it is a small one, like a new customer or a great review, then you are more likely to burn out. If you constantly check in on the successes of your business, then you will enjoy the ride much more.

Don't try to rush ahead to quickly with your brand. The challenge is not how quickly you can grow your business but how well you can grow it. A business needs to grow efficiently and effectively. Fast growth isn't always a positive thing. I have seen many brands run into problems, or fail, ,because they tried to grow too fast without the structures and systems in place to manage the growth. So enjoy and celebrate the process of setting up your business and putting the systems in place, as this will lead to greater success in the future.

Don't only measure yourself and your brand against other labels, as you have no idea what is going on behind the scenes of their business. Set your own goals and build your business in the way that is best for you and your brand. Set yourself realistic goals and remember 'why' you are starting your own label.

Finally, the reality of the changing fashion industry is that successful start-up fashion labels are doing things their own way. They are taking success in their own hands and creating brands that they love as much as their customers do. They have recognised that the traditional fashion rules are broken and have taken back the power to run genuine, authentic businesses with new goals, values and ethics. And they are enjoying the ride!

Chapter 2 – The Business Structure

Setting up a business can be daunting and many designers have no idea where to start, or don't consider some of the really important and legal elements. There are some essential areas that you need to work through to make sure your business will survive. Before you rush ahead, make sure you have reviewed these elements and have set structures and systems in place. There are real benefits in setting up your business in the right way from the beginning, as it will save you time, money and problems later on. Many designers just start making clothes, begin telling everyone about them and try to sell them, before they have these basics in place. This nearly always results in disaster later on.

In this chapter, I am going to look at the really important aspects of deciding on your brand name, making sure you have a legal company structure that will enable you to grow later, writing a useful and effective business plan, legal issues concerning protecting your name and designs, and where to base your business and find mentors to help you. You need to ensure that you are in the best position to make your business a success, as well as ensuring that no-one can jeopardise this success by using your name or stealing your designs.

Your Brand Name

A name is for life. It can be really hard to change your brand name later, so it is important that you make the right decision at the start. People may say "It doesn't matter it's just a name" but it is never just a name. The success of your brand could rest on it.

It may be that you are considering using your own or family name, or have come up with something creative and you love it. You may personally think it communicates everything you want to say about your brand, but what about everyone else? Your brand name may make sense to you, or be simple to say, but to your customer it may not make any sense at all. Can your customer say it? Does it translate well in other countries and languages? Are there any negative connotations, or does it evoke a negative emotion or memory?

Before you finally decide on your name you need to do some research.

Is your name already registered?
First of all, you need to check your name is available as a domain name and also that no one else has registered or trademarked your name. You can check registration and trademarks on sites such as United States Patent and Trademark office www.uspto.gov or on the UK government site www.gov.uk

For domain name searches, be wary of searching on a lot of registration sites, as your name can be lost if you don't buy it straight away and then held to ransom to make you pay a lot more for it. Be prepared to buy it quickly if it is available. It is worth taking the risk even if you don't use that name later. One of the safer sites to check domain name availability on is www.whois.net.

If your domain name is not available, then be wary of picking something similar but not the same as your brand name, as this can badly affect your e-commerce sales later on. Customers need to find your company site and more importantly your shop very easily, as they will only spend a few seconds searching. Be careful of unusual domains, as most customers still search for .com or co.uk so these are still the best domains to buy.

Google it
The next stage is to Google the name – is there anyone out there already with the same name or something similar? You don't want to pick a name where there is already a lot of competition, as it would make it harder for your customer to find you. Also, what type of companies are the ones that have similar names? Make sure there are no negative connotations that could have an impact on the perception of your brand.

Language and translation
Check in the dictionary for all the meanings of your name and associated words. Consider what your name means in other languages, as names don't always translate well. For example, if you are a brand who decides to call your brand 'Minga,' then you need to consider that in the UK Minga also means unattractive or horrible person, and in Sicilian culture Minga means a man's penis. Would you want these connotations with your brand?

You also need to consider if international customers can say the name, as some words and names are much harder to say or understand in different cultures and languages.

Emotional Value
Think of the emotional value of your name, as it is important to think what it will mean to your customer, and consider what type of products will they imagine. Could there be any negative associations or emotions with your name. The more luxury your brand, the more important that your brand name reflects a luxury image.

Design it
As you get nearer to the end of the process, then start to design a logo for your brand name and consider how it will look on all your marketing materials and also on the labels in your clothes or on your packaging. It is

really important to make sure customers can easily read your name and recognise it.

The logo needs to create the right impression and have longevity, as you will use it as your mark for years to come. You need to consider how your customer will perceive the logo and the types of symbols, fonts and colours they connect and want to be associated with. Imagine in the future you might choose to put your logo on a piece of clothing in the way that Gucci, Nike or Supreme do. Would it have impact? Would your customer want to walk around with your logo on their shirt or jacket?

It is possible to design a logo yourself, but I would recommend commissioning a designer or using a specialist agency. It is such an important element of your brand that you need to get it right. If you are going to commission someone to design the logo for you, start to put a mood board together which includes examples of your competitor's logos and other examples of ones you love. Also ensure you write a full brief explaining what your product is, the price point, a description of your customer and target market and an explanation of your brand values.

Test It
Before you make a final design, test it, test it, test it! Ask friends, family, people from different places and different languages if possible to make sure there are no problems with it. As I said at the start of this section, it is very difficult to change your name later, so it is much better to take some time now to make sure you get it right.

Register and Protect
Once you have decided on your name, then register it and protect it as soon as possible. If you have the options, then buy all the best domains for your name such as: .com, .net and .co.uk. You can then direct all the addresses to the main site you chose to use and this also stops someone else setting up with something similar to you.

We cover trademarking and company registration in later sections within this chapter, so please read these for advice on making sure you are protecting your brand name.

Your Legal Company Status

You may be ready to start your new business but some decisions you make now could affect the growth of your business in the future. You need to decide on the structure of your company and consider the implications of the different types of company format.

A lot of designers who start up on a small scale, without a lot of cash or likelihood of raising investment in the near future, then they just start their business acting as sole traders without creating a formal or legal company. This can be Ok, but it may hold your business back in the future. Below we look at the different options for setting up your company.

Sole Trader

As a sole trader, you are your business. You can make instant decisions, and everything belongs to you. It may also seem easier in the beginning to just set up as a sole trader as there is less administration. There is the advantage that many of the expenses, such as business travel and a portion of the costs of your accommodation, are tax deductible but you do still need to register as self-employed for tax purposes.

However, on the flip side you also have all the liability for the business. If it has bad debts then those debts are yours, and you will have to pay them if the business fails.

Other problems can arise as a sole trader when you start to grow the business. Rising finance can be very difficult for sale traders as banks and investors prefer to work with limited companies. Many suppliers and manufacturers also prefer to work with registered limited companies only, as they see sole-traders as more of a risk and there is a perception that sole traders are less credible.

Partnership

Partnerships are usually similar to a sole trader set-up but with more than one owner. Partnerships work well if it is someone you really trust, but choose your partners carefully. Experience shows that close family members, or life partners coming together to run businesses can be absolutely disastrous. The break up can be worse than a marriage breakdown, with the risk of you losing all your personal wealth, if the business doesn't work. Also, if one of the partners cannot pay the debts or just disappears, then the other partner is left to pay the full amount of the debts alone.

You can create a limited liability partnership (LLP) which would offer more protection to individual partners, as it limits liability to what each partner has invested in the business. For this you have to create a more formal company by registering with Companies House and putting information about the company and its partners on the public record.

For a partnership, you need to generate a written agreement with the details of how the liabilities, ownership and profits of the business will be split and what happens if one partner wants to leave.

Limited Liability Company

Incorporating means registering a limited company (LTD) or LLP at Companies House in the UK or similar organisation in your own country. Each country has their own version of a registered company. Registering your company as a legal entity is usually the recommended approach, as it protects you as an individual from greater financial risk and also enables you to grow your business in the future.

Registering your company is a simple process and will add more credibility to the business. It also makes it easier to find suppliers to work with you and raise money in the future. Many fabric suppliers and manufacturers will only work with registered companies, as they can check your legal status and review your likelihood of paying their invoices.

The advantage of limited liability is that there will be a firewall between your money and the company's money. The business is a separate entity and therefore the company bills are owed by the company, not you as an individual, and your personal assets are not at risk.

Some people consider registering a company negatively as you will have a lot more administration to complete and will need an accountant to help you complete your end of year accounts. However, if you are looking at growing your business in the future, then this is a necessary step.

Registering your Trademark

Registering a trademark is one of the most effective ways to protect your name, brand and work. A trademark is a symbol used to distinguish the goods and services from your company against your competitors. The trade mark refers to your brand, such as Dior, and can include individual words, logos, a sentence, a phrase or even a shape or sound.

In most cases you can register your trademark yourself using an online site, which saves legal costs, but also helps you really learn about the intellectual property protection process. However, it is essential to get it right, so if your case is complicated, or you are looking for international protection outside of your own country, or are just unsure, then it is worth getting legal advice.

This is a quick guide on trademark but it is not in any way detailed or complete, nor can it be classed as legal advice, but it is a starting point for you to consider your Trade Mark process.

Firstly, you need to search to make sure nobody else has registered your trademark and there are numerous websites that you can do this on. This is a good starting point, but it is advisable to use a specialist legal company to provide a full clearance search. In order for your trade name to be registrable it must be able to distinguish the goods and services from others. You cannot register a trade mark if it describes a product such as DRESS, or a generic term in the fashion industry such as MACKINTOSH, or too descriptive such as SILK.

The next step is to consider the registration territory (or countries) and you will need to file applications for each of the territories or countries you wish to trade in. As global registration is expensive, designers usually have to prioritise the territories according to their budget and where there is most risk. Speculative trade mark registrations are common in areas such as the Far East, where they will advise you that they wish to file your company name to see if you will counterclaim. They may then take your trademark and hold it to ransom to make you buy it back. This can be very expensive to resolve, so you need to be sure you have cover in this territory if you wish to sell in the Far East.

It is really important that you understand that by having a trademark in one territory / country does not protect you from someone using your brand name in another country that you have not covered.

Your trade mark is also by 'Class,' which is the industry grouping your trade mark will come under. There are 45 classes listed by number and covering certain products and service such as Class 14 Watches and Jewellery; Class 25 Clothing, footwear and headwear. You can be classified under more than one class.

Trade marks typically take three to six months to process and are covered for 10 years initially. You can then use the registered trademark symbol ®. The trade mark can last forever as long as renewal fees are paid and the mark continues to be used for the products and services covered by the registration.

Once you have the registered trade mark, it will stop others using the same or similar marks in the classes and territories you have covered. The trade mark also adds to the brand credibility and can be used to generate income through selling or licensing it in the future.

Whilst you are applying, you can use the symbol ™ to provide notice of a claim of common-law rights. A ™ is usually used in connection with an unregistered mark, to inform potential infringers that a term, slogan, logo or other indicator is being claimed as a trademark. Use of the ™ symbol does not guarantee that the owner's mark will be protected under trademark laws.

SWOT Analysis

One of the most useful business tools that all entrepreneurs or start-up businesses can use is the SWOT analysis. It is an easy to use, basic tool that we use for many aspects of building and growing a business and we will revisit it again in the marketing section.

The SWOT analysis is a framework that you can use to evaluate your business idea at the beginning of your journey. It is also a tool that you should use on a regular basis in your business to continually measure your position in the market,

In the SWOT framework you measure the strengths, weaknesses, opportunities and threats for your business idea, assessing what your brand can and cannot do and how you will stand against your competitors. Using the format of a table, as shown below, the SWOT analysis can be used to quickly scan the brand to realistically analyse each area. A SWOT analysis should be short, simple and not over analysed, which is why it is a useful tool to revisit time and time again.

Strengths	Weaknesses
What is the brand good at, what does it offer that is unique, customer base, skills, funding, brand perception and image etc.	What could stop the brand from achieving success, what do the competitors do better, debt, supply chain problems, lack of staff/ skills etc.
Opportunities	**Threats**
What other markets could the brand look at in the future, what else could be brought into the brand to make it more successful, such as skills, money, staff etc. Are any of the weaknesses an opportunity for the future?	What could affect the business such as competition, loss of suppliers or manufacturers, rising costs, changing market etc.

The SWOT analysis will lead you smoothly into the business planning process.

The Business Plan

You have decided to start your own label and you can't wait to see your completed collection hanging on a rail, take part in your first catwalk show or see your collection in that big department store. You can already imagine how awesome that will be! So probably the last thing you want to do is sit down and write a business plan.

You may be asking is there any point in writing a business plan when you are not sure what your brand will look like in the future, or how your business will progress? We have all heard people say how much they hate writing business plans and most of the time the business owner just makes up what they put in it, coming up with numbers that sound great with no idea if they are realistic. And then who will even read the business plan – as the banks won't lend money to you anyway and an investor won't be interested yet in your start up business?

You also may not know what to include in the business plan. Writing the plan would mean you need to find the time to do more in-depth research on the market, competitor analysis and consumer profiling and that would slow you down from starting your label.

All these reasons may make you decide not to write a business plan, but having no business plan is not a solution either. You may think that a plan isn't important as you are carrying around all your business ideas in your head, but sometime in the future as your business starts to grow and your days get busier and more stressful, you may forget some of your original plans and aims.

I constantly see brands who run into problems further down the line because they didn't have or use a business plan. Problems include: -

- Designers and brands who forget what they originally set out to do and have found themselves a few years down the line running a completely different business than the one they intended, one they no longer enjoy or have pride in.

- Brands that fail because they haven't done enough research on the market, competitors and realise too late that they do not have anything unique to offer to the market.

- Brands that have no clear idea of who their customers are or how they reach them.

- Labels who, when questioned by buyers or press, are very vague, flaky and unfocussed in their descriptions of their brand. They don't have a well-defined description of their brand, have no strong brand story telling messages, nor a clear vision of where their brand is going.

- Partnerships that break down as the partners in the business have very different ideas of where the brand should go and what it should achieve.

- Start-up brands that run out of cash at a critical moment, because they hadn't developed a cash flow forecast or had no idea of how much money it would take to start their label.

- Designers that get disheartened, as they have no system for checking their own progress and seeing how much they have achieved.

Many of these problems could have been avoided or resolved if the business owner had started off with a business plan.

Whilst it is a waste of time writing a complex and lengthy business plan, it is of great value to have a document that sets out your basic aims. This would be a plan that you can regularly review to see what goals you've reached or missed, what challenges you have won or lost, and give you an opportunity to celebrate your growth and achievements.

Your business plan does not need to be complicated, it just needs to be a few pages in clear language that sets out your ideas and plans such as: -

- What the company name is, who owns it, where it will be based.
- What your product is, a description of your design aesthetic, what your brand signature is and what you offer that is unique.
- Who your customer is and where they are.
- How you plan on selling your collection through wholesale and/or direct to consumer.
- What your goals and milestones are.
- Your financial needs – how you will manage your cash flow.

There isn't any golden formula for writing a business plan as each business is different. Your business plan is yours, it is personal to you and should include the information you will need to help you run your business.

The business plan will help you: -

- Be really clear on your business idea.
- Give you chance to consider what is unique or the signature of your brand.

- Spot any potential problems you may come across.

- Set out your goals.

- Ensure you have systems in place to measure your progress and successes.

Business Plan Format

Whilst there is no set formula for a business plan, as it can be as unique as your brand, here are some ideas of what you can include. As the Business Plan is personal to you, then you can change headings, move things around but it is worth considering having these elements in your plan in some way.

Executive Summary
The Executive Summary always comes first in your Business Plan but is the thing you write last. It is a statement that gives the first impression of your brand and should include a quick snapshot of all the key ideas, plans and objectives of your label. This executive summary can act as your elevator pitch, so it should be interesting, memorable, and concise and explain what makes your brand and your product unique.

Company Overview - Vision
Detail the background to your business in depth: what it is, what does it do, what is the advantage of it, how will it stand out, what will make people buy your product and where are you already with the business? This section is very important as you look for finance or investment as it helps the reader understand the particular market you are going for and what makes you unique and different from your competitors

Customer and Competitive Analysis
This is the section where you put all the research you have done into your customer including who the customer is and a detailed customer description; the market, how this market is growing and how big it is; who your competitors are and what makes you different to them; why this market and consumer is viable for you.

Sales Plan
You need to determine how you are going to sell your product and this is where you detail your sales strategy. You need to detail the approach you will take for each sales channel such as: -   • **Wholesale** - *the stores you will be targeting and trade shows you will participate in to reach the wholesale buyer*

- **Direct to consumer** – *online thorough your own e-commerce site and through pop up shops, trunk shows and consumer shows and through social media*

Marketing Plan

In this section, you need to be sure to detail your unique selling proposition (USP) with what makes your company different from other brands and also a value proposition, which details the tangible and intangible benefits a customer gets from your product. Your marketing plan will include the 7 P's of marketing product, price, place, promotion, process, people and physical environment.

Your marketing plan also has to detail how you will communicate with your customer through Public relations, advertising and events. It would also include how you would work with stylists, loan collection pieces to magazines, influencers and brand ambassadors

Organisation and Management

Outline your brand's organisational structure and include the directors or owners, as well as all staff. Also include anyone else the business will need or work with such as mentors, professionals including lawyers and accountants, and freelancers such as pattern cutters. Include the different roles each person will take in the company and how all administrative tasks will be completed such as accountancy, ordering etc.

Include the legal status of the company and the details of registration, the registered business address and trading address, the address the business will be run from. Also include the details of how you will protect your Intellectual Property such as registering your trade mark and design rights.

Product development

Describe your line in detail and include your product offer, your range plan, where you will source your fabrics and trims, how you will manufacture your collection, the stock levels you will hold, and your pricing.

Implementation plan

Detail the specific actions you will take to design and develop your product, market and sell it. Include a timeline or critical path analysis for the next three years stating what activity will be done when – this will connect with your cash flow forecast later.

Financial Projections
In your financial projections, you need to include various elements: -
• *The costs of starting the brand including all equipment costs*
• *A detailed cost analysis for your products.*
• *A cash flow forecast including all projected income and outgoings such as rent, product costs, marketing, fashion shoots, influencer costs etc.*
• *Projected balance sheet*
• *Projected profit and loss*

Additional Information
This section is to cover anything else that you have not been able to include in other sections

Once you have written your business plan, don't just put it on a book shelf. Use it to review your business every six to twelve months to see if you are still on target, have achieved your goals and are still running the business you set out to run at the start. It is ok if you have moved off plan a bit, a business needs to be flexible, but don't go so far off plan that you no longer recognise the business from the one you started.

On my website www.startyourownfashionlabel.com you can download a fantastic Business Plan template, which you can easily adapt to your needs.

LEGAL ISSUES

Intellectual Property Protection

One of the crucial parts of running a successful fashion brand is understanding how to protect your business, your designs and brand. When it comes to intellectual property protection if you create something new, whether it is a new product or service, a new logo or design, it is important that you protect it so that no-one else can steal it from you. There are different methods of protection for different elements.

In this section, we will look at copyright, patents and design rights. I covered Trade Marks earlier in this chapter. If you didn't read it earlier, then I recommend you go back and have a look at it. To give you a quick understanding of the different elements, the trade mark refers to the brand such as 'Chanel'; copyright protects your 2-dimensional drawings or prints; and the design right may protect the appearance and shape a garment 'the Chanel style jacket' and finally a patent, which covers an innovative function, construction or operation of a product, or a new type of material.

COPYRIGHT

Copyright relates to two-dimensional work and unlike other forms of intellectual protection you don't need to register copyright to gain protection in the UK. However, in some other countries such as the USA you can formally register your work. In the UK, copyright will arise automatically as soon as you put pen to paper.

For a fashion brand, copyright can apply to your images, your website and content, your patterns, drawings and unique prints. In order for the copyright to be yours, the work must be original. It does not need to be creative or innovative, but the designer must have used his/her own skill and effort to create the work, they must not have copied it from someone else.

Copyright lasts for 70 years after the death of the designer, however if the work is put into production through an industrial process, then the copyright only lasts 25 years from the end of the year that the piece was first marketed.

If a designer/ brand wants to claim copyright infringement, then they must be able to prove they did the work first. You will have to provide proof of origin, date of creation and where you were working at the time. It is essential that from the very start the brand keeps clear records so that you can quickly prove ownership of the copyright. It is recommended that you declare your copyright clearly on all two-dimensional works by applying the copyright symbol © and your name and the date. This will hopefully also act as a deterrent to any potential infringers.

Patent

If you have created a totally new product, design an innovative construction process or fastening or a unique fabric, then the best way of protecting this is to get it patented. A patent gives inventors a monopoly on their products for up to 20 years, giving them the right to stop anyone else from making it or using it without their permission. The patent will establish the invention as being yours, which means you can sell, rent or license it to others.

Design Rights
A designer has an automatic 'Design Right' that protects their design for 10 years after it was first sold or 15 years after it was created, whichever is the earliest. You can use your automatic design right to stop someone copying your design, as long as you can provide evidence of when you created the design. Your design right relies on very good record keeping. You could sign and date copies of your drawings, patterns, spec sheets and agreements with suppliers and manufacturers to prove your case.

The design right can apply to the shape, structure, look, and design of the fashion piece such as clothing, shoes, handbag, or accessory. The design right can apply to the whole or part of the product, such as the design of a dress or a unique collar detail can be covered by design protection.

It is also possible to register your design for better protection, provided it meets the eligibility criteria. The application to register a design can be made at any time in the first 12 months of the design first being shown. Registered design rights are usually sought for a core product that has longevity, a product that you will produce many times in future seasons, such as the Chanel style jacket, rather than a one season trend piece.

In fashion, all the different intellectual property protections can cross over and can co-exist, so that a brand can seek protection from copyright, trade mark and design rights if infringement has been made.

The fashion design industry is based on the reinterpretation of styles and concepts, so there is always the potential for copying. For young designers who struggle to finance litigation against bigger brands who steal their designs, then the only option is to stay ahead of this by constantly innovating and ensuring you protect yourself as much as possible by keeping detailed records of all work.

Confidentiality and Non-Disclosure Agreements
One way you can protect yourself and prevent someone from stealing your idea, is by asking people to sign a confidentiality agreement or non-disclosure agreement before revealing details of your proposed business, brand or design.

The agreement should clearly state what information you want to talk about and declare that both parties will agree to keep it confidential and only use the information shared for the purposes of that discussion.

I would recommend that you ask for non-disclosures to be signed by all suppliers, manufacturers, freelancers and staff before you start any conversations. If the person won't sign it then find someone else to do business with, as this is an indicator that the person does not value your intellectual property.

On my website www.startyourownfashionlabel.com you can download a fantastic Business Plan template, which you can easily adapt to your needs.

GDPR – Data Protection

On 25 May 2018, the General Data Protection Regulation (GDPR) was enforced across Europe, including the UK. The law aims to give citizens more control over their data and to create a uniformity of rules to enforce across the continent.

As you are starting your brand, it is recommended that you are GDPR compliant from the beginning. As you start to gather data for potential and current customers, staff, press and buyers, you need to set up the systems to protect the data and gain consent from the individual that you can hold their data in the first place. A failure to do so could result in heavy fines, such as €10 million (£7.9 million) or 2% of your global turnover– whichever is greater.

GDPR means that if you have ANYONE's contact details, such as customer email addresses, addresses for orders, email addresses for press, buyers etc. and you email them, send them newsletters, or keep a mailing list, then you need to be work on your GDPR!

If you are a UK company then the first step is to register your company with ICO who will be managing GDPR https://ico.org.uk. Under the Data Protection Act it requires you to register with ICO and pay an annual subscription. The next step then is to begin auditing your business, reviewing every aspect of data collection. You need to understand and record what personal data you hold as a business, how it was captured, how it is held, how you use it, and where it is going. GDPR defines 'personal data' as: "... any information relating to an identified or identifiable nature person such as a name, an identification number, address, email address."

The way to document the data is to create a Data Protection Schedule, something like the table below, but you do not need to go into fine detail.

TYPE OF DATA	WHERE	HOW LONG FOR
Customer email addresses	Mail chimp Dropbox	For as long as the customer stays subscribed to mailing list

Staff contracts	Dropbox – GDPR file	Two years after staff leave the organisation
Customer invoices and delivery information		

You also need to consider the data your website collects through cookies, registration and contact forms, and you need to include a cookies policy and privacy notice on your website.

You need to place all personal data in a safe place, that is not easily accessible to anyone who could take this information. If you back it up on the cloud, then it needs to be on a cloud server in Europe or one that is GDPR compliant.

You are allowed to contact new people if it is a legitimate business interest, such as store buyers, but once you have made contact you will then need to explicitly ask them if you can continue to contact them. Under the GDPR, businesses will need to obtain explicit consent, a clear affirmative action from website visitors or contacts that signifies their agreement to their data being processed. Individuals must know what their data is being used for and what they are agreeing to, therefore it needs to be explained really plainly on your website!

Also, consent is specific to the type of communication in question, so if an individual opts in to cookie tracking, they have only given their consent for cookie tracking; whereas if they've given consent to be communicated with over email, they've only given their consent for email communication. You must get consent for each element of your marketing activity. Consent cannot be implied or inferred from silence, pre-ticked boxes or inactivity. Data subjects must take some form of clear affirmative action, such as an opt in, to indicate that they are indeed happy to hear from you. Businesses must allow website visitors, leads, contacts and customers to withdraw their consent and opt out of specific marketing communications and their data being processed. Consent must be demonstrable, and therefore an audit trail of obtaining an individual's consent and the process used must be available. You will need track and keep examples of consent so that you can prove it within 24 hours if asked

Another aspect of GDPR is the right of individuals to request information on how their personal data is being processed, including where and for what purpose. The information must be provided to the data subject free of charge and in a machine-readable, electronic format. For marketers, this means having a complete record that includes all of the data you currently have on that individual. I strongly recommend that you use a system which makes it easy for you to export this data and share with an individual who has requested it.

The right to be forgotten, also known as the 'right to erasure', enables individuals under the GDPR to request the deletion or removal of personal data where there is "no compelling reason for its continued processing" – essentially when that data has no real use to the business.

Insurance

One area that designers often neglect is taking out insurance, usually because they feel they cannot afford it. You need to take out insurance as soon as you start your business to protect and cover your property, computers and collection from fire, theft and water damage etc. It is also worth taking out business interruption insurance so that you are covered if you have to stop trading due to fire or flood etc. Disasters do happen and all your hard work could be lost and without insurance to cover your loss, then you may not be able to start all over again.

A business should take out liability insurance to protect yourself in case your product, or something at your place of work, pop up shop or trunk show causes injury or death. This may seem ridiculous in the early stages but even the simplest accident can end up in court in the modern litigious world.

You also have a legal requirement to tell your landlord or mortgage provider if you plan to run your business from home, as this affects their insurance, as the property would be insured as a residential property only, not also as semi-commercial premises.

Health and Safety

Health and safety laws apply to all businesses and as an employer or a self-employed person, then you are responsible for health and safety in your business. Health and safety laws are there to protect you, your employees and the public from workplace dangers. For most small, low-risk start-up businesses that have fewer than five employees you don't have to write down your risk assessment, or your health and safety policy, but this is something you need to consider as your business grows.

Banking and accounting

Before you start trading you need to set up a business bank account, as the company is a separate legal entity to you. It's not strictly required if you are a sole trader, but it is highly recommended, as it is very easy to muddle up your personal and business expenses and income if it all goes through the same account.

You also need to start keeping clear accounts from the day you start, so keep records of all costs, expenses and income and set up a system to manage it all. There are now numerous online book keeping tools that can help you such as QuickBooks, Sage and Xero.

Home versus Studio/Office

With everything else in place to start your label, one of the next decisions is where to base it. Many designers, due to limited cash flow or for ease at the beginning, start their business working from their own home. This means you have lower overheads, but you need to think about the long term, ensure that you are covered legally to work in your own home and also consider the pros and cons.

Starting from home means, as well as having no rent to pay, that you can have more flexibility in the hours you work, particularly good if you are working with overseas suppliers who you need to call late at night or early in the morning. You will save time not having to participate in the morning commute, and you have the options to go out to meetings in different locations such as private members clubs and coffee shops.

The downside to working from home is that meetings in clubs and coffee shops become expensive after a while and you always have to travel to your client. It can be quite lonely working from home and it can be difficult to separate home from work, so you end up working all hours or your business starts to impact across your home. There can also be numerous distractions from family, children and pets as well as the neighbours popping by for coffee as you are now home during the day! You need to consider if it is appropriate to have staff or interns working out of your bedroom and whether you can hold client visits and receive deliveries without your neighbours complaining about the number of visitors you have. There are also legal requirements, as you are required to tell your landlord or mortgage provider that you are running a business from home, as it may be necessary to take out additional insurance.

Taking a studio can be a big financial investment and many leases require large deposits and long-term lease commitments, which can be very restricting for a start-up brand. If you decide to work from a studio initially you don't want to commit to a long lease, as you don't know where the business will be in 2- or 3-years' time. You may need to get out of the lease due to cash flow problems or if things go really well then you may need to expand into a bigger space. So, with any lease you need to take legal advice to make sure you have the best deal for your business.

One way that many designers and new brands take on an office or studio space, is to move into a shared working space or a building that specialises in start-up creative businesses. There are lots of companies all over the world that now offer flexible work spaces to start-up entrepreneurs and businesses. These are ideal, as you can grow your business with the option to increase or reduce your office space, as you need it in the future, as the spaces are often offered on a month-by-month lease. Another benefit is that you can be in a space where you can network with other creatives, relieving the loneliness of working from home and also building a community with other likeminded start-up and established businesses. These shared workspaces often attract other businesses that could benefit your label as you grow, such as graphic designers, web developers, IT companies and app developers amongst others.

Business Advisors and Mentors

As you start to set up your business, remember that you do not have to do it all on your own. If you are going to run your own business then you need to assess your personal skills. Recognise what areas you are good at and what you are not good at, then ask business advisors and mentors to help you learn, find the information, or provide help for those areas that you are weak at. You do not have to be good at all the business aspects of running your own label, but you do need to know where your weaknesses are and ask for help. Designers are often not very good, or are not interested in, the business aspects of running a fashion label, so need to find people who will help them set the structures and processes that will keep the business on its path to success.

In the early stages, it will be unlikely that you can afford to hire and pay a permanent team of consultants and advisors, but you may need to pay for some professional services such as legal and accounting. The best way to find these people is to ask for referrals and look for professionals that understand or specialise in fashion businesses, as this can save you costs. Don't rush into taking on staff, as this can be a huge cost pressure on the business, instead buy in freelancers and consultants as you need them.

A good accountant right from the start can really help with the development of the business. It is best to get one who specialises in start-up businesses, as their advice can save you money and also, they will ensure you are being legally compliant. The accountant would also be able to advise you on when you need to file tax returns or register for VAT, or whether you benefit from registering for VAT registration before you meet the threshold.

An extensive network of mentors and advisors can be instrumental in making the business a success. They bring in a wealth of knowledge, contacts, connections and industry experience that it could take you years to build. It can be very difficult to keep your eye on all elements of the business when you are doing it all on your own, so these mentors can help you keep on track and identify the areas you need to focus on. When you are looking for advisors or mentors you need people who have been there and done that, have the connections and can open doors for you.

To find your mentors and advisors, first of all look at the network you already have and then look at who they are connected with. Ask people for help and ask for introductions. People are often waiting to be asked! If you don't have anyone in your current contact list, then start to network at industry events, meetups and talks or reach out to people through Linked In.

Finally develop peer group mentoring, as many designers are in the same situation and you can all share experiences, advice, support and learn from each other.

If you don't already have a network of business advisors, then you can connect with some great mentors, who are all industry experts, through my website www.startyourownfashionlabel.com On the website there are also opportunities to network and chat with fellow designers.

Resources

Don't forget that on my website www.startyourownfashionlabel.com you can download loads of great resources to help you set up your business, including Business Plan template, Non-Disclosure Agreement and Intellectual Property Protection.

Chapter 3 - Who is Your Customer and Competitor?

During the many years that I have worked with start-up fashion labels, I have seen a lot of brands that have already designed and made their collection before they think about who their customer is. It is only when they discover that no one rushes forward to buy their garments, that they panic and think, "who is my customer?".

These brands usually don't know who their competitors are either. They often declare that they have no competitors, or believe that what they do is totally unique. Yet they have no research or evidence to prove that this is true. Other brands will only identify leading luxury, heritage brands as their competitors, but fail to compare themselves against more direct competitors such as other smaller emerging labels.

There are plenty of reasons why a brand might not know who their customer is, or who their competitors are. The first reason is that many fashion schools encourage designers to push the boundaries of design and be as creative as possible, without considering the customer, competitors or the realities of trying to sell their creations. I personally believe that this limited education method or attitude is damaging and can set the designer up for failure. It can also cause conflict between a designer and the store buyers, or can result in a designer establishing a brand or product that is too similar to what is already available in the market.

I often hear store buyers define start-up designers as "hopeless idealists," and the designer who wants to focus on the shape, construction and aesthetic of their design feels that the buyers lack imagination, creativity and are only interested in profit. Both points of view are true in some ways. The designers want to create something that they feel passionate about and not create to a brief. The stores want to offer unique garments to their customers, but they also want ones at the right price. Therefore, the store buyer needs to offer pieces that meet with consumer needs, rather than fill their stores with 'art pieces' or the same products as their competitors.

Other reasons why designers don't consider the customer include:

- The perception that their creations are so amazing that of course people will want them.

- That their design skills would be restricted if they considered and had to meet a customer's needs.

- That their design aesthetic could be comprised by considering competitor brands.

Again, all these views have some merits but are not realistic in a modern, crowded marketplace. Designers are often misled into thinking that if they create extreme designs that get attention from the press, then this will lead the customer to wanting their brand more than other labels. This is not true, as the customer is only interested in brands they can connect with and can see themselves wearing. Every brand has to have a balance between creative and commercial pieces in their collections; otherwise amazing creations only flourish in the designer's studio and never see the light of day. This leads the designers to feeling disillusioned that no one appreciates their art and/or they quickly go out of business.

My experience over sixteen years has shown me that none of these perceptions are a good business strategy. I have met many amazing designers who have created outstanding garments and designs but no one buys them. Or I have had to break the news to brands that there are numerous other labels already out there successfully selling similar products, therefore there may not be a need or a customer for their collection. You can only be classed as a business if you sell something, so I have met many designers who would be classed as running expensive hobbies rather than businesses.

Having an outstanding talent for design is a great start, but to turn your passion into a business you have to learn how to either persuade the customer to buy your designs or adapt your design philosophy to meet the customers needs. Either way you have to understand who the customer is and what they want. There is no place in business for ignorance or arrogance. Every successful fashion brand owner has had to learn, adapt to and understand the market and the customer. This is what has helped them to succeed. The brand is not about you, it is about the customer. You have to step out of your own head and into the mind of the customer and think about what they want, what they care about and what they are already buying.

When I meet a new brand one of my first questions is always "who is your customer?" It is a very simple question but one that most start up brands can't answer eloquently. What I hear in reply is usually a vague ramble such as:

"Designing for myself" or "Designing for my friends"

"Designing cool street wear like XX brand but more accessible prices"

"Creating pieces that empower women" or

"Designing pieces for 24 – 40-year-old women looking to buy high end emerging designer brands"

These are not adequate answers and don't give enough detail for the brand to be able to create pieces that sell. Nor does it give you enough detail so that you understand how to connect with and talk to your customer through social media, or promote your product to them in a way that will appeal to their needs and desires.

To be successful you have to identify customer segments, splitting your target customers into groups and understanding why they would want your collections. You need get into their minds to understand who they are, what they want, what motivates them and what inspires them. You need to know what they already wear, where they go and what they want from a garment. To be successful you need to know the fine detail about your customer's life.

Consumer Profile Exercise

Below are some examples of customer segments in the UK from Experian (you can find more details on www.experian.co.uk). Look at the descriptions below and think about what type of fashion products they buy? Which brands they choose and why?

Jessica

Impulsive, fashion-conscious Jessica is likely to be a full-time student. With an average overall spend and household affluence, she favours mid-market brands and can be swayed by a celebrity endorsement or two. Aged 18 to 25.

Francesca

With a high disposable income, urban dweller Francesca indulges her love of fashion with a high spend on shoes, clothes and personal care. She's drawn to luxury and doesn't mind paying more for quality. Aged 26 to 35.

Jodie

Fashionista Jodie's looking for style on a budget. Special offers will appeal to her, as will celebrity endorsements. Mostly she sticks to more affordable retailers, but she can't resist an occasional expensive treat or impulse buy. Aged 18 to 25.

OLIVER

Fashion-conscious Oliver is a full-time student living with his affluent parents. He likes to shop online, favours mid-market brands and premium products and does a lot of his shopping online. Aged 18 to 25.

TOM

Ambitious Tom is doing well in his career and likes to spend his earnings on quality products, including impulse purchases he doesn't strictly need. He mainly chooses mid-market brands and would be more likely to buy from retailers whose ethics he agrees with. Aged 26 to 35.

RYAN

Despite having a low disposable income, Ryan is spending beyond his means. He buys shoes and clothes online and mainly sticks to affordable brands, but can't resist a more expensive product or celebrity endorsement. Aged 18 to 25.

In many books the competitor and customer are included in the general marketing section and there is very little detail. I feel that every brand needs to be very clear on who their customer and competitors are, therefore the subject is too important to lose within a general marketing chapter. There is no business without a customer, therefore I am writing a whole chapter on this alone.

In the rest of this chapter I will discuss the methods you can use to research and identify your competitor, your customer and create segments in order to target your designs and marketing to particular customer groups. The information you gather through this chapter will inform the rest of the development of your brand, including your product development, building your brand, creating a marketing plan and promoting your label.

Understanding the market

The fashion industry is highly competitive and it is a very saturated market. It is essential to conduct research into the size of the market, to see whether it is feasible for you to enter and succeed with the concept you have for your brand.

The fashion industry is also moving and changing at an incredibly fast pace and it is really important to stay ahead of the changes and adapt to them. These changes could affect the type of product you make or the way you promote or sell it, so it is essential to keep up to date and remain relevant.

Your business will be at risk if you don't understand your competitors, what they create, who their customers are and why they buy from them. If you don't have this information then how can you compete?

To understand your market, you need to learn the following:

- Your customer, who they are, their mind-set and buying behaviours.

- Your competitors and what makes you different/ better than them.

If you get a good understanding of your market and competitors, then you can find your point of difference, and build a realistic strategy to grow your business.

Pre-launch Research

Research is an essential part of launching a fashion label and that research includes determining who your competitors and target customers are. Understanding your customer will help you create the product, uncover the language you will use to communicate with them, explain how you will sell to them and guide the brand development. There can be no short cut in this process, as your business success is reliant on identifying and selling to a customer segment. You need to put significant time into your research.

You need to include research into the fashion market as a whole, as well as identifying and reviewing your competitors to understand what they offer and their strengths and weaknesses. This will enable you to find your point of difference. You need to do the initial research before you design or manufacture your first product, otherwise you may start off on the wrong foot by creating an unsuitable collection for the market.

Some designers think it would be too hard to do the research before designing the product, as they will not know what the exact product will look like, the price or the value of it. However, if you are thinking of starting a label, then you should have an idea of what you want to create, so your initial research is to understand whether there is a place in the market and a customer for your concept. As the brand develops you will continue to research and will be able to refine your range using direct feedback from customers, as well as the actual experience of what sells and what doesn't.

Your initial stage research should help you develop a general understanding of:

- How the market works.

- What motivates customers to buy?

- What problems customers want solving?

- What product attributes customers look for.

- How buying behaviours have changed.

- What the customer wants to experience during the buying journey.

This general research will help you identify where there are gaps in the market that you could step into, if there is a niche product you can develop to solve a particular problem or how you could offer your customer something new in their buying journey.

Types of Research — Primary and Secondary

To understand your market, your competitors, find out more about fashion consumers and identify your target customer, there are two types of research you can conduct, primary and secondary. Most start-up brands do not do enough research, either because they think they already know the market, are too keen to jump straight in, they may be lazy or because they think they can't afford to do it.

It can be costly to conduct research, but it is also easy to do a high level of research even if you have limited resources of time and money. It may cost your company much more in the long run if you don't do the research. Without the research you are likely to create the wrong product or will have no idea who the customer is and not know how to talk to or sell to them.

Don't make assumptions, as it is very likely that you will get it wrong. Observing customers in real life is essential for success, so go and do the research. You might be surprised at what you find out, or identify a gap in the market that you can develop a niche product for.

Primary Research

Primary research is often called field research and involves practical, observational research of customers in their natural environment, the stores. I am always shocked by the little amount of primary research designers and start-up brands do. If I ask them if they have been into the stores they say they want to be stocked in, most times they haven't. If they have been in, then they have not actually done any real research, just wandered around looking at the other brands in the shop. The research has to be focussed to gather the right information.

You can conduct primary research for your indirect customer (the store buyer), the store and the direct customer in the same way. Prior to starting your primary research, you should prepare a list of questions that you can use as prompts, to ensure you find all the answers you need.

Here are some examples of the types of things you should be looking for when you are doing your primary research in stores:

? What brands does the store carry?

? Is their product trend focussed or classic?

? What sizes does the store carry and how many of each product?

? What types of product does the store hold? Do they specialise in particular types of product, such as occasion or street wear, jackets or dresses? What types of colour and print do they carry? Do they focus on particular fabrics?

? What departments does the store have, such as contemporary, designer, international brands? What are the differences between the products in each department?

? What price points does the store carry? You will need to look at different product categories to have a good understanding of pricing across the store, as you may find some stores carry very expensive handbags but limit the prices on clothing.

? Who is the customer in the store? This means who is the actual customer, the person at the check out buying product in each department, as many stores have tourists or window shoppers wandering around and you need to identify the person who is actually buying product similar to yours.

? How does the customer move around the store? What do they stop to look at or touch? Do they read the tag, look at the price first or look inside at the finish of the garments? Do they wander round all the products or head straight to a particular brand?

? How are the garments merchandised and packaged?

? What are the customers wearing, what bags or carrier bags are they carrying?

? What type of customer service or in-store experience does the shop offer, such as shop assistants helping the customer, talking them through the product or explaining about the brand?

When you are in the store, also take advantage of talking to the shop assistants, as they are a valuable source of information on what works well in store and what customers look for. They can have invaluable knowledge about what customers say they want or like about different brands and also what products are most popular and why.

Start-up brands can also find great benefits from the primary research they get from hosting a focus group. This may sound daunting, but I have worked with many start-up brands that have tried this approach in quite a low-key way, yet derived huge benefit from it. A focus group can be something as casual as gathering together a group of your family and friends who could be potential customers. Invite people to join you for a focus group over a cup of tea or a glass of wine/beer and ask them questions about what they buy, why they buy it etc. Tell them that you are doing some research for your brand and would value their input. This has proved a really successful approach for some of the brands I work with, as the people who got involved in the focus group often proved to be their first customers. They also became great promoters of the label, as they felt a sense of accountability for the success of the business.

Secondary Research

Secondary research is often called desk research. In other words, you can sit at your desk and do it. There is a lot of information widely available that can help you with your research, such as:

Public sources — There is a lot of information that is available for free from government departments on industry statistics and research. Most libraries hold a lot of information that is free to access. Ask the librarian to help you to find up-to-date information that is relevant to your business in your area.

Commercial sources — It can be expensive to access commercial data from companies like Neilson, Mintel or financial institutions but sometimes on-line searches can provide a certain level of data for free. Financial companies like Experian gather big data on fashion consumers when they use debit and credit cards in store. This data can include demographics, types of product purchased, when they purchased, examples of average shopping trips, buying behaviours and profiling.

Educational institutions — Many fashion colleges have great libraries, which hold valuable information about the industry and brands. Again, the librarian can be really useful in helping you source appropriate research findings and documents.

With all these types of research, it is important to ensure that it is relevant and informative for your brand and not too generic so that it has no use.

Your online secondary research can also include checking to see what brands feature on online platforms, as well as the types of products they stock, as this can be very different from the product offer in store. You can also research your competitors' websites to understand their positioning, brand storytelling and product details, as well as research the physical stores they are stocked in globally.

One of the easiest and most successful ways of doing secondary research is through social media, which has opened up a new world of opportunities for start-up brands to understand their customers. Social media is a much more relevant approach to understanding consumer behaviour and many successful brands are now using the platforms as an efficient and effective research solution. Consumers now vocalise their opinions and thoughts openly on social media and are much more eloquent in sharing their feedback, likes and dislikes. Through platforms like Instagram and Facebook you have access to authentic information and insights into the demographics, geography, lifestyle, buying behaviour and brand loyalty of customers. You can also follow your competitors' social media accounts to understand how they connect and engage with their customers, learning from them what works best in images, hash tags and story telling.

I often joke with my clients that in order to run a successful business you have to learn to be a bit of a stalker! Call it stalking, research or social listening, you have to spend time really digging deep to find the information you need about your customers and competitors. You will not gain any advantage in the market by skimming over the research. Success comes from conducting intensive primary and secondary research to get an in-depth understanding of customers and competitors.

Direct and Indirect Customers

Fashion brands have two routes to market and two different customer groups, as they can sell through wholesale and/or sell direct to their customers.

Your indirect customer could be a store, an agent or a distributor. They are third parties who buy your product to sell to their customers. As a start-up fashion brand, you should have a really clear understanding of the needs of this third party, as well as the person they are selling to. You will need to research the store, what they sell and who their customers are. Stores are not all the same, nor do they have the same customer base. I often hear brands list a wide range of department stores and say they want to be stocked in all of them. This is not realistic! The stores will all have their own customer base and the brands and/or product they carry is different and they will be looking for brands that will help them attract their target customer.

Your brand can choose to sell direct to the customer through your own e-commerce shop or through pop up shops and events. Your direct customer is the person who will wear your garments and this is the customer that you really need to understand. You need to try to get inside their minds to find out what they buy and why, what types of brands they like and follow, as well as the type of content they engage with.

Initially, you need to target your research and focus on one or two customer groups, because you can't appeal to, or offer something to every customer. It is also likely that you do not have the resources to market your brand to different market groups or produce a big enough collection to appeal to all. It is much better to initially focus on finding your niche and target this specific group to develop a loyal customer base there first. It takes time to build a brand that can offer products to a wide range of customers from around the world, so you need to identify your one customer group and target them first. Then once that strategy is working, you can add in new customer groups to target. Working with different customer groups can be similar to the spinning plates trick at the circus, each plate is like a customer group and you have to work out a way to keep all the plates spinning. If not, one may fall as you focus on a different plate or group. As your business grows you will take on more people to help with keeping the different plates spinning.

It can be beneficial to your brand to focus on your local market first, as it is much easier to understand and connect with this customer and reach them than it is to work with an international customer that you may not understand so clearly. Once you have successfully sold to this local market, then you can grow your brand by scaling your business to reach out to new markets and customer groups.

Competitor Analysis

I will remind you again that it is essential to have an accurate understanding of your competitors. Competitor analysis helps you develop your brand with a point of difference. You need to look at your competitor's strengths and weaknesses and what makes them successful. This analysis will help you identify customer behaviours and gain insights into how brands and customers communicate and engage.

Through primary and secondary research, you can look at the competitor's product, quality, price, marketing and branding as well as who their customers are. Through research in stores or on social media, you can see who their customer is, what they like and comment on, which posts get more engagement and what the customers say. On their social media accounts, you can dig deeper by following through to their customer's own pages, to see what they talk about, their lifestyle and what other brands they follow. This can take time but it is really valuable research that gives you a very genuine insight into real customers, rather than basic generic classifications.

Your starting point for competitor analysis is identifying which brands to analyse. You need to find competitors of different sizes. Look at smaller and start-up brands as well as the more established larger, well-known brands. It can be challenging to find which brands to analyse, but that doesn't mean you don't have competitors. Your customer is already spending their money somewhere, you need to find out where.

Here are some of the basic steps to take in analysing your competitors:

1. **Identify your top ten competitor brands**
   As a fashion brand you will compete with thousands of other brands creating fashion product, but you need to refine the list of competitors to position your brand against to a manageable level. Look at indirect competitors such as the big-name labels as well as direct competitors, who will be other small, start-up brands. I would recommend as a starting point that you select ten brands that are your most realistic competitors.

   You can identify these ten competitors through primary and secondary research. You can check in stores to find brands that have a similar aesthetic, product, customer base and price point. On-line searches can help you refine the list of brands to ones that are your more direct competitors. Every brand has direct and indirect competitors and start-up fashion brands often make the mistake of only researching indirect competitors, which can lead them to building their business on a level of inaccurate research.

   Direct competitors will be brands that offer similar products and prices. They may also be emerging labels that have been established for a short time. These are more realistic competitors as they will be targeting the same market place as you, and will also be struggling with similar challenges, such as producing smaller quantities of product. Their prices will be more comparable and they will be in the same position of having limited brand awareness and a smaller customer base.

The larger, well-known labels will be your indirect competitors, but may become your direct competitors in the future. It is harder to compare your brand and prices with these larger labels as they have history, brand recognition, economies of scale in their production and established market share that you won't be able to compete with initially. Don't discount them as competitors but only include a few of them in your competitors list.

Indirect competitors also include any other place that your customer may spend their money and one of the biggest competitors for fashion is 'experience.' Many people now look to spend their money on activities that make memories such as eating out, travel, or spending time with friends and family rather than buying fashion. To appeal to this new type of consumer, fashion brands have to consider how to create experiences and not just sell product.

2. **Analysis of competitors' product and price**
   Once you have identified your top ten competitor brands, you need to analyse their product and price in detail. Your criteria for analysing the product includes the quality, uniqueness, design features, signature, finishing, fabrics, embellishments and hardware. Look for their size ranges, how many different stores carry each product, then try to anticipate how many of each product the brand produced. Finally analyse the price of the product and the pricing architecture of the brands full range, researching if the stores tend to carry particular priced products from within the range.

3. **Analysis of competitors customer**
   Using in-store primary research, or secondary research on the competitor's social media platforms, you need to research and analyse their customer. Do they seem to have a particular type of customer, does the customer live in a particular country, do they tend to be within a consistent demographic, do some of their customers engage more with the brand than others?

4. **Analysis of Competitors social media**
   On your competitor's social media platforms research what their customers are talking about, what they like, what they comment on, how they spend their time, the kind of language they use and what other brands their customers follow. You can also use social media to research brand sentiment and perception, analysing brand awareness and influence. There are numerous apps that

you can use to interpret data such as Hootsuite, BuzzSumo and Brandwatch, which can provide consumer insights on areas such as competitor content and product categories.

I would recommend creating a document that lists all the details of each competitor including their product, brand signature, services, customer profile, language, branding and hash tags. This document will be really valuable as a resource to refer to throughout the development of your branding and product.

Consumer Motivation and Buying Behaviour

The success of a fashion business relies on its ability to understand consumer needs and offer merchandise that will satisfy those needs. Too often, start-up brands are unaware of the fundamental principles of customer needs assessment, so they launch businesses that are destined for failure.

Many of the changes happening in the fashion industry have arisen due to the changing buying behaviours of consumers. Today's customer has access to a global market at the click of a button. They have access to more information than ever before about products and brands, and they can purchase product in numerous ways. This has led to a change in the relationship between brands and consumers, with the customer having much more control on what they want and when they want it.

One change has been that customers are moving away from shopping in brick and mortar/ physical stores. Many shops fail to deliver an 'experience,' so there is no incentive for the customer to visit and they choose instead to buy online. Online sales can lead to the brand and the customer becoming disconnected, resulting in less brand loyalty. It is easier to be distracted online by alternative offers or discounts. The online fashion market is very crowded and a brand needs to find unique ways to stand out to the customer.

Your brand must understand consumer motivations and buying behaviours to keep ahead of industry changes. If you understand what motivates a consumer to buy, then you can create the right product, present it in a way that appeals to the customer's motivations and ensures they buy your product rather than your competitors.

There have been several motivations identified which make customers buy fashion including:

- **Getting a Bargain**
  With so many sales happening continuously on the high street, the consumer now has become a bargain hunter, aware that the brands and stores will have sales and discounts so there is no reason

to pay full price. These consumers track products, seek discounts and follow the sales.

- **Standing Out from the Crowd**
  Some customers want to create unique looks that express their personality, so they seek statement pieces, or latest trend looks, that they can style in their own way. This customer is an innovator, wanting to buy fashion pieces before they become widely available or get copied by fast fashion brands.

- **Fitting in and Belonging**
  Many customers use fashion as a way of fitting in and belonging to a peer group. They are less confident in their ability to style their own looks, so seek guidance from the brand, peers and media to advise them how to put an outfit together. Peer pressure in dressing happens at all life stages, whether it is a child wanting to wear the same sneakers as all their friends, or the city worker who chooses to wear the same suit brand as his colleagues.

- **Trying to Avoid Clothes Shopping**
  Some customers don't enjoy clothes shopping, so either choose a 'uniform' such as jeans and t-shirts, or will want to shop quickly and easily. They will choose to shop in stores that offer a consistent style or shopping experience, such as John Lewis, Next or Gap.

- **Looking like a Celebrity**
  For young females, one of the biggest drivers for fashion sales over the past decade has been celebrity. Many brands take advantage of the power that celebrities and influencers have over young fashion by working with the celebrities on campaigns. Young consumers often want to buy fashion pieces that they feel will make them look like their favourite celebrity. The influence of celebrity has less impact on a mature consumer.

For all types of fashion product, three core motives have been identified as reasons that make consumers act and react in a particular way when purchasing, these are:

Rational   A rational motive is when the customer considers factors such as price, care, serviceability, practicality and warranties when making a purchase. If the customer has limited money, then they are likely to be more rational in their purchasing behaviour. They will ensure that they are spending their money wisely and either getting something at a good price or garments that will last well.

Emotional   Fashion purchases are often emotionally motivated. The customer seeks prestige, status, romance, and social acceptance that will come from their purchases. Fashion is usually promoted and merchandised on the basis of emotional appeal. Brands do this by creating stunning inspirational imagery, using celebrities in their campaigns or creating an inspirational in-store display to make the product look aspirational.

Patronage   Patronage motives relate to brand loyalty. A customer chooses to return to a particular retailer or store because they believe the company will offer them the best service, price, customer service, personal shopping availability, convenience, and product assortment. The more of these features a retailer or brand offers, the more likely it is that shoppers will return to the business in the future.

Consumer Analysis

Now that you understand the types of research and the basic consumer motivations, it is time to start analyse consumers in detail. It is imperative that you have a complete understanding of the characteristics of the marketplace in which you want to attract consumers. This includes analysing population shifts, market size, family status, nationalities, age groups etc. but you will need to do more than just research and find data. You need to analyse the information you gather, to ensure you choose to target appropriate customers for your brand. By studying people's lifestyles and attitudes, you will be able to get even closer to your target market.

The purpose of consumer analysis is to discover which customers are most likely to buy your products. If you understand what motivates your customer to make a purchase, what inspires them, how they will use the product and what benefits they seek from it, then you will know what to make and how to sell it to them.

Once you have a general idea of the fashion consumer through your primary and secondary research, you then need to segment them into groups. It is important to have as many details as possible and no aspect is irrelevant. The fine detail may make a difference in how your brand connects with the customer. As well as information on age, location and demographics, you also need to gather psychographic details including the customer's personality, lifestyle, attitudes and values.

In order to segment your customers, you should list all the characteristics of fashion consumers according to geography, demographics, behavioural and psychographics. Let me break this down into more detail:

Geography

Geography refers to where your customer is based, the country they live in, whether they reside in an urban or rural environment, in a hot or cold climate as well as their housing type and location. The purpose of this research is to confirm that your product is suitable for different climates and living conditions. Customers from different locations can have different needs, such as the customer who lives in a rural area is less likely to buy trend focussed product than someone who lives in an urban city.

Demographic

This is the simplest type of segmentation and sometimes the only one that fashion brands use, as they only look at their customer according to age. Demographics need to be more detailed than just age, so a brand needs to also group customers by gender, occupation, income, religion, nationality and race. Demographics will also include the life stage of the consumer, whether they are a dependant or have a family, as this impacts on the disposable income they may have. Marketing specialists define customers into generational groups such as Generation X or Y, the Millennial, Generation Z or Generation Next, which is the new consumer who shops for experience over product, and looks for authenticity and transparency from brands.

Behavioural

This segment divides the population by their behaviour in how they use the products and what benefits they seek from it. This could be used to divide customers who buy a lot of occasion wear, from someone who buys an occasion dress once every few years. This segment would also look at pricing consistencies, brand loyalty and volume of purchases.

Psychographics

Psychographic segmentation is really important in today's digital world, as this is the segment that will impact on how you connect and engage with your customers. Psychographics refers to lifestyle and buying behaviours. For this segment you need to consider what your customer does on a day to day basis, 365 days of the year, as well as the customers social aspirations, value perceptions, interests and hobbies, attitudes and opinions and their self image. Without this information your brand won't know what content to post on your social media, which celebrity to chose for campaigns or the style of aspirational imagery to create. I discuss the psychology of fashion in a section below, which connects to this area, as you also need to gather research on how your customer feels, their emotions and emotional triggers as part of your research.

Once you have segmented your customers, you will need to put them into groups whose members are homogenous in their behaviours and type. From these groups you will be able to determine that each segment is:

- **Distinguishable:** Defining each segment by the points that make them different from other segments.

- **Substantial:** Determining if the group is big enough to be worth focussing on.

- **Financial:** That the costs of targeting a segment will result in a positive return on investment.

- **Accessible:** That your marketing messages and content will result in positive engagement from the segment.

Targeting

Once you have identified all the segments, you next step is to decide which segments and groups you will target.

Many start up brands try mass marketing to reach consumers, trying to sell their products to a really wide market. This is not an effective strategy for any fashion brand, never mind a new one. Instead it is recommended that you consider niche marketing, where you target a specific, defined market with a product range that is the right design and price for them. Target one group only at the beginning, then as your brand grows you can include different groups of customers.

Creating Customer Profiles

From your research into your competitors and consumers you should now have a considerable amount of data to convert into consumer profiles for your target customer. The more data you have gathered the easier this will be.

You need to develop detailed written profiles for your ideal customer, one document that catches their key demographics, characteristics and lifestyle. This information will inform your product development and help you develop an effective marketing plan, which I will discuss in a later chapter.

Despite your primary and secondary research, you are not going to be one hundred percent sure on all the details, as your brand hasn't started talking to customers yet. You will have to make some assumptions, but you have to start somewhere. As your brand grows you will be able to develop a better understanding of your customer and then you can update your customer profiles to make them more accurate.

Using all your research, select and start to pull together information for your core target customer including their demographics, geography, behaviour and psychographic. This is not the time to be talking in generalities; your customer profile needs to be really detailed and specific. Give the customer a name, a specific age, a job, a lifestyle and the details of their life 24 hours a day, every day of the year. Identify and list the needs of this customer, such as the particular clothing they wear for work, hobbies or their lifestyle. Think about the other brands they buy, where they spend their disposable income. What magazines, music, celebrities and influencers do they like? You need to think about every small detail.

I have met many brands that build their consumer profiles around themselves, or declare they personally are the ideal customer, but this often leads to inaccurate assumptions about the brand and the product. It is essential to distance yourself from the brand and identify a real-life customer, based on the evidence you find in the stores or through the desk research you do. Be wary of drifting into creating fantasy figures with unrealistic lifestyles, as this will also hamper you from reaching authentic customers. The profile needs to be specific as you cannot appeal to everyone and without a targeted customer profile you will struggle to be heard in a crowded market place. With a targeted customer profile, you will be able to focus your activity on developing a loyal customer base rather than just chasing random customers.

On the following page is a brief example of a customer profile for a young, fast fashion customer for a high street womenswear brand.

Customer Profile 1

Gemma is a 20-year-old student who shops on a budget but likes to buy the latest fashion trends.

Gemma still lives at home with her parents and younger brother in a suburban area outside London. She is studying beauty therapy at the local adult education college and works part time in a bar at weekends. This job gives her some spending money.

A happy go-lucky girl constantly surrounded by friends, Gemma likes to go shopping every Thursday after college with one or two girl friends to buy herself a treat for the up-coming weekend. She is passionate about beauty and skin care and usually shops in Superdrug or Lush for beauty products every week and her favourite purchases are lipsticks and bath products.

For clothes Gemma looks in Topshop and River Island but rarely buys anything, as she feels she can find similar pieces elsewhere at a better price. She will always look in New Look and Bershka but her favourite shop is Primark. She likes to buy cropped shirts and t-shirts to wear with jeans for her bar job. She likes to constantly be seen in new things and this is the easiest and cheapest way for her to do it. When she goes out with friends she likes to wear playsuits or cropped tops and mini skirts. Gemma also buys lingerie and shoes in Primark but she aspires to buy designer shoes in the future. She rarely makes big purchases but asks family for birthday vouchers from Top Shop and River Island, and likes to shop their sales to get good bargains and always asks her mum to buy her nightwear for Christmas presents.

Gemma's biggest expenditure goes on beauty treatments at the nail bar or brow and lashes bar, but once she is qualified will be able to do these treatments herself.

Gemma rarely buys magazines but keeps up to date with fashion trends through sites such as Who What Wear and through Instagram influencers like Little Magpie. She loves reality TV programmes including Love Island and Towie and knows all the latest music through the DJs that play in the bar she works in. Her celebrity crushes are Kylie Jenner and Shawn Mendes and she likes to try and copy Kylie's style.

Gemma aspires to run her own beauty salon in the future, she is happily single at the moment but her dream is to be married and have a baby by the time she is 30.

This customer profile identifies many elements that a fashion brand could use to connect with Gemma and create product for her, such as her need for regular small fashion purchases, beauty products and the influence of the celebrity.

Your customer profile has to be very detailed, so that you can really envision the person who will want to buy your product and become a loyal follower of your brand. At the start of your brand you only want to create one or two profiles, as you will not be able to target lots of different customers, therefore make these profiles very specific. A more detailed profile will make it easier for you to develop a marketing strategy, brand storytelling and create content for your social media that will connect with this customer. Your customer profile will help you pinpoint the who, where and how to reach potential consumers interested in the product your brand will offer.

Psychology of Fashion

There is a growing interest in the psychology of fashion. Although at the time of writing this book research is still limited, there have been some works written about how fashion affects our psychology. Understanding consumer psychology is not a fad. It is essential for a brand to get inside the mind of their consumers and understand how to use emotional triggers to increase sales and build customer loyalty.

It is widely understood that what we wear affects us psychologically, affecting our mood and feelings of self worth. We know that some people may judge us on what we wear. These judgements may not be based on fact, or even be a conscious decision, they are usually an automatic snap judgement based on past experiences, education or familial upbringing. There is also some evidence that what we wear can impact on our success at getting a job, finding a mate and have an impact on other people's perceptions of us.

When people buy fashion, they are buying more than a product, they are buying into a dream or a lifestyle. I know there have been times in my life when I have bought dresses to impress a potential boss, a hot guy that I have fancied from afar or a statement piece to wow my friends. However, if I was unsuccessful, either in getting the job, winning the guys attention or worse yet my friends don't comment at all about my dress, then I no longer have positive feelings about that dress or the brand that made it. This might not be rational, but it is a realistic part of many customers' connection with a brand that the business may not be able to do much about. There are many areas, however, that your brand can work on to market your product to appeal to the customer psyche.

In the section about consumer motivations and buying behaviours earlier in this chapter, I mentioned that a lot of fashion is bought on an emotional basis and this is connected to the psychology of customers. Your customer makes decisions according to both conscious and subconscious emotional triggers, drawing them to products that make them feel an emotion such as self-esteem, satisfaction or power.

Our senses, sight, sound, touch, taste and hearing, play an integral part of our emotional processing, which impacts on what we buy. Brands need to consider these emotional triggers when creating their brand and product. Brands and stores that are moving towards experiential retailing, look at how they can appeal to the five senses, creating immersive experiences that generate emotional responses in their customers that then increase sales. A customer may think that they favour a brand because of the quality or price, but it is more likely that it is their emotional response, how they 'feel' about the brand that has a greater influence. If you want to appeal to your customer, you need to create an experience that makes them feel good, not just create product.

I will revisit psychology in the marketing and branding chapter, when I will discuss neuromarketing, which is a process of promoting a brand based on the psychological traits of a target audience. The research you have done as part of this chapter will help when we move to the marketing section.

Positioning

Once you have completed your consumer and competitive analysis, you will be able to decide which brands in particular to position yourself against, as well as focus on positioning your brand in the mind of your customer. From your research you should now have a good understanding of how to occupy a clear, distinctive and desirable place relative to competing products in the mind of the consumer.

There are several steps to the process of positioning how the customers perceive the product including:

- Understanding what a target customer expects from a product.
- Understanding what a customer feels are the most important points when deciding on a purchase.
- Understanding what your brands capabilities are for producing products that meet your customers' needs and expectations.
- Evaluating how your competitors are positioning their brands.
- Positioning your brand with messaging, brand storytelling and products that will resonate with your consumers.

A successful positioning occurs when the target customers find that the product or brand satisfies their expectations and desires.

Building the relationship

As it may have taken you considerable time and money to attract a customer, you will want to ensure that you can keep them. Your aim should be to create a close relationship to grow the lifetime value of your customers. This close relationship will improve the products that you produce, as you can respond to customer needs, as well as making your marketing and content development more effective.

Today's consumers are highly educated and cognisant, aware of poor products, cheap quality, mass production and fake advertising promises. There are many disenchanted consumers looking for more authentic, transparent brands that want to build genuine relationships with their customers. It is strong relationships with your customers that give you a competitive advantage in a saturated market. Good relationships result in lower customer turnover and higher customer satisfaction.

In a crowded market place, you will have to work hard to build affinity with your customer, as they have endless options and will always gravitate more to a brand that cares about and relates to them. You have to do more than sell them amazing products. You need to give them a great experience that makes them feel happy, satisfied and loved.

If you give your customers a great experience and stay connected with them, then they will remain brand loyal and also act as your biggest advocates. I always advise my clients that one happy customer makes another and word of mouth is your best promotional tool. Remember that the customer can also share negative experiences, which can be very damaging for brand awareness, as bad reviews tend to be more public.

Your aim, therefore, is to research your customer, find them, build and maintain the relationship, sell to them and continue to show them you love them! Over time your customers buying behaviours may change, so through on-going research you need to ensure you stay relevant to them and adapt to their changing needs.

Ongoing research

Research is not just for the start-up stage, a brand needs to continue to do research as it develops because the market, competitors and consumers do not stand still and will all change over time. Undertaking on-going research will make sure your brand stays healthy and help you identify opportunities and threats. I always recommend that a brand sets up the systems, from the beginning, to track changes and continually monitor customer's experiences, perceptions and brand awareness.

One of the easiest ways to set up on-going research is through Google Analytics. This free tool is one of the best resources to uncover trends, data, and insights about the consumers who are coming to your website and helps you continually improve and grow your business. Through Google Analytics you will be looking to find information on your dashboard such as:

- **Users**: You can choose to look at the people who have visited your site within a certain date range; these will include new and returning visitors.

- **Dimensions**: These are ways to view and segment qualitative data, describe who the users are, such as male, from London etc.

- **Metrics**: Metrics measure what the users do on your site, such as page views, average session time etc.

- **Bounce Rate**: This is the percentage of single-page visits, meaning that someone left your site from the same page at which they entered and didn't interact with your site.

- **Sessions**: A session is the period of time that a user is actively engaged with your website.

- **Traffic Sources**: Tracks where your users are coming from, such as direct by typing in your URL, through organic search, paid search through something like an Adwords campaign, email, social media or referral from another site.

- **Audience Profile and Demographics:** This section provides insights into your website visitors and can help you find out a bit more about them such as gender, age, location. This is essential research to see if the users match who you think your target customer is.

To increase your chance of building your brand and growing a consistent, loyal customer base, your ongoing research needs to include measuring brand awareness and brand perception. Measuring brand awareness will tell you if people know your brand. You can find this by monitoring your website traffic through Google Analytics as well as using Google Adwords Keyword Planner and Google Trends. With these tools you can check the number of searches for your brand name and keywords, as well as compare search terms or searches for your competitors against your brand.

You also need to measure brand perception, which will tell you what people think of the brand, your products and customer service. You can monitor brand perception through social listening. Using social listening tools such as Brandwatch, can help you track conversations around your brand, your competitors, keywords and phrases, understand sentiments and see if your customers are aligned with your values. By analysing social conversations, you will be able to understand what aspects of your brand or storytelling are working, or not working, with your target customer. You can then use these insights to increase positive brand perceptions.

Your research strategy can be as simple as asking your customers for feedback. Do not be afraid to ask your customer simple questions, but make them easy to answer and seek both practical and emotional responses. Asking your customer for feedback can lead to greater customer loyalty, as it shows that you care about their opinions.

As well as on-going research of your customer, you also need to continually review your competitors, as their brands won't be standing still. They will also be researching and adapting to customer needs. Over time some of your competitors may no longer be relevant as they pursue new customer groups, but there may also be new competitors who join the market. Your research strategy should include regular industry scanning to search for new brands and industry changes, as well as reviewing your competitors to see whether their brand has made any considerable changes.

Recap - Researching your customer and competitor

The success of your business relies on one thing, customers! You need customers who are willing to pay money for your products, but they will only buy products that meet their needs. You need to totally understand your customer, every small detail about them, in order to understand their needs and meet them. You also have to identify and understand your competitors to ensure that you build a brand with a point of difference, so that your brand attracts the customer instead of them. In the next chapters I will show you how you can use the information about your competitors and target customer to design your product range, create your brand and market your business.

If you haven't thoroughly researched your competitors and developed detailed customer profiles then you will struggle to build your business and make a success of it. So before you rush on to the next stage of your business development, make sure you have a clear strategy of how you will develop your competitors and consumer profiles.

Here is a quick recap of the steps you need to take:

- **Get out and about**
  You can't find all the information you need about your customer and competitors sitting in your studio. You need to get out and

about to do some primary research. It is really valuable to have first hand experience of watching the fashion consumer in their natural environment, the store. You can learn so much watching how they shop, which products they look at and touch, how they move around the store, what they are already wearing and what bags they are holding. You can also use visits to stores to research your competitors in depth, looking at their product range, quality, pricing, displays and branding.

- **Dig deep**
  You can find information on your competitors and consumers through secondary research, but you need to dig deep and analyse the data you find. There are lots of third parties who have researched the fashion market, brands and consumer behaviours and this information can be very informative. Your secondary research can also involve social media monitoring of your competitors accounts and their consumers to understand what they are talking about, care about and type of content they connect with.

- **Tap your networks**
  You can use your own networks to do your research, asking your friends and family about how they shop, what benefits they look for in products, how they feel about certain brands and what types of content they engage with. You can ask your own contacts to take part in simple focus groups, which can help you form your business.

- **Active looking and listening**
  Don't make assumptions or base your research on your own style or lifestyle, it is really essential that you start active looking and listening. When you are in the stores don't just wander aimlessly, set yourself some questions that need answering and be systematic in the type of information you gather about competitors and consumers. Get involved in social listening on social media platforms, to understand what people are talking about and how the customer feels about certain brands.

- **Create a detailed consumer profile**
  When you develop your consumer profile, make it very detailed so that you totally understand what your customer needs, cares about and aspires to. The fine detail will help you create the right product and content that will guarantee a loyal customer. Be specific in your profile, considering who this customer is and what they do 24 hours a day, 365 days of the year and include every detail about what they like, dislike, need and want.

- **Never give up**
  As you build your business you need to keep up the research, as the market is constantly changing and consumer buying behaviours change over time. In your business strategy you need to include on-going primary, secondary and social listening research into your plan. Your business will change as it grows and you will need to ensure that you are taking advantage of new opportunities, are aware of any threats and are staying relevant to your consumer.

Chapter 4 – Product design and development

In this chapter I will be sharing ideas on how to increase the chance of your designs selling, rather than trying to teach you to be a designer.

Many people who start their own fashion label have graduated from a fashion school or trained as a designer. However, there are also labels that are started by someone with no design experience at all. This person may have spotted a gap in the market, or identified a great concept for a brand, and then will hire a designer to bring their vision to life. Later in the chapter I will discuss how you find designers and the areas you need to consider when hiring one.

It is essential that a new brand designs a commercially viable collection, and doesn't get carried away creating pieces that are either unwearable or don't appeal to the brands perceived customers. The collection needs to sell, either by wholesale or direct to customer, but either option means the range must be cohesive, have a recognisable signature and meet the needs of an identified customer.

I always recommend that a designer conducts significant research before starting to design the collection. The research will include current and future trends, the zeitgeist, changing consumer demand as well as new technologies.

As the brand grows, the pressure to design and create more collections at faster speeds will increase. Therefore, for a start-up brand, it is worth taking time at the beginning to really refine your design aesthetic and determine your signature. These are elements that shouldn't be left to chance, as they will affect the success of the brand in the long run.

There are four areas of development in the design process, which I will discuss in the chapter:

1. Inspiration.
2. Development of trends, colour, shape, silhouettes and textures.
3. Developing the brands signature.
4. Creating and editing a range plan to satisfy the customer need.

I will also discuss how your selling strategy will impact on the collection you develop. You may need to produce a different collection if you are selling wholesale, on consignment and direct to consumer. Your selling strategy may determine whether you do a seasonal collection or use the drop model.

Inspiration

A question often asked is, when designing a collection where does the inspiration come from? For some designers the starting point will be the fabrics, but for others they will find inspiration from history, the current populism or arts, nature or music.

Inspiration can sometimes come from very random sources, but inspiration doesn't always come easily. I have found that many designers are inspired by travel destinations, local cultures and traditional crafts, but others struggle to find their own inspiration and seek ideas from other brands or designers.

It doesn't matter what you are inspired by, all great collections are the result of research. The research will help you investigate the idea, gather materials and images and set the concept. Detailed and in-depth research can lead you to discover a unique signature, discover your point of difference and can lead to market innovation.

As you conduct your research, you can start to bring elements together to create a mood board. This can include numerous elements such as:

- **Trends.** Looking at trend forecasts, determining which elements of the trends you will adopt.

- **Colour.** This can include the trend colours or a colour palette that connects with your inspiration.

- **Fabric.** Certain fabrics may inspire the collection, or you could be influenced by new sustainable or technical material options.

- **Construction.** The inspiration can come from different shapes or silhouettes, such as structure, tailoring, draping, and leisurewear.

- **Trims.** What trims, such as buttons, zips, lace etc. would add unique detailing to your collection?

- **Art.** Will you include prints or embellishments that add artistic elements to your designs?

The mood board is the next step in the design process to help you refine your concept and ideas. Once you are happy with the mood board, you will start to sketch the shapes and silhouettes of your pieces. These first sketches are quick ideas that will block the basic shapes and colours of the collection. This will help you determine which pieces to take forward for the final line up of designs.

The Customer

Many designers start designing, and sometimes even produce their collection, without thinking about their customer. I have always found it surprising that in the fashion industry so many products are created with no idea of who the customer is. In every other sector, a business would do it the other way round, they would identify a customer and what that customer wants, and then create the product for them.

The customer should be at the very core of your business, as a business without customers is not a business! It is a hobby! To build a fashion business without customers would be a very expensive hobby at that! There is often a perception in fashion that if you create an amazing collection then the customer will automatically come, but that is rarely the reality. Your brand stands more chance of success if you identify and understand the customer. The simple truth is, that no matter how amazing your designs, if the customer doesn't need it, want it or understand it, then they won't buy it.

I have covered how to find and identify your customer in Chapter 3, so if you haven't read that yet, go back and read it first.

As you start to design your collection, you need to know who you are designing for. Your collection won't be suitable for everyone. Fashion isn't a mass-market product like an iPhone or a can of beans, which can be sold to anyone whatever their gender, age, home country and meets a range of needs. Fashion is much more personal and the needs can be very different depending on age, size, shape, culture or desires.

Follow the guidance in Chapter 3 in identifying your customer and creating a consumer profile. Then as you design, you can consider if the product you are creating would be suitable. In the beginning you need to create a very specific target market to help you hone your collection. If you have a very broad customer target market, then you are likely to create too many different options and the collection won't be cohesive or appeal to individual customer groups.

Trend Forecasting

The fashion industry has historically been based on trends. Whether it is the latest checked cape, the white ankle boot or the velour tracksuit, suddenly the product is everywhere, compelling us to buy it. How is it that suddenly every store has the same product or trend? Did all the designers and brands suddenly have the same idea at the same time? Did they all get together and decide to go for the same thing?

This certainly doesn't happen, as brands are naturally secretive about their collection developments. They all have the same idea and create similar products because they are all exposed to the same influences and seek inspiration at the same time. The industry talks about these influences coming from numerous sources including the runway, street style, celebrities and influencers, history, cultural changes, and the leading fashion houses and capitals. This may be true in some ways, and was definitely true in the past, but with the speed of the fashion industry now it is a different matter.

The bigger brands normally buy into a subscription based fashion trend-forecasting platform. These agencies and platforms offer different levels of service depending on fee levels, but generally the information they provide is:

- Long term consumer trends.
- New and breaking trends.
- Reporting from catwalk shows and trade fairs.
- Street style coverage.

The trend-forecasting platforms provide information on trends 2+ years ahead, helping brands to enhance their planning and sourcing, ensuring they create relevant and profitable collections.

The leading fashion trend-forecasting agencies are major powerhouses, heavily leading the trends and the fashion industry. My personal opinion is that these agencies almost create a fear factor! Their approach is that you have to buy their service and follow their trends, or you will risk having a collection that won't be on-trend, commercially viable or press worthy. If you listen to the promotions from these agencies, they say that they will 'tell' you what trends are coming. It is obviously to their benefit to tell all their clients about the same trend, as this then reinforces their power. If they tell you 'this blue' is the blue of the season, then you know that you will be making pieces in the right trend colour. You will be safe in the knowledge that they will also have told your competitors that 'this blue is the blue of the season.'

The problem with these big trend-forecasting agencies is that now every brand and designer ends up creating the same or similar product. The brands are scared that if they don't buy into the trend service, then they will miss the key trends that all their competitors are working on. There is a reality too for an independent brand that if you don't follow the trend, then the store buyer may not buy and the magazines may not write about your new collection. The downside of all the brands buying into the same services is that everyone is now creating the same product. This is counterintuitive, as the brands have no point of difference, yet the consumer is demanding pieces that are new and different.

Trend-forecasting agencies can be very expensive and start-up brands rarely have enough money in their budget to buy into them. This leaves a brand with the challenge of considering how they manage their approach to trend forecasting. It is not something you can ignore. As a designer or a brand, you may have your own design aesthetic, however you also need to consider trend forecasting in order to understand what customers may be seeking, store buyers purchasing and magazines featuring in the coming season.

For your brand, you may decide not to follow the trends, or may choose not to create seasonal collections, but I would still recommend that you are aware of what the trends are. If you don't follow the trends, then you may choose to set them instead! Perhaps your brand will be a leader rather than a follower, or be a disruptor, shaking up the industry by innovating the way you create or market your product.

Whichever path you choose, you should still have an understanding of what is popular, what new opportunities and innovations are going to come on the marker and what is coming next. Therefore you still need to understand trend forecasting.

Another element of trend forecasting to consider is how trend-focused is your customer? Customers can buy into trends at different times, and you need to determine if your customer is:

- **An innovator.** Someone who is a bold leader in fashion, looking for something before anyone else gets it and not scared to challenge perceptions of what is in fashion.

- **An early adopter.** Someone who buys into a trend early, having had some knowledge about it. This person can be influential in helping the trend spread further.

- **An early majority.** Someone who buys into the trend as it starts to appear all along the high street and everywhere in the media.

- **A late majority.** Someone who doesn't buy into the newest trends and fashion and takes their time to accept new ideas.

- **A laggard.** Someone who would say they don't buy into trends at all. Someone who may dress in classic pieces that last for years and rarely buy new trend-focused clothes.

Having decided how trend-focused your customer is, you now need to find out information on the upcoming trends without having access to a trend-forecasting agency. For a start-up brand to take trend-inspiration from the street or a catwalk show for example, then it can be too late, as by the time you source the fabric, book your manufacturer and get the product to market the trend may have finished. A brand therefore has to make sure it works on the trends at the right time.

One easy way to research and identify upcoming trends in fabric, colour, print and embellishment, is to attend the big fabric fairs. When you attend the trade fairs you will see that most of the suppliers have the same 'blue' at the front of their stall, or that lots of companies have unicorn prints highlighted for example. The fabric suppliers will also have bought into the trend-forecasting services, as they need to provide the trend colours and fabrics that the brands need.

Other research can include following very trend focused brands that are a season or two ahead. You can also follow the new travel destinations that everyone is going to, or have awareness about political climates, global, social and cultural changes and trends. There are also many free industry blogs and newsletters that write features and posts on upcoming trends.

Trend versus Classic

It can be very difficult for a start-up brand to compete with the high street on introducing new trends. Smaller more luxury brands now work months behind the mass-market ones. There is also a change in the demands of the fashion consumer who is now looking for more sustainable, timeless product rather than fast throw away fashion. This customer will not buy into trends that could quickly look dated, instead opting for more quality, timeless, classic styles that will be worn for years to come.

As trends can be very risky for start up brands, my recommendation is to always act on the side of caution. If you get the timing or the trend wrong, then there maybe a chance you won't sell anything from the collection.

Therefore, I recommend that brands introduce elements of a trend rather than fully engaging with it. This can be done by adding spots of the trend colour or only creating a small percentage of trend pieces within the collection. You will then have a larger percentage of your classic or core design pieces to sell if you have mistimed it.

Many start-up brands now create really strong classic, core or basic ranges within their collections and these often prove to be the strongest sellers. Your core collection would be in classic colours such as black, navy, white or grey and would be more classic silhouettes and shapes that have longevity. With these pieces you have no time pressure to sell, so could still be selling them for years to come.

Seasonal collections

I have identified in Chapter 1 that seasonal collections no longer make sense for many fashion brands.

There have been many global changes that have affected or should affect how and when fashion is produced. These changes include:

- Weather changes mean there are no guarantees anymore when the weather will be hot or cold. A customer may want a warm coat one day and the next day a sundress.

- Customers are now international travellers so they need different clothing at different times.

- Changing consumer demand that means if they see a collection they want to buy it now, no longer prepared to wait for months for it to arrive in store.

- Overproduction, which is creating a huge environmental impact. This is often due to seasonal collections being produced but not sold within the limited time frame, and then having to be disposed of because the next collection is due in store.

- A smaller brand that creates seasonal collections will have very limited time to try and build relationships with stores and sell the collections before the end of the buying period. Many start-up brands have not even started to sell their collection before the season is over and they have to move on to the next one. This is not an economically viable way to grow a business.

- Consumer interest in more sustainable, timeless collections rather than seasonal trend focused garments.

- Seasonal collections lead to seasonal sales. The consumer is now savvy that if they like a new season piece, they just need to wait a couple of months or a few weeks and the product will be marked down in the seasonal sale. So customers are now tracking products and waiting for discounts.

Seasonal collections are necessary if a brand wants to wholesale their range to stores. As stores are still working on seasonal collections, they will want to work with a brand that produces exciting new collections for them each season. This puts the brand and the designer under huge pressure to design and produce a new range every six months, this can be very difficult for a small brand with limited cash flow and few resources including team and time.

More and more brands are moving away from the traditional seasonal collections and using the 'drop' model. This model is based on small production runs or capsule collections that are dropped monthly.

There are many benefits of the drop model including:

- Small production runs to avoid overproduction and also help cash flow.

- Regular drops of new product encourage the consumer to regularly visit your website or shop, as there is always something new.

- No need to have a 'sale' as the product is core product and not seasonal, so the brand doesn't have to have an end of season sale. Discounting devalues a brand, so this is a good way to avoid it.

- Limited edition, small production runs incentivise the consumer to buy now before it goes.
- The drop model offers stronger 'sustainable' storytelling, as your brand is not following the seasonal, throwaway model, instead creating pieces with a longer life span than a season.

There is one final bonus of moving away from seasonal collections and that is about protecting a brand's intellectual property. In the old model, when collections were shown during the fashion week season but then didn't appear in the stores for six months, it meant the fast, mass market fashion brands could take ideas from the catwalk and quickly flood the market with copies. With the 'see-now buy-now' model, or the drop model, there is no opportunity to copy, as the brand instantly has their product available.

Sustainably focused design

There are an increasing number of customers who seek brands that offer sustainable products and transparency in how products are made. Today's customer is much more knowledgeable about sustainable fabrics, ethical working conditions and the impact of fashion and overproduction on the environment.

Your start-up fashion label should consider sustainability as a core part of your business development. It should be embedded in your business model and be part of the brand DNA, rather than using sustainability as a marketing tool. As you develop the business, you can provide transparency by taking your customer on the journey with you, as you develop the design, sourcing and manufacturing steps of taking your product from concept to consumer.

Even in the design process you can use strategies and techniques that offer more ethical and sustainable practices in your business. These can include:

Zero Waste
Zero waste is a design process that eliminates fabric waste at the design stage. This technique means that you will use your textile effectively creating a cutting ticket, a bit like a jigsaw puzzle, that uses all the material. Zero waste can also be achieved in your designs by including the use of any surplus fabric to create buttons, pockets, trims, edging and smaller goods etc.

Upcycling
Upcycling includes transforming materials or waste products into something new. Brands are upcycling all kinds of materials to create their collections and this can save energy, water, chemicals

and other resources. Other brands are upcycling dead stock fabric from factories and mills, or using vintage clothing to make new fabrics.

Multi-functional

This approach involves creating garments that are multi-functional, reversible or can be transformed into a different piece, making it wearable in more ways, so that the consumer can buy fewer pieces.

Timeless Design

Timeless designs or slow fashion refers to the design of classic pieces, ones that are not trend focused instead designed for longevity. Some slow fashion brands say they are now designing pieces that can be treasured for years to come, creating future heritage pieces. Consumers looking to buy slow fashion garments seek to buy timeless pieces that with care would last for years and be pieces that they would in time either repair, resell, update, recycle or upcycle.

Circular fashion

Incorporating circular fashion into your brand DNA involves designing, sourcing and making garments with the intention that they will be used for as long as possible and then returned safely to the biosphere when they no longer have human use. A brand would need to consider designing pieces that have longevity and are created from sustainable fabrics and trims that can be repaired, redesigned, swapped, rented or at the final stage returned to the earth without creating damage to the planet.

As a start-up brand, you should be considering all these elements, along with seeking more ethical fabrics and manufacturing, to ensure your brand can offer full transparency to your consumer in the future.

Your signature

In a fashion market that is full of product, many brands are creating the same or similar product with very little to differentiate it other than price. As a start-up brand you don't want to end up in the same position, creating the same product as everyone else. In order to stand out and have a point of difference, a brand needs to have a signature. I advise start-up brands that without a signature they are just producing product. This product has to compete against the product that the thousands of brands out there are already making. If you are just creating product, you have very limited chance of success.

Developing a signature style for your brand will help it stand out and helps you develop brand awareness with the consumer. Many people in the industry talk about brands always needing to create new and different products each season. This is not the best approach for an emerging brand looking to find a place in an over populated market. A strong signature is what will make your brand stand out and bring the customer back to you time and time again.

Great examples of strong brand signatures can be found at luxury brands, such as the Burberry trench, the Chanel jacket, the Maison Martin Margiela stiches or the Louboutin red sole to name a few. With these brands, the signatures vary between those like Louboutin who include the signature in every piece, or Chanel and Burberry whose signature is a statement piece, which is replicated, with slight adjustments, in every collection.

In the beginning, a signature needs to be more than your brand name or logo, as this has no brand value until you become a better-known name. The signature needs to be something that will always be present in all collections. Then in the future it will be identifiable without the consumer having to look at the label.

I advise brands that if they do not have a signature, then they are not ready to launch their businesses. Without a signature you have nothing that will make you stand out.

This signature can be an element that runs across every piece, or a statement piece that you will repeat in each collection until it becomes your iconic, signature piece in the future.

A strong signature will:

- Make your brand unique and differentiate your product from the hundreds of others out there.

- Build a buzz around your brand that connects with your target consumer.

- Help to create a community, as your signature can have an emotional connection with your customer and help you build a tribe of loyal followers.

- Add value to your product outside of your brand name and encourage sales.

Too often, start-up fashion brands try to create a bit of everything in their first collections and try to satisfy the needs of lots of different customers. This usually fails in its attempt and all the different pieces just detract from the brand's signature. This makes their collection end up looking like all the others. Greater success will come from developing a small capsule collection with a strong signature that is instantly identifiable.

When trying to find your signature, you may need to play around with various design elements, such as a bold print, a particular fabric or trim, a unique silhouette or design feature, a way of blocking colour, embroidery or embellishment, or a unique customisation. Whatever you decide on, it needs to be a one-of-a kind element that makes your brand stand out.

Product Development

Bringing your ideas to life is a huge task for every emerging designer and one that can seem mysterious, as if it is some insider secret that you just can't access. As a designer or brand owner, product development is the process you have to go through to realise your ideas into actual products that appeal to and meet customer needs.

Many designers create a full collection, or detailed range plans, without thinking of each product as an individual item on its own. However your customer is likely to only buy one product at a time, therefore each product needs to offer your customer a unique experience and value, whether it is a simple top or a statement coat.

Product development can easily become complicated, so it is important to take time to plan each product carefully. Before you take your pieces to a manufacturer, you need to ensure you have a concrete idea of what you need each piece to look like, the quality, style and functionality or you risk the end result not meeting your needs.

Each garment in your range needs to be reviewed to ensure it meets your targeted customers requirements, such as fabric, colour, cut, style and design details.

Emerging designers often struggle with the realisation that their product is very expensive, due to the smaller minimum order quantities from suppliers and manufacturers. A brand may then attempt to lower their prices to match their competitors but are unable to achieve the right price point without crippling their profit margins. I always advise brands to stop looking at lowering their price, instead looking at increasing their perceived value, so that the consumer doesn't query the price. When you are designing the product and your range, you should add elements that increase the perceived value of your product.

Total Product Concept

A brand can increase the perceived value through adding in elements from the total product concept. This is a process that is used to design all kinds of products but is just as relevant for fashion.

A brand can increase the perceived value through various steps:

- Unique design elements.
- Colour, fabrics and trims.
- The quality of the workmanship.
- The functionality of the garment.
- Sustainability and transparency.
- Unique features and brand signature.
- The brand story telling.
- Experiential packaging such as scented tissue papers or thank you notes.
- Good delivery terms.
- Any elements of customisation or personalisation of products.
- Any warranties or after sales services such as care, cleaning or repairs.
- Credit terms.

The more tangible and intangible elements that a brand introduces into their product, the more it will encourage the customer to pay the extra, as they perceive the product to be of greater value. Each brand needs to determine how many extra benefits and values they need to incorporate into their products to meet the needs and desires of their customer. For a start-up brand, as their name isn't recognisable and has no perceived value on its own, then they may need to add in more values to appeal to the customer.

The Range Plan

Developing the full range of pieces you will have in a collection takes careful planning. You need to decide on the type and number of pieces you will develop dependent on your selling strategy, budget and the consumer's need.

I am constantly asked how big a collection should be for a start-up brand? This can depend on the budget you have or the type of pieces you are creating, but a start-up brand should no longer be creating and manufacturing a big 24+ look collection. It is better to focus on creating 6 amazing looks that have a strong signature and point of difference. There are some new brands that create one amazing distinctive piece and build their business on that, with a few options in colour or size as a starting point. Other brands create a 6-12 look collection but don't release it all in one go, instead 'dropping' in new pieces each month to inspire the consumer. This can be a good model for a start-up brand as it helps to drive your customer back each month to see what new pieces have launched. Smaller collections and regular drops can also help you manage your cash flow, as you don't have to put a whole collection into manufacture in one go.

The collection needs to be easily merchandised. When the products are displayed they need to look cohesive, exciting and entice the customer to buy. The main thing that your range plan should do is to tell your story. Across the collection you should be able to see the story of the range by seeing elements of the same colour, shape, fabric or print appear across the collection. For example, to tie a collection together a print fabric could be used in a full piece, as well as a trim, pocket or belt on a block colour item. This makes the product easier to merchandise, makes it look more cohesive, as well as appealing, with the added bonus of it offering a way to work towards zero waste.

Your signature should be easily identifiable in the range and you should ensure you are offering a consistent product range every season that the customer will recognise as your brand. If you create a strong range of products that are good quality, great fit and value for money, then your customer will return to the brand again to buy more pieces.

Your range plan should be drawn out before you purchase fabrics or make pieces. This will help you ensure that the collection is cohesive, has a strong brand signature, you have used fabrics efficiently and the collection can be beautifully merchandised both on your website, as well as in a store.

A range plan needs to consider numerous elements as detailed below:

- **Cohesive**

  The consistency of the quality and presentation of your collection is what will make your brand stand out and will set you apart from the competitors. A cohesive collection is one that looks great on the rail, all the pieces make sense, that the colours and prints work well together and the range can be easily merchandised. One weak piece or conflicting colour garment can throw off the whole rail, making it look cheap, incoherent or detract from the brand signature.

- **Signature.**

  As identified above, the signature of your brand is crucial for success, as this makes you stand out from your competitors and gives you a point of difference. The signature should be always present and easily identifiable within the collection. When drawing out your range plan, you need to check that the signature, or signature piece, will stand out and be instantly recognised.

- **Range width.**

  The width of a collection refers to the number of different styles you are offering. A more established brand may have a collection width of 100 pieces, but this is unfeasible for a start-up brand. Many start-up labels start with 6-12 styles initially to test the market, and then their collection will grow as they get more established. If you are creating separates, you will need to ensure you have a balance between tops and bottoms in your collection.

- **Range depth.**

  The depth of your collection refers to the variations you offer. This could mean that you have one style but produce it in different colours, prints or fabrics. Emerging brands need to be wary of offering too many variations within a collection, as this can make it lose the cohesiveness and it could look messy on the rail when you are merchandising it. Most small brands create a signature piece in one colour way or fabric as a limited edition piece and then offer the same piece in another colour or fabric in the next drop.

- **Pricing Architecture**

  Within your collection you need to ensure that you have a realistic pricing architecture. This means not having lots of pieces at a lower price and then one really expensive piece, or the other way round. For example it makes no sense to have 10 pieces at around £100 and then 2 pieces at £700. There needs to be gentle increments between your prices.

It is also likely that you will offer more options on pieces at the lower end of your price range, such as 6 colours of shirt, as you would hope to produce more of these so you could warrant the expense of different fabrics. Whereas an expensive dress may be only offered in two colours, as you will sell less and it would not be cost effective to offer too many fabric options.

- **Balance editorial v commercial**
  It can be very beneficial to have a statement 'WOW' piece that draws attention to the brand. This may not be a commercial piece, but one that gets attention from press, buyers and customers and gets people talking about the brand. The statement piece draws the customer in, but then they are likely to buy more commercial pieces, therefore you need to have a balance in the collection of creative, impact pieces with more wearable and saleable ones.

- **Hero Product**
  It can be a commercial advantage for a brand to have a hero product, the bestseller that showcases your signature style and holds the collection together. The hero product is the one that is the well-known instantly identifiable signature piece that frequently draws the customer back to your brand. A hero product may take a while to develop, as it will be based on customer desire and feedback.

- **Sizing**
  When designing a collection, the brand normally creates the collection around a 'sample size' or 'fit model.' However you also need to consider the sizes of your actual customer and whether this design will work the same for them. One size does not fit all. Customers from different continents have different body types, shapes and sizes, whether that is around height differences between many European and Asian customers, or an older customer who may want longer sleeves or hem lines.

The best way to ensure that you have a cohesive and realistic range is to create a template that details the total number of pieces you will make. This template will include each of the styles with fabric, colour options and estimated price points. A good template will help you ensure that you are making efficient and effective use of fabrics and styles and that you will be creating a balanced collection.

Style	Red cotton	White cotton	Black cotton	Horse print	Floral print	Black jersey	Grey jersey	Total option	Est. RRP
Shift dress				X	X			2	£150
Midi dress	X		X					2	£120
Maxi dress	X		X					2	£175
Mini dress	X		X	X	X			4	£120
Shirt with collar		X		X	X			3	£90
Sleeveless shirt		X		X	X			3	£75
Mini skirt	X		X			X	X	4	£70
Midi skirt	X		X			X	X	4	£95
T-shirt						X	X	2	£55
TOTAL	5	2	5	4	4	3	3	26	

Once you have created the template, you should then review it to make sure that you have made efficient use of all fabrics to limit your costs and risks. In the example above, you may decide that only making two pieces out of the white cotton may not be a good decision, particularly if you have to purchase a high minimum order quantity of that fabric.

It is also time to review the size of the collection and whether it is feasible and sensible to put it all into production. If the collection is too large, or not cohesive, then it can be disastrous. Too many brands don't realistically consider the cost of buying all the different fabric options, or putting a large collection into sampling and then production. I see many designers and brands that blow their entire budget on creating a large collection, but then have no money left to market it.

A designer needs to be strong and be prepared to edit their designs, cutting back on any pieces that are weak or don't fit with the rest of their collection. Designing a strong commercial collection is not the same as creating a personal wardrobe. When the range ends up on a rail it needs to clearly show the signature, the core product and the point of difference. Editing the collection is as important as designing it.

Developing your range for wholesale

A designer often wants to design a large collection with a range of detailed and conceptual pieces, but if you want to see your brand stocked in a well-known retail store then you need to create collections that they can sell. The first part of the process of designing for wholesale is to research and understand the type and style of product the store carries, who their customer is and the price points they offer. You need to consider how the store would merchandise the product, which means them having a range of styles that look cohesive and will appeal to their customer.

When designing your range plan, you need to consider your selling strategy and whether you will be able to deliver orders to wholesale buyers under their terms. Wholesale store buyers now usually want to take on newer brands on a consignment or sale or return basis. This means that the brand has to cover all the costs of buying their fabrics and trims, paying their manufacturers and shipping the goods to the store and then wait for sales to be made before they get any money back. This means that you have to be completely sure that you can afford to make all the options you are offering to the store.

It might be more astute to carefully plan the range you would offer to a wholesale buyer looking for consignment, to ensure you don't cripple your cash flow in the process. The range for consignment orders should not include too many trend pieces, as you risk being stuck with out-of-date stock if the store can't sell it. You would also want to limit the more complex construction or more costly to produce pieces, as these would also damage your cash flow. You need to think about a piece that may get damaged whilst on the shop floor that then doesn't sell, so garments on consignment shouldn't be too delicate or easy to damage.

A final consideration would be, can you offer an exclusive range to a store to incentivise them to purchase from your brand. Stores will look to have exclusive product that their competitors aren't selling, as a way to ensure customers visit them first. A big brand will have larger collections with broad depth and width, which means a buyer can make an exclusive selection from within the range. This isn't possible for a small brand, but you can still offer a store buyer an exclusive by offering them pieces in a particular style or colour that would unique in their territory for them.

Developing your range for direct to consumer

When developing a range for direct to consumer, there are also considerations on the type of product to create that will increase sales and manage costs. If you are going to sell direct to consumer, then you need some inventory that you can sell through your website, pop-up shops or trunk shows. Many brands used to avoid this model, as they thought they had to carry huge quantities of stock and they didn't have the cash flow to be able to produce this. There were also concerns that if they didn't sell products then they had to discount them heavily. These problems can be avoided with careful management and good product.

The same as with wholesale, when designing the collection for direct-to-consumer you need to consider the costs of producing the stock. You will need to manage your cash flow and plan on producing simpler, more cost effective pieces. Many of the brands I work with will make small product runs of 10-20 of a style and then when it sells through introduce a new piece, or the same piece but in a different colour or print.

A big consideration when selling through your own e-commerce website, is the type of product that sells best. You need to limit the number of returns that you will get, and there are always greater returns if product is very tailored, sizing and fit is incorrect, and the product is poor quality. When designing collections for online sales you will need to consider these elements, research what type of products are selling best online and then ensure your product is the best quality and fit.

On your own e-commerce website you have the potential to sell a very strong curated collection that promotes your signature and brand story telling, that engages with the consumer and invites them into your brand's lifestyle.

Hiring a designer

If you are starting a brand but are not a designer, then you will need to hire someone who will be bring your ideas to life.

When looking to hire someone, you should consider the following questions and decide what important skills you are looking for: -

> ? What budget do you have?

> ? Do you want someone full time or freelance?

> ? Research the type of experience you should look for?

> ? Have they had experience of designing the kind of product you are planning on making?

> ? Do they have sewing skills and can they make samples and toiles?

> ? Can they use design software such as CAD?

> ? Do they have good fabric knowledge?

> ? Do they have relationships with suppliers and manufacturers?

The ways to find a designer can vary but you can use recruitment companies, ask for referrals, talk to design schools, or approach small brand designers you like to see if they take on independent freelance work.

It is worth hiring the best designer you can afford, and not recommended to hire someone cheap. Your whole fashion business is reliant on great product, so you need a good designer to create this for you. An experienced designer can do more than sketch out your ideas, they may also be able to create all your technical documents, advise on fabrics and trims, understand the industry and also have connections with suppliers and manufacturers. An inexperienced designer may have great ideas but they could cost you more money if they make mistakes due to lack of experience.

Once you have decided on the person you want to hire, make sure you have very clear contracts and also a signed non-disclosure agreement to protect your brands intellectual property and to ensure any designs created belong to your brand not the designer.

Final top tips on creating a commercial collection

1. Do you really understand your customer and know the person that you are designing product for? Research your target market in detail.

2. How are you going to sell your product? Your sales strategy will affect what you design, the product range and when you will create new collections, such seasonal or using the drop model.

3. What is your signature? Have you developed a strong brand signature that will make your collection and brand stand out from all the competitors?

4. Plan on your product niche. Don't try to create every type of product for every type of customer. In the beginning you should concentrate on one product category and one customer base.

5. Don't create too large a collection that would affect your cash flow and limit your chance of success. Focus on developing a small capsule collection that stands out as being cohesive, with a strong signature and clear brand story telling.

6. Do more research than you can possibly imagine before you design anything. You need to make sure you are not duplicating what is already out there and know that you are taking advantage of new opportunities, fabrics, trends and ideas.

7. Review each individual product to make sure it meets customer need, expectations and desires.

8. Don't buy any supplies until you have finished your range plan and considered the efficiency of fabric use in your range.

9. Edit, edit, edit! Just because you came up with idea or drew the design, doesn't mean it should be in the collection.

10. Look at how you can add value into every product to create an amazing brand experience.

On my website www.startyourownfashionlabel.com you can find more resources and information, such as how to sell to wholesale buyers, and templates including range plans, line sheets and a non-disclosure agreement.

Chapter 5 — Sourcing, Manufacturing and Fabrics

If you have finished designing your collection, you will now be at the point where you should be looking to source your materials and manufacturing. In reality many brands start off by sourcing their fabrics first, as they find that a certain fabric or trim inspires them and this acts as the point that kick-starts the design process.

My recommendation to all start-up brands is to refrain from purchasing bulk supplies until after you have finalised and edited your range plan. If you purchase all your fabrics in advance, then you risk overspending on materials that you may not use in the final collection.

After months of thinking only about designs, your signature, colours, textures and trends, you now have to switch your thinking to the more business focussed and challenging element of finding and working with suppliers and manufacturers. Planning and managing your production process is vital.

It is a well-known fact in the industry that sourcing manufacturers and suppliers is a problem for all fashion brands, yet the challenges often take designers and start-up brands by surprise. Sourcing is a much more difficult task than it sounds, and is likely to be a headache throughout your brands journey. It unfortunately does not get any easier the bigger you become, there are always new challenges to face in finding more or different suppliers and manufacturers as your business grows.

Sourcing Strategy

Before you start talking to suppliers and manufacturers there are some primary questions to ask yourself, then you will be sure you are looking for the right partners and suppliers.

? How much do you have to spend to bring your products to market? Set yourself a budget and don't blow all your money on your first collection. You will also need money for marketing and selling, and it may take time for the first collection to start to sell.

? What do you want the end product to look like? The type of fabric and quality of finish you need for your product will determine whether you can sell in the luxury or fast fashion markets. For example, does your product need to be created in silk or natural fibers, or have French seams or over locking? The higher price the product, the more detail you need to pay to these elements to ensure you meet the customer's needs and expectations.

? What is the timeframe you need to work to? You should work out when you need fabrics by and how far in advance you need to book your manufacturer. Small labels usually need to book their manufacturing slot six months in advance. How long will you need to deliver production orders to a store? You have to create a critical path/ timeline to ensure you stay on track and that all the different elements of ordering supplies and manufacturing product are executed efficiently.

? What is your strategy to find reliable, high quality suppliers that fit your requirements such as budget, personality, location, skills and minimum order quantity?

? What is your sustainability policy? Will you seek sustainable and ethical suppliers and manufacturers? How can you track your processes to offer transparency to your customer?

? Do you understand the logistics of shipping fabrics and goods around the world? There are many elements to logistics, including tracking your purchase orders, customs clearing, quota numbers and containers? Many designers run into problems, as they don't understand the laws around international shipping, don't know about different labels or paperwork requirements, and have no idea where to go for support.

? Last but not least, how will you keep track of your finances? You need to develop a strategy that deals with your payment terms and requirements. You will need a cash flow forecast to ensure you don't run out of money at a critical time, such as getting your product from the manufacturer. Most start-up fashion businesses find it impossible to get credit terms from suppliers, so you will need to carefully consider your cash flow as well as the payment terms you offer on wholesale orders.

I will cover many elements of these questions in the following sections of this chapter.

Local versus Global

As you start to develop your strategy, one of the first areas to consider is whether you will work with local suppliers and manufacturers in your own country or source your supplies from global ones.

There are pros and cons with both options and it will be up to you to determine which option is best for your business and best suits your brand's resources, time and ethics. With more focus now on developing conscious collections and ethical production standards, it has meant more brands are seeking suppliers and manufacturers in their local market.

If you are based in Europe or the USA, then it is likely that your local suppliers and manufacturers offer higher quality product. However, it can be more expensive to work with your local market. Working with local suppliers can be part of your brand storytelling, which can help justify the higher price. Another benefit of working with local suppliers is that you can reduce shipping and production times, and also have better control of the production process. If your suppliers and manufacturers are local, then you can easily check on their working conditions, communication can be better as you speak the same language, and you can visit them to ensure you stay on schedule. The downside of local, as well as the higher cost, is that it can be difficult to find companies to work with. The good companies may have limited capacity, so might not be looking to work with new start-up labels.

Once you start your label, you are likely to be bombarded by international manufacturers who want to partner with you. Most of these suppliers will be based in China, India, Vietnam and Cambodia etc. These manufacturers can usually offer you much lower prices but there are disadvantages to this. The lower prices are usually dependent on high minimum order quantities, which are unrealistic for start-up brands and could lead to damaging over-production issues. The overseas manufacturers often produce much lower quality products, may not offer ethical working conditions to their employees and there would be longer shipping times. In addition, one of the biggest issues is that, unless you stay in the country during the manufacturing process, you may lose communication, have no idea of what is happening, or know where and how your product is actually being made. These disadvantages mean that the initial lower cost may not be an advantage. It may end up being costlier to produce, if the result is a poor-quality product, or you have to visit the manufacturer to sort out issues.

Finding fabric and trim suppliers

Having decided whether you will be looking for suppliers and manufactures locally or globally, your challenge will now be finding them. Designers who are struggling to find suppliers regularly approach me to ask where they go to find them. They often express shock that they are not getting answers from companies they have reached out to, and have been unable to find recommendations from other designers.

You need to find reliable fabric suppliers who will offer good quality materials and trims, and supply the goods in the quantity and time you need. If you are going to wholesale to stores, then it is essential that you find suppliers who can guarantee the stock you need. Store buyers will not accept changes to fabric and trim after orders have been placed.

Sourcing your fabrics and trims can be overwhelming and time consuming but finding the right ones can improve the profitability of your brand. As a start-up brand you will be looking for low minimum order quantities, a good variety of materials, the ability to re-order if necessary and the opportunity to get fabric swatches without paying a fortune for them. You can find fabric and trims through numerous ways including retail, jobber, fabric importer, converter and mill.

Retail

A mistake start-up designers often make is purchasing their first fabrics from a retail store or market. Although this means that they can buy a small quantity, it is not an efficient way to purchase suppliers. Through a retailer you will usually pay much more for the fabrics and trims, but this also means that you usually cannot replace the materials once the store sells out.

Wholesaler

There are wholesalers where you can go to buy different quantities of materials, some may only consider high minimum order quantities, so you need to find ones who work with smaller quantities. Some wholesalers sell 'stocked' fabrics, such as silks, lace or cottons in standard colours that they always keep in stock, meaning you can buy a small quantity but buy more of the same one again later. If you are working with stocked fabric ensure your wholesaler is reliable and can be trusted to have it in next time you visit. Also remember that dye numbers may not be the same across new rolls of fabric, so there could still be slight variations.

Jobbers

There are fabric suppliers called 'fashion jobbers' or 'textile jobbers' who carry a limited stock of end-of-runs from mills ends, odd lots or seconds. As they only carry limited stock, once it is gone they cannot repeat it.

Mills

A mill can provide made-to-order fabrics, but these are usually based on a minimum order of a thousand yards or more. However, sometimes start-up brands can work with mills by buying limited quantity, end-of-run lines or over-production, but not all mills offer this facility.

Converters

A converter is a secondary source that processes unfinished products from mills to produce printed fabrics, specialty effects, and/or different colours.

Online

You can search for suppliers online but you will need to be careful to find reliable ones. You should consider whether you could trust them to deliver the quantity and quality you order at the right time. There are also platforms such as the Sustainable Angle, Let's Make it Here, Foursource, Sqetch and Makers Row to name a few, where you can search for suppliers.

Trade Shows

Emerging designers tend to favour trade shows as their favourite place to research and source fabrics and trims. There are lots of shows all around the world from large ones such as Premiere Vision and Tex World to local supplier's trade fairs. These fairs can be great for research but many of the exhibitors will only sell high minimum order quantities.

Fabric Challenges

Fabric sourcing can be a challenge for a start-up brand. There are some questions that you need to ask to make sure that you have chosen the right supplier. Wherever you are purchasing the fabric from, here are some key questions to ask:

- What are the minimum and maximum order quantities?

- What is the wholesale price and is there tiered pricing for different quantities? Are there any additional costs for shipping, taxes and import duties etc.?

- What is the lead-time, so how long will it take for the product to be made and shipped to you?

- What is the fabric width? This can vary greatly with no standard widths from some suppliers, so an essential point to ask.

- Can you place a repeat order for the fabrics and trims? You need to check whether the supplier will carry a stock of the fabric or replenish it if sold out.

With high minimum order quantities being one of the biggest challenges, many younger fashion brands are being creative to get around this problem. They are working with end-of line fabrics or off-cuts to produce small limited-edition collections. They may have a standard pattern, then produce small runs of the piece in different colourways, prints or fabrics which they source. This can be greatly beneficial to a start-up brand, as they don't tie up their money in having excess fabric sitting in their studio waiting to be used. Small limited-edition collection runs can incentivise the customer to buy the product quickly as it might sell out, rather than waiting for it to be discounted or put in the sale later.

Other start-up brands look to recycle or upcycle fabric, both for environmental reasons as well as getting around the challenges of purchasing large minimum order quantities of fabrics and trims. Some brands will source their own fabrics to upcycle, others will use one of the increasing number of production businesses that take left over or used fabrics and turn them into new ones.

Although it is good to have an idea of what you are looking for when you start sourcing your fabrics and trims, you may not always find exactly what you want, or at the price you need. Therefore, you should be prepared to compromise. You do not want to waste time and money chasing an elusive fabric when a suitable one is more easily available.

Fabric Options

The types of fabrics you choose can be dependent on your brand ethos, storytelling and customer need. Your choice may consider the fibres, colours, weight of the material, price, and sustainability. Fabrics are an intrinsic part of your brand's quality and storytelling, as well as having an effect on the customer's perceived value of the pieces.

A designer needs to understand about different types of fabrics and their suitability for different uses. The fabrics need to be fit for purpose, and be functional for the design you are creating. When selecting supplies, a brand needs to consider the increasing focus on the environmental impact of the fabrics used in the fashion industry. Customers are now more knowledgeable, and seek more ethically produced materials, so there are a growing number of new sustainable fabrics coming on to the market that offer new opportunities. It is impossible to include an exhaustive list in this book, but here are a few examples to consider:

Cotton
There are currently great concerns around the environmental impact of the increasing cotton production due to the high use of water, high levels of pesticides and chemicals as well as issues around workers rights. There are more sustainable alternatives including organic and Fairtrade cotton, recycled cotton, as well as cotton in more natural colours to reduce pollution.

Polyester
Polyester is cheap and versatile, but there are environmental impacts due to it being made from carbon-intensive non-renewable resources, as well as shedding harmful microfibers. There are some more sustainable options on the market, including polyester fabrics made from recycled plastic bottles, industrial plastic waste and ocean plastic.

Wool

Although wool is a natural fibre, there are now concerns around animal welfare and environmental impact. There are producers looking to counteract any negative elements, as well as recycled wool and animal free alternatives such as Tencel.

Silk

There are concerns over child labour and workers rights, as well animal welfare rights and high use of energy. New options are being developed including organic production, peace silk and plant-based alternatives, as well as synthetic spider silk.

Leather

In an increasingly vegan society, the use of leather is changing due to the environmental and animal welfare issues. There are a number of leather alternatives on the market including vegan leathers, and leathers made from fruit skins or grown in labs.

Denim

Denim has a huge impact on the environment due to the water used to manufacture it. Many brands now use recycled denim or alternative fabrics.

Lycra

Lycra or elastane are the most commonly used stretch fabrics that are usually blended with other fibres. Lycra is very difficult to recycle and takes the longest time to biodegrade, if ever! Alternatives can be recycled polyester or plastics.

With more consumers demanding fashion that is ethically produced, a brand moving towards sustainable production will need to understand the different fibres and their environmental impact, as well as possibilities for circular fashion models. The industry is renowned for its excessive chemical and water usage, overproduction that ends in landfill and poor working conditions.

New sustainable fabrics that are available come from a range of sources, including hemp, banana, coffee grounds and stinging nettle fibres to name a few, along with fabrics made from pineapple leaves, orange and grape skins, as well as lab grown leathers.

Other sustainable elements that brands are considering in their fabric sourcing include zero waste, upcycling and recycling. Zero waste means the brand looks to use the entire piece of the textile in their collection, creating their range plans based on ensuring they use all the off-cuts of fabric, for example as trims, pockets or binding. I also discuss zero waste in the design process, as well as considering it in the manufacturing process when determining your cutting guide to the factory.

There are also brands that use upcycling and recycling as part of their sustainable practises. The difference between the two can be explained as: upcycled clothes have been made by creatively using waste clothes to turn them into something new; whereas recycling means the fabric is broken down first before it can be used.

Brands are also looking to implement circular fashion systems, where product is sourced, produced and sold, with the concept that it will be used for as long as possible before being returned safely to the earth when no longer useful to humans.

Manufacturing Options and Challenges

Having sourced your fabrics and trims, you now have to move on to producing the collection. Working with clothing manufacturers is risky. It doesn't matter whether you are a major high street label or a start up brand, the one thing that is guaranteed in the fashion industry is that you will always find the manufacturing process challenging.

The challenges in the manufacturing stage for all brands include: -

- Always needing to find new or different manufacturers to find better prices, different order quantities or better quality.

- Not being able to find factories that will produce the minimum order quantity that you need.

- Overproduction. This happens when companies produce more products than they need or will be able to sell. The brands produce more because they have to order a higher quantity to get the factory to work with them, or to get a better price per piece from the factory.

- Protecting your designs during the manufacturing stage, because this when designs are often stolen or copied.

- The difficulty of managing production to ensure your product is produced on time and at the right quality.

- Difficulties in tracking the supply chain process to offer your customer transparency in how, and by whom, your pieces are made.

- Sub-contracting, where the factory you have selected to work with subcontract your job to another factory, one that may not have good working practices or has less ethical processes.

For a start-up brand, the challenges are even greater. Just finding a manufacturer when you are starting out can be a huge challenge and then you have to convince them to work with you. Even if you meet the factory at a trade fair or they answer your email promptly, they may still not want to work with you! I know this may be surprising, as surely they want good, paying customers, but most factories are not excited to work with start-up brands! They find newer brands more challenging to work with for several reasons, including:

- Lack of experience, so you may not understand how the factory works.

- You may take more time when sampling, due to your patterns or specification sheets not being correct.

- You will only place very small orders.

Therefore, factories only choose to work with a few smaller brands and may have already decided on the start-up brands they will work with, and won't be taking on any new ones in the foreseeable future. There are far more designers and brands than factories, particularly factories that work with small minimum order quantities, so it can take a while to find the right factory that has a gap to work with you.

A small number of brands avoid the challenges of manufacturing by producing their collections in-house, employing their own team of pattern cutters, seamstresses and tailors to make their garments. The benefits of this can be that the brand has control of the process, can guarantee quality and finish, and also produce the number of garments they need. The downside can be that the in-house staff are not working at full capacity in the beginning, and it can take a while until you make enough sales to justify paying a full-time team.

If you decide to work with a factory rather than make the collections yourself, then you will need to find the contact details for possible factories that you can work with. However, before you search for, or talk to a manufacturer you need to work out what you want them to do? Do you want the factory to simply cut and assemble all the materials and trims you've bought to a pattern you've designed? Or do you want the factory to source all materials, create a pattern and assemble it all from your sketch?

The first model mentioned above is a Cut Make and Trim (CMT) factory and the second option is a full package manufacturer: -

- Cut, make and trim (CMT). A CMT factory will cut the fabrics you supply, and then make and trim your design. They will not assist with the design process or sourcing fabrics and trims. CMT factories can work to different size orders, from making 1 piece or sample to 100 + pieces

- Vertical or Full Package manufacturer. This type of factory also sources the materials and trims for your designs as well as making it. Some may offer design services and pattern cutting. They can produce an initial sample from your sketch, image or text description and then produce a bulk order based on that sample. This option is usually not suitable for start-up fashion brands, as they work to high minimum order quantities, but also because there is a chance that the quality would not be as high as needed. I believe for a start-up brand it is essential that they source and choose all the fabric and trim elements. There are also concerns that the factory will create a pattern that makes manufacturing easier and cheaper, rather than creating the patterns to ensure the best fit for the customer.

If you are growing your business on a shoestring, then you need to manage the production process to make sure you don't end up with overproduction that eats into your valuable business funds. There are no guarantees that your first collection will sell, so you need to limit your risk by only producing small quantities. The worst thing you can do for your brand, and for your cash flow, is to have excess inventory that you need to sell off at a discounted price. Having to discount excess stock is a damaging strategy for a start-up brand, and can be detrimental to your brand value.

Another reality is that as a start-up brand you will be placing a small order, so you will not be classed as high priority or of great importance by the factory. This may mean that they put junior or new members of staff on your job who have little or no experience. Or they fit your job in between other more important clients work. This can result in poor quality or inconsistent quality product, or your collection being 'bumped' down the list and not being completed at the time you initially agreed.

There are a million things that can wrong at the manufacturing stage, and believe me over the years I have seen many of them! In order to limit your risk, you need to be prepared for all eventualities, maintain clear communication with the factory, put detailed quality control and supervision systems in place to keep control of the process. I also advise all brands that I work with to remember this is a business relationship. Even if you build a great relationship with the factory and they treat you like friends and family – you aren't! Keep everything on a business footing and maintain a professional approach, as then everyone will be sure where they stand.

As a small start-up brand, you need to make an amazing first impression, which means you will be reliant on the quality of your product. You can not risk mistakes with poor quality finish, late production deliveries or dropped lines.

Finding Manufacturers

Having decided what type of factory you want to work with, then it is time to find the perfect one for your brand. This can be much more difficult than just searching for factories on Google or looking them up in a directory. Research is essential and you need to plan time for it. Don't just jump at the first factory you find, or offer that is made, as you may get a better deal elsewhere, or find someone with whom you can have a better relationship.

Often the research starts with asking friends, colleagues or other brands for recommendation but in the fashion industry this rarely works. It can be really difficult to get recommendations from other designers and brands, as they will not want to share their contacts if they have found one of the best factories to work with. They will be worried that if they shared the contact with you, then the factory may choose to work with you instead of them, particularly if you have a bigger order, a more interesting design or the factory thinks you have more potential for growth.

So how do you find the perfect factory?

There are some online platforms that can help you search for manufacturers by keyword, category or location such as Let's Make it Here, Makers Row and Foursource amongst others. I have listed some of these in the Links and Resources chapter. These platforms list a full range of suppliers and factories, but they do not endorse the companies listed, so you will still have to research how appropriate and trustworthy they are.

Tradeshows are a great resource and an easy way to meet several factories in one place at one time. There are lots of tradeshows around the world, from big international ones to local trade fairs that promote local manufacturers. Again, I have listed many of these shows in the Resources and Links chapter.

When you are looking for factories either online or at tradeshows, remember to try first of all to find ones as local to you as possible, so that you can make frequent visits if need be. Once you have a list of potential factories, you need to contact them initially to see if they can make the style of garment you need, at the right minimum order quantity and price.

To convince a factory to work with your brand, you will need to be very professional in your approach, be respectful and there are some basic tips I can advise when you make that first email contact with a factory: -

- Keep the email short and simple and make a good first impression by being polite and respectful.

- Provide all your contact information.

- Give a brief description of your brand and a link to your website if you have one

- Clearly state what services you are looking for such as cutting, sewing or production management. It can be worth stating the types of fabrics you are looking to use, as well as whether, for example, you work with draping or structure. This helps the factory determine if they have the right facilities and skills to make your collection.

- State the number of items you are possibly looking for, this is something you can change later, but don't overestimate your numbers, as this could waste everyone's time.

- Don't initially ask for pricing, as they will not be able to tell you this until the see your designs.

- Do not send them any examples of your designs at this stage, as you need to protect your intellectual property. Only send designs once they have signed an NDA.

Finish the email by asking if you can book a meeting to visit them.

You can download a template for an email to send to a manufacturer and an NDA template on my website www.startyourownfashionlabel.com

Once you start getting replies from potential factories that can meet your requests, then your next step will be to visit and start to build the relationship with them.

Selecting your manufacturers

It is essential that you visit factories before deciding on, or contracting, a manufacturer. A factory visit will help you decide if you can work and build a relationship with them, as well as assess the capabilities, physical and working conditions.

To make the relationship with the factory work, you need to make sure that your contacts speak the same language and have clear communication skills. During your visit you can ascertain what other brands or designers they work with, their specialist skills, and agree your minimum order quantity, production slot and delivery dates.

Before confirming your arrangement with the factory, you also need to check the working conditions and procedures to make sure they are organised and efficient. This is important because a dirty or disorganised factory could damage your fabric, they may lose your patterns or trims, and unhappy staff may not provide good quality work. Old machines can lead to oil spots on fabrics, poor stitch tension or skipped stitches.

Prior to your factory visit, plan the questions you want to ask and create a checklist to make sure you don't miss anything that could be important later. Here is an example of some of the areas you may want to check:

Factory Checklist

? Good communication.

? Clear minimum order quantities.

? Specialist equipment.

? Area of specialisms such as tailoring, draping.

? Ability to work with different fabrics such as silk or denim or leather.

? Age of equipment.

? Pressing machines.

? Technical skills.

? Pattern skills.

? Good health and safety.

? Happy staff.

? Staff canteen or rest area.

? Cleanliness.

? General tidiness and organisation.

? Protection of client's intellectual property.

? Easy to travel to.

+ Any other areas that you are personally looking for.

When you attend the meeting at the factory, you will need to be prepared and take along samples of your work, fabric swatches etc. or clear ideas of what you need, so that the factory knows what they would be working with. Be wary of showing your designs unless you have a non-disclosure/confidentiality agreement signed beforehand and do not leave anything with them.

Once you have decided on your factory and are happy with the services they supply, then you will need to get a quote from them with the price, minimum order quantity, and payment and delivery terms. It is essential to get this in writing before starting to work with them. You will need to ask the factory if they will provide, or sign, a contract that agrees all the terms. Contracts are not widely used in the fashion industry, but a brand should push to have one, as a written agreement helps should there be any dispute at a later date. A contract can include a statement about discounts for late delivery. This is a standard problem for newer labels who get their orders "bumped' down the priority list and this statement may ensure the factory keeps to the agreement.

Booking your production space and docket

Once you have decided on your factory and confirmed that you will be working together, then your next job is to book your production space.

The booking will depend on how long it will take you to get delivery of your fabrics and trims, as well as when the factory has a space. A good factory will get booked up quickly, so sometimes start-up brands will have to book their production space six months in advance.

As you near your factory booking date, it is advisable to get all elements of your production, including patterns, fabric and trims, collated together in one place and not sent in multiple deliveries to your factory. It would be better to collate everything in your studio and then pass it all on to the factory in one package with the docket (their purchase order). This improves the chances of production being made on time, as well as ensuring nothing is lost.

The docket will be the order to the factory that tells them exactly what to make including the style, how many of the style to make in which sizes, the different fabrics, trims etc. to use, the factory price based on the sample and delivery dates agreed.

There is a downloadable example of a production docket available on my website at www.startyourownfashionlabel.com

Patterns

Pattern cutting is a skill that takes years of practise to perfect, therefore unless you are a trained and talented patternmaker, you will need a professional to create your patterns for you. A start-up brand may try to cut corners and costs by trying to produce the pattern themselves, but it isn't worth the risk. The pattern is considered to be the most critical part of the pre-production process, as the whole product depends on it. A poor pattern will result in a poor product. Therefore, many designers who do not have the skills to create their own patterns will employ a third party to do this for them.

Most factories offer pattern cutting, but I always advise a brand to be wary of this. Firstly, there is the issue of who owns the pattern if they create it using your designs, because you need to make sure they can't use the pattern again or sell it to other clients. Secondly the factory may make a pattern that focuses on easier production, rather than the emphasis being on an excellent fit for your consumer.

There are freelance pattern cutters that you can work with, and these can be found online, through trade press or word of mouth. With either the factory or a freelance pattern cutter, you need to ensure that your design is protected and you have full ownership of the use of the pattern.

A pattern cutter will turn your sketches into patterns, which are then used to make first toiles and then samples, as well as production once the sample has been approved. A great design needs a great pattern to make it a good seller. Bad fit is one of the biggest reasons fashion products don't sell, so a good pattern cutter is essential.

A pattern cutter will create patterns for each piece either from paper or digitally using specialist software and Computer Aided Design programmes. A brand can create a pattern block, which is their custom measured, basic pattern from which lots of different styles can be created. The pattern cutter can also provide the brand with pattern grading, which is creating other sizes from the master pattern.

Building a relationship with, or recruiting, a great pattern cutter will be an essential part of the production process, but it can be difficult. There are not many freelance pattern cutters and the good ones get booked up very quickly and can charge high fees. If you are forced to use your factory to make your pattern, ensure you carefully communicate what you want. It is also really important to determine who owns the pattern they create, as you need to protect your designs and you wouldn't want the factory using your pattern for other brands. Therefore, ask for confirmation in writing who owns both the pattern and the intellectual property for it.

Samples

Once the patterns are cut, then some brands will create a toile, a prototype of the design. This is a sample made out of cheap material to test the pattern, so that alterations can be made without the risk of wasting money on the actual sample fabric.

A manufacturer needs to create a sample so that they can assess how the garment needs to be made. By making the sample, they are then able to cost the production, and provide the brand with the price. The sample is an opportunity to make the final small changes to fine-tune the garment and fix any problems before putting the garment into production.

Before signing off the sample, you need to make sure that it fits perfectly, so it is better to do this on a fit model rather than a tailor's dummy. That way you can also check that the garment is wearable and moves properly. A fit sample may not have all the final trims etc. added to it, as it is looking purely at the fit of the garment. A sales sample will be an exact version of the final garment, with all labels, trims and finishing's, to show to buyers. At the sample stage the amendments should be minimal, this is not the time or place to start making major changes to the design and you should remember to add any changes to the pattern and spec sheet.

Tech Pack and Specification Sheets

A tech (or technical) pack is a detailed document pack that the brand gives to the manufacturer, which includes all the instructions on how to make the designs. The more information that you put into your tech pack the better, as that way there is less chance of mistakes. The manufacturer needs the fine details of all the elements of creating the garment from start to finish.

The tech pack needs to be detailed, accurate and include the following elements:

- Detailed front and back technical drawings of the garment including dimensions and measurements.
- Pattern.
- Graded spec with points of measurement for the different sizes.
- Details of prints, logo, embellishments.
- Colour and fabric references.
- Any reference materials or details of finishes.
- Spec sheet.
- Sizing.
- Quality control.
- Packaging including how the garment is folded and what it is packed in.

Within the tech pack will be the specification, or spec sheet as it is more often called. This is a document that provides the fine detail for a garment to be made. On the spec sheet you will include:

- The garment name or number.
- Description of the piece.
- A technical line drawing of the front and back of the garment.
- Details of all fabrics, trims, threads, colours to be used.
- Types of seams and stitching.
- Labels.

- Detailed construction notes such as seam and hem allowances.
- Positioning of pockets, prints, logo etc.
- Finished garment measurements.
- Some brands choose to include the costing information on this too.

You will need to create a tech pack and spec sheet for every new design and need to update them if any changes or alterations are made. In the tech pack add revision notes documenting the development of the piece. Ideally you should attach a sealed sample (one with a red tag that notes it has been approved by the buyer) to the tech pack.

Below is a simple example of a spec sheet:

Brand Name	Date
Garment Description	Garment Name or Style Number
Garment Sketch	 Front Back
Fabric 1	
Fabric 2	
Trim 1	
Trim 2	
Zip	
Button	

Tread type and colour	
Interfacing	
Shoulder Pad	
Binding	
Brand Label	
Care Label	
Seam type	
Seam Allowances	
Key measurement 1	
Key measurement 2	
Key measurement 3	
Key measurement 4	

If you get your tech pack right and communicate clearly and concisely with your manufacturer, then there is less chance of mistakes. Inaccurate tech packs and spec sheets can increase production costs, result in additional samples having to be made, or can affect the quality, fit or delivery schedule.

Production Plan and Management

For a start-up brand, one of the aspects of the business that they find the most difficult is managing the production side of making their collections. There are so many different elements to consider from ordering fabrics, tracking supplies, negotiating prices and minimum order quantities to booking production slots. If a brand doesn't have good management systems in place, then things can start to go wrong very quickly and they can find that they have incurred very costly mistakes.

The things that go wrong during the manufacturing stage are often due to the brands lack of experience in working with manufacturers and suppliers, poor communication between the brand and the factory, or a lack of organisation and planning to ensure everything is in place at the right time. There are many steps to monitor in the production process and it is easy to miss something vital, or lose control due to timings slipping.

The Steps of Production

1. Collection concept.
2. Research materials, shapes and trends.
3. Develop designs.
4. Select fabric and materials.
5. Order sample cuts of fabric.
6. Create first patterns.
7. Make toiles.
8. Cut and sew the sample.
9. Edit final collection of samples.
10. Photo-shoot for the collection.
11. If wholesaling, sell collection and finalise orders.
12. Order production fabric and materials.
13. Finalise production pattern.
14. Finalise production sample.
15. Grade pattern for sizes.
16. Create marker for cutting fabric.
17. Oversee the manufacturing or Cut, Make and Trim.
18. Garments packed and shipped.

As your business grows, you may have orders at various stages of completion and your collections will start to overlap. You may be sourcing new fabrics, making samples and producing stock all at the same time. Therefore, you need to develop a system to keep track of every stage of the production process. This will help you monitor designs waiting to be made, one's that are in process, and others that are ready for delivery to your customer. A really simple system such as a checklist can be a good start, then as you get more experienced, you can develop Excel spreadsheets or use production management software tools, but these aren't needed in the beginning.

For the production steps above, you also need to plan how long the whole process is going to take to get your products to market. Timing is crucial and most start-up brands completely underestimate the time it takes to start a fashion label. They try to rush through the processes, which means they often end up making mistakes that can be costly in the future. I would recommend planning on an initial 18–24 month schedule, to allow you to find good manufacturers and suppliers, make your first samples, put your collection into production and set up all the systems you are going to need as your business grows. A realistic timeline will give you the time to build a strong brand with a beautifully made collection that customers will want to buy.

When creating a timeline or critical path for the development of your business and collection, then you need to capture all the key tasks you have to complete. Below is an example of a timeline for a brand that is wholesaling two collections a year.

Month	Spring Summer	Autumn Winter
January	Design concept, trend forecasting	
February	Research fabrics Start designs Production plan created	
March	Order sample fabrics and trims	
April	Range plan completed	
May	Patterns cut Toiles made Samples started	

June	Finish sampling Edit collection Shoot the look book	Design concept
July	Wholesale selling season starts	Research fabrics Start designs Production plan created
August	Selling	Order sample fabrics and trims
September	Selling	Range plan completed
October	Selling season finishes Collate orders Confirm manufacturing Order production fabric and trim	Patterns cut Toiles made Samples started
November	Oversee production Chase payments	Finish sampling Shoot look book
December	Oversee production	Wholesale selling season starts
January	Oversee production	Selling
February	Deliver to store Chase payments	Selling
March		Selling season finishes Collate orders Confirm manufacturing Order production fabric and trim
April		Oversee Production

This example may not be appropriate for your brand but it gives an example of how to create a timeline plan. The critical path or timeline will help you keep control of the production process and keep you on track, making sure that something important doesn't get forgotten.

Avoiding mistakes in sourcing and production

There are a million ways that things can wrong with production, but here are a few examples of areas that tend to effect start-up labels that you need to avoid.

NDA and Manufacturing Agreements
Before showing any supplier or manufacturer your actual designs, you must protect your intellectual property by getting them to sign a Non-Disclosure Agreement. They will then be unable to share your designs with other people. As there is a history of manufacturers failing to sign or agree to contracts in the fashion industry, many designers don't even bother to ask for one. This is a mistake. You should insist on developing and getting a manufacturing agreement contract signed. Without a contract the manufacturer can 'bump' you down the list, provide poor quality products or fail to deliver the collection at all.

Quality control
Start-up fashion brands often presume their manufacturer will provide the best quality product or service, but this may not be the case. The designer or brand has to instigate quality control processes and inform the factory and suppliers what they expect. The brand also needs to have quality control checklists to ensure nothing is missed in the production process.

Staying on schedule
Emerging brands place an order with a fabric supplier or manufacturer and then just expect them to deliver on time. With suppliers you need to consider lead times, as a supplier may give you a date when the goods are ready to leave them and you need to factor in shipping time. You should also remember that in some countries the factories close for several weeks for holiday periods, which will delay your order. You will need to keep in regular contact with suppliers and manufacturers to make sure your order stays on schedule and that you are not 'bumped' down the priority list.

Tracking production materials
With most brands now working globally, production supplies such as fabric, buttons and zips can be shipped from all over the world. Brands need to have a detailed plan and timeline to ensure all their supplies arrive at the right place at the right time, so that your manufacturer can start the production run. As you will have to pay your manufacturers and suppliers in advance, you need to ensure that what you ordered is delivered. When tracking your production materials, you also need to put quality control systems in place prior to production, to ensure the manufacturer has received the right product,

Tech Pack

The biggest mistake I regularly see is that brands haven't created professional and detailed tech packs, which results in production mistakes. Without an accurate tech pack, you can waste time and money, as you have to keep returning to the factory to fix problems and make alterations. An inaccurate tech pack can lead to poor products being developed that you are unable to sell. The lack of a professional style tech pack can also mean that the factory has not been able to provide an accurate quote, and if they have under-quoted, you can be hit with high additional costs later.

Grading for Size

For start-up companies, the freelance patternmaker you hire will most probably also grade your patterns. A pattern grader will use a set of mathematical formulas that are designed to increase or decrease each pattern piece and they should advise you on how to establish your brand's basic sizing policy. They also develop several kinds of grading styles, so that the sizing is consistent with the fit and type of fabric used in the design.

Pattern grading isn't difficult or expensive if produced using an appropriate software programme, but it does need an expert who understands the process. Start-up brands that try to grade patterns themselves often end up with mistakes and problems when compiling the garment and pattern pieces don't fit together. Poor grading also results in garments that don't fit the customer.

There is no standard garment grading system in the industry, as there is no standard body shape. It is up to you to determine your brand's grading in relation to your customer, taking into consideration their age range, preferences and buying behaviours. It is also sensible for your brand to closely align your sizing with your competitors. This means their consumer can also easily buy from you and successfully select a size that fits without having to try on numerous pieces, which can reduce returns of online sales.

It is essential when you are hiring someone to grade your patterns that they understand who your customer is, as well as the competitor you are aligning your sizing with.

Marker Making / Lay Planning

After the pattern grading, then the next step is the marker making, or sometimes this is called lay planning. This is the process of arranging the pattern pieces on the fabric, to make best use of the fabric and incur as little waste as possible. For a start-up brand that has limited resources and is only producing small quantities, marker making is essential. Marker making takes time and skill and not all designers are capable or want to create the marker. The fabric needs to be carefully cut depending on the grain lines, patterns and stripes etc. and if it is poorly done then it will result in a bad quality product. A poor marker will frustrate the factory cutter and can result in time being wasted and increased charges.

Some brands will use the factory to create the marker, but as with pattern cutting, to personally ensure your quality, it is recommended that you use a freelancer, or ask your pattern cutter, or an independent pattern grading service to do this rather than the factory.

Samples
The sample is essential to ensure your factory can produce the garment to your specifications, provide a cost for the manufacture of the piece and ensure that your product will be a great fit and good quality. It is at the sample stage that you can tweak the pattern to perfect the design. It is the opportunity to make sure that the design works with the fabric you have chosen. Factories can tend to rush the first sample, so there will be mistakes. Therefore, it is important to make sure you have checked the sample thoroughly and checked the fit on a model, or the mistakes will be carried through onto the production run. A brand should never sign off a sample until it is 100% accurate.

Garment Labels
An area that is often forgotten is the labelling and many start-up brands don't understand the legal side of the care labels. Along with the brand label, on every garment there needs to be clear garment labelling, which must adhere to local regulations and laws in the country you are selling the product.

The label will detail the fabric composition and country of origin, along with the care instructions to the customer. It is necessary to consider the differences in legal requirements for products sold in the US and Europe, as each country imposes penalties for failure to comply with their laws. I would recommend seeking advice from the fashion export department of your governmental body to get full advice and support.

Cut and Sew
When you have booked your production slot at the factory and have confirmed the date, you will need to ensure that every element of your production is at the factory for that date. A CMT factory cannot start your production run if elements are missing such as a zip or buttons. If deliveries are late, then you will be bumped down the list until everything has arrived. Another mistake that happens is when a designer fails to ask the CMT factory if they supply threads, shoulder pads, interfacing etc. Do not presume that the factory will automatically supply these.

Too much product

Overproduction is a huge problem in the fashion industry, with nearly all brands producing more products than they can sell. For start-up brands, overproduction can have a huge financial impact, pushing many of them into bankruptcy.

There are several reasons why brands end up with overproduction. It can start at the design process, where the brand creates a large range plan and then samples all pieces, rather than focussing on designing a small capsule collection with a strong signature. It can be the result of brands producing seasonal collections that they don't have enough time to sell before the next one drops. Or, the brand puts a large collection into full production, presuming they will sell large, unrealistic quantities of their product.

For a small brand, overproduction can also arise if they cannot find a manufacturer who will work with them at the minimum order quantity they want. It is a really big mistake for a start-brand to agree to a higher number of pieces, just so that they can work with the manufacturer. The start-up brand may also agree to produce higher numbers of pieces to get a better price from the factory, but this short-term win can turn into disaster if you can't sell the quantity of pieces you made.

When developing and manufacturing your collection, you need to produce only what you can realistically expect to sell, based on research and engagement with your potential customer.

Subcontracting

Finally a big concern in the manufacturing process is the hidden issue of subcontracting. I have never met a fashion brand that wants to produce their collections in unethical factories, but sometimes their collections end up in unregistered, informal workspaces where there are unregulated working conditions. This happens due to manufacturers subcontracting to other suppliers, without the knowledge of the brand.

If subcontracting takes place, not only are your products being made in awful working conditions, it is also likely that your product will be poor quality or damaged. These unchecked and unregulated workspaces would not meet the conditions on your factory checklist, such as clean works spaces, modern machines etc.

One of the benefits of working with a local manufacturer is that you can check that your product is being made where you booked it. If working overseas you should consider hiring an independent production manager who can monitor where your collection is actually being produced.

Quality Control

I have mentioned quality control throughout this chapter, but it is such as important element that I am highlighting it again in a separate section.

A start-up brand is reliant on good quality products to build a customer base, sell the product and minimise returns. Yet quality control is often left to chance, with the brand 'presuming' that their suppliers will offer them the best quality product. I constantly hear from designers who have experienced disasters with their production runs. They have usually lost a huge amount of time and money and ended up with products that are not suitable to take to market.

It is the brand's responsibility to set up quality control checks throughout the production process, to minimise the risks and identify potential problems. Suppliers will not necessarily offer quality control systems, so you need to instigate them. If you are working with local suppliers, then you can visit them and approve fabrics, trims and manufacturing quality before paying for them.

The biggest problem comes from sourcing overseas. As a start-up brand your suppliers and manufacturers will all demand that you pay in advance. This is where most problems occur. I meet many designers who have paid for goods in advance, and then when the product or the collection turns up, it is poor quality, faulty or damaged. They then have to fight to get their money back, which many of them fail to do! If you are working with overseas suppliers then you may need to find a freelance production manager to oversee quality on your behalf. If this isn't possible, then you will need to ask the supplier to take pictures/ video for you to see all the product before you pay for it, but this is still very risky.

Others ways that you can manage quality control are:

- Detail your requirements in your purchase order with the supplier or manufacturer.

- Have a quality control checklist that starts pre-production with timeline to make sure nothing is missed.

- Only approve a sample that is 100% correct. A factory may say the last few changes will be fixed in production, but never allow production to start until the sample is perfect.

- Check 10% of the order to make sure quality is consistent rather than accepting a Top (or Top of Production) sample.

- Do not stay with a factory that continually makes mistakes or produces poor quality pieces. If you have tried to work out quality issues with them but they continue to make errors, then it is time to move on to work with a new factory.

Even with a quality control system things can still go wrong, but it will seriously reduce the risk.

Sustainability and transparency

Sustainability has become increasingly important for consumers and they demand more information and transparency about how ethical brands are. Today's customer is much more knowledgeable and wants to connect with more environmentally conscious fashion brands. The customer is demanding provenance, clear information on how brands source their fabrics, the impact of fabric and production on the environment, as well as the ethical employment and working processes used in making fashion. Brands of all sizes, from high street to high-end, are looking at introducing more sustainable practices and product.

Sustainability isn't a replacement to great product. The design is still the most important element, as the customer won't buy an ugly product just because it is sustainable. So the brand design aesthetic comes first, but a new brand coming on to the market should be looking at sustainability and how they can meet ethical standards as part of their brand's core DNA.

A start-up brand has the opportunity to create ethical processes throughout their business as they set it up, starting their production and sourcing strategy with clear ethical standards in mind. It may be impossible to address all sustainable issues at the beginning, but you should have a clear idea of what standards you are working towards and communicate this with your customer.

Transparency is an important element of the sustainability process. There are lots of different terms being used such as ethical, conscious, sustainable, local, organic, animal friendly and vegan, and the customer wants to know what these mean and how brands are meeting various standards.

I have met hundreds of start-up fashion brands that use the terms 'sustainable' or 'ethical,' without clarifying what they mean or how they are being sustainable. When challenged, these brands are often only considering one small element, such as using organic cotton or they are working with a local factory. In the worst case, a start-up brand that described themselves as an ethical label, were actually only using a paper recycling bin and long-life light bulbs. If a brand is using any of the sustainability terms as a marketing approach, then they need to be prepared to explain how and why they are ethical.

In the beginning, it can be very difficult for a brand to be sustainable across all your working practises, but you have to start somewhere. You can look at adding more sustainable elements as the business develops. My recommendation is to clearly communicate with your customers that you are working towards more sustainable practises and where the challenges are. This transparency can build brand loyalty, as you can take the customer on the journey with you, as you research and seek more environmentally and ethically conscious working systems. This honesty and transparency can help your brand stand out from all the others and helps attract consumers who are looking for authenticity.

In order to be transparent in your story telling to your consumer, you will need to find trustworthy suppliers and manufacturers who can offer you transparency by clearly stating their working practices. As you work through your production process, you will need to track and note where all the different elements of your collection have come from and how they were made. You will then be able to share this with your customer through pictures, text or video showing the factory, the person who made the piece or the design and production process.

Blockchain

One of the coming changes in the supply chain will be Blockchain, which at this point is a little hard to define, but relates to proving exclusivity and supports anti-counterfeiting. Blockchain is talked about in a range of technical buzzwords that mean very little to most of us, such as it is a decentralised, frictionless, way of permanently exchanging value between two entities on an open ledger. I can honestly say I don't know what that means!

In simpler terms for a fashion business, Blockchain is a technological process that will help companies exchange data. This will be a key element for brands looking to offer transparency in their supply chain to their customers. Today's customer increasingly wants to know where their clothes have come from and who made them, but many companies find it hard to find, never mind share, this information.

Blockchain will transform the fashion supply chain by offering a type of track and trace management system. This system creates a link or a serial number, which records every time the product changes hand, tracking it from the raw material, through the design process to the factory and finally on to the customer. This process will result in a type of passport for each garment, showing exactly where it has been and when it has changed hands from one supplier or owner to another. This Blockchain process will allow the customer to fully trust where their garments come from and how ethically they were made, rather than rely on a brand's vague 'sustainable' statements.

An added bonus of Blockchain is that brands will be able to protect their intellectual property better, and the system should reduce counterfeits, as the customer will be able to trace the authenticity of a product.

Recap on Sourcing and Manufacturing

Just to recap the main points covered in this chapter, below are the key elements you need to understand when producing a fashion collection.

- The initial sourcing and production process can take 12-18 months. It is vital to give yourself enough time to source your production properly.

- You need to carefully research your manufacturers and suppliers and understand what areas they specialise in, find different suppliers for different jobs, and start to build a relationship with them.

- You need to find factories and suppliers who can work with your minimum order quantities.

- Look as locally as possible to find your suppliers and manufacturers to make it easier to oversee the production process.

- Remember more customers now look for sustainable fashion products from authentic brands that offer transparency in the manufacturing processes.

- Protect your intellectual property by making suppliers sign an NDA before showing your designs.

- Not everyone will want to work with you, so you may need to contact hundreds of suppliers before you find the right one.

- Sourcing and production is not an easy task and it can easily go wrong. You need to have a very strict production timeline and management plan to minimise the risk of mistakes

- Don't make assumptions! Check every small detail.

Resources

Don't forget that on my website www.startyourownfashionlabel.com you can download loads of great resources to help you set up your business, including Production Docket template, Non-Disclosure Agreement, Factory Checklist and Quality Control Checklist template.

Chapter 6 — Branding and Marketing

When you launch your label, you will probably be in a hurry to get out there and start telling people about it. However, before you do that, you need to hold back and make sure you are ready. Remember that you need to launch more than just products, you need to launch a brand.

Before you jump into marketing and putting the messages about your brand out there in the wider world, you need to create your 'brand,' one that has a concise story and clear messages. You need to ensure that the whole presentation of your brand is cohesive.

I am constantly approached by brands who tell me that they want to start their marketing and PR, but 9 times out of 10 they are not ready because they do not have a clear brand strategy. Marketing your label without a brand strategy can result in you giving out mixed messages that will damage your reputation. The industry and consumers may only give you one opportunity to create a great impression; you need to make sure you get it right from the start!

A brand, no matter whether start-up, large or small, needs to focus on both branding and marketing. Branding and marketing work together but it is imperative that you approach them in order, as branding begins within your company and marketing begins with the consumer.

Many start-up brands confuse their 'brand' with just their logo, company name or website, but a brand is much more than these components. Your product, website and content show the world what you look like, not who you are. A brand needs to be much deeper than this.

Changes in consumer behaviours have meant that the customer now seeks new experiences, authenticity in their relationships with brands and transparency in the design and making process, not just product. Today's customer is marketing savvy, not easily fooled and tunes out many elements of promotion and advertising. They are looking to find more genuine brands to connect with, ones that share their values, ethics and personality. You must invest time into building a brand with valuable experiences that connect with your consumers on an emotional basis, so that they become and remain loyal customers.

If successful, your brand will live inside the hearts and minds of your consumers. Seeing and hearing your brand name will prompt positive perceptions and emotions leading to an engaged, loyal customer base.

Branding also becomes important when you are pricing your product. If the buyer says the price is too high then this is an indication that you haven't created a strong enough brand. If the buyer understands the brand and the brand story, then by the time they hear the price of the product they will think it is good value. It is better to add 'brand value' rather than try and reduce your prices and lose profit.

In this chapter, I will talk you through the differences between branding and marketing, exploring the elements of developing your brand and creating a marketing strategy. I will show you how your brand is your promise to the customer and marketing is what you do to attract customers to your brand through your product, messaging and delivering those promises.

What is branding?

There isn't a clear definition for branding. Many describe it as a marketing process that creates a set of perceptions about your business. I have always liked the CEO from Amazon, Jeff Bezos's definition, "Your brand is what people say about you when you're not in the room."

Many start-up brands get confused and think their brand is the name on their label – it is not! Branding is essential for a fashion business. Branding is how you will tell the world about your company and why you are different. Your brand is not just your logo, your name or your trademark; it is much deeper than that.

Branding is how your customer perceives your label, how they feel about it, and the emotional connection they have with the business. It is about creating such a strong identity that when your customer sees your brand, your product or hears your name, they instantly know what the brand does, what it stands for and how they feel about it.

Branding has to be established from the start of your label, as it involves everything from the look of the product, your language, images and social media content to how customers experience and shop the brand. It all needs to be consistent from the very beginning. If you develop a strong brand with a compelling message, it will help your customers connect with the clothing when they wear it. If your consumer relates to your brand, then you will create a connection so that they feel that the brand is an extension of themselves, or how they would like others to perceive them.

Elements of a brand

Branding is complex and people often get confused, but there are some key elements that are widely used in developing a brand, they are:

- **Brand Identity** is how people recognise your brand. This can be through your logo, your signature design, and your aesthetic or image style.

- **Brand Image** is how your customer perceives the idea of your brand in their mind and what they expect from it, such as luxury brand or fast fashion.

- **Brand Essence** is a promise of specific values and benefits, one that has meaning and relevance to users. To consumers, these promises differ from those of the competition. It is the consumer's gut feeling about your company, service or product.

- **Brand Loyalty** results in customers who will consistently purchase products from their preferred brands, regardless of convenience or price.

- **Brand Value** or Equity enables a company to generate more money from products with their brand name on it, as consumers believe that a product with a well-known name is better than products with less well-known names.

- Brand Personality is the way a brand expresses and describes itself such as sexy, fun, feminine, chic.

Developing your brand strategy

You can approach an agency to assist you with developing your brand, but you cannot just hand over the process to someone else. Your brand is something you need to develop yourself, as it is your voice, your heart and soul, your story. So even if you go to an agency for help, you will still need to guide them on what your business is about.

When you create your brand, you need to decide what you want to tell the world about why your business is special and what you do that others don't. The customer needs to understand your brand through the words you use, your images, your product, your events, your storefront and your social media.

Building a strong brand doesn't happen by accident, you need to put time and effort into it, but it will be worth it. Consumers will pay more for their favourite brands, they are more likely to be brand loyal and they will also tell others about brands that make them feel great.

There are various steps to developing your brand which include:

1. Identify your target customer and research your competitors and their brands.

2. Determine the key qualities and benefits your brand offers the consumer.

3. Form your brand voice.

4. Build your brand messages.

5. Determine your brand experience.

6. Create your brand logo and brand image guidelines.

7. Integrate your branding across all elements of your business.

Identify your customer and competitor

I have covered this first step about identifying your customer and competitor in Chapter 3. If you still haven't clearly identified your target customer and competitors then go back and work through this part of your business development.

It is really essential that you understand your customer and competitors in order to develop and build your brand. You need to understand what the consumer will want from your brand including the qualities and benefits they will get from making a purchase from your company. As a start-up brand you are not able, nor should you try, to have more than one target customer. It is really important that you develop a strong customer segment. This will enable you to market your product to them because they have a similar age, gender, interests and spending habits.

Once you have identified your competitors then you can determine your **BRAND POSITIONING**. This is the position that your brand will hold in the mind of the customer. Brand positioning is the strategy used to set your label apart from the rest of the brands, making the customer perceive your brand as different, more favourable and credible than the competitors.

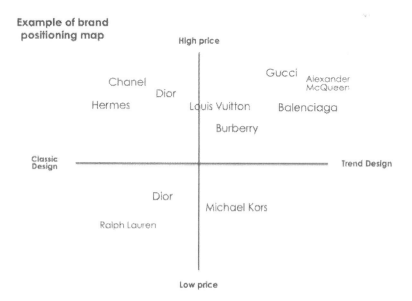

Brand Qualities and Benefits

Once you know what sets your brand apart from the competitors and understand your customer, then you can identify the qualities and benefits you can offer the consumer.

You need to develop a set of benefits that become your **BRAND PROMISE**. This is the message that speaks to your target customer and tells them what they can expect when they choose to purchase your product or follow your company. The brand promise includes the tangible benefits, the things the customer can see and touch, as well as the intangible benefits, which are the things the customer feels and experiences.

Every brand needs to develop the range of benefits that they offer, such as quality, value, and unique design. It could be that your product solves a problem, or makes your customer feel better than other brands. These benefits can come from your **BRAND VALUES** and will help build engagement with your customers. Your brand values are the promises about how your company will act, such as being more environmentally conscious or supporting ethical production. To determine your brand values, you should consider what matters to you but also your customer, decide what your business stands for, and be consistent, ensuring your brand meets your value promises.

Brand storytelling is a powerful technique that you can use to connect with your customer and communicate your values and how your brand is different. If you don't have a story to tell, then you are just selling product, and that really limits your chance of success. The brand story is important to make sure people care about your brand, want to support it and buy into it. Your brand story is not just a tag line, it is the very foundations of your business.

Your brand storytelling and brand values needs to be authentic, you cannot just add in buzz words or key phrases and not deliver on them. There are currently many brands that throw the words sustainable or ethical into their brand storytelling without explaining how and where. Or others who state they donate money to certain charities with no evidence of the value of this. Today's modern consumer is very marketing savvy and knows when a brand is being false or misleading with their descriptions, using terms, phrases and even charity giving in an unauthentic way. If you want to build a strong brand with greater value, then you need to be transparent and genuine in your ethos, descriptions and attitudes.

Form your brand voice

Your brand voice defines your personality and how you speak. Brand personalities are just like the personality of human beings, they have certain emotional or personal qualities that attract us and make us like them. To develop your brand voice, you need to consider again who your customer is, how they talk, what personalities they connect with and how you will talk to them.

Build your brand messages

Brand messages refer to the value propositions you use in your images, language and content. A **VALUE PROPOSITION** is the promise of the value you are offering to the customer, such as the qualities and benefits we discussed above. You need to use the value proposition in your brand messages to inspire, persuade, motivate, and ultimately make the customer want to buy your product.

Brand messages must resonate with your customer and make your brand memorable. **BRAND PERCEPTION** is how your customers view your brand. Whilst you can't control this, you can influence how the customer perceives your brand by understanding their values and beliefs and matching your brand messages to these. You will need to communicate the messages you want to be heard and repeated.

To develop your brand message, you need to consider how you can easily capture what you do and what benefits you offer within one or two sentences or within an image style. The message needs to be simple and in the language that your customer uses. Many brands make the mistake of describing their brand in too much detail or using industry language. Here are a couple of examples of ideal brand messages:

- "Quintessentially English brand creating timeless, luxury womenswear. Each piece is lovingly made in the UK and is designed to be cherished for a lifetime."

- "Every one of our garments is 100% sustainable. Working with local craftspeople and artisans every piece is handmade in the UK."

Your core brand message will shape all the content and marketing materials the brand creates, so it is important that you get it right.

Determine your brand experience

Customers now look for more than product, wanting instead to connect with a brand and have engagement with them. You need to consider what brand experience you will offer your customers. **BRAND EXPERIENCE** comes from all the interactions a customer has with your product, website, social media and customer service. The brand experience is everything you know about a brand, which is why it is essential to make sure your brand messaging is consistent and cohesive.

Can you offer your customer a better experience than your competitors? Can you offer something that makes the customer feel amazing? These elements come down to how you make your customer feel and emotion is a critical element in the selling of fashion. You need to consider how you can make your customer feel about your company and your product and how you can create a positive and consistent emotion in your consumer.

A huge part of brand development in the current market place is to develop an authentic brand. In a crowded market, customers can be overwhelmed by the noise and choice, yet they are not easily fooled. A brand needs to be authentic and honest, creating a genuine brand proposition and experience that it will live by.

Brand logo and image guidelines

To create your brand identity, you will develop a range of visual devices that you will use to determine the brand's image. These visual devices include:

- Logo
- Product label
- Website design
- Packaging
- Social media
- Look books and campaign materials
- Store design and displays

Your visual imagery is an important part of your communication and connection with the customer. Your brand image needs to be designed with the customer in mind. To create strong visual devices, you need to create style guidelines taking into consideration fonts, colour palettes and styling. The more distinct, specific and cohesive these elements are, the more likely you are to shape a differentiated brand that is recognized and admired.

In an increasingly visual world, the need for powerful, impactful images has never been more important. Too often designers are only focussed on the product and the images are an after-thought and subject to limited budget. The images for your brand need to tell a story, relate to your customer and speak to them. Images bring your brand to life, giving the brand a personality and added value.

Integrate your branding across all elements of your business

A strong brand is a consistent one. If your messages and branding are consistent, then you will create greater awareness and build more trust and loyalty with your customer.

To ensure your branding remains consistent, it is advisable to create brand guidelines. This will ensure that as your business grows, your branding will stay on message. This can be a simple document that details the specific colours, type, font, use of logo and imagery styling that the brand uses, which every member of staff can use as a guide.

All your documents, images, social media platforms, website and marketing materials need to be consistent with your brand messages and match your brand values. I would recommend planning regular reviews to ensure everything is cohesive and consistent with the brand guidelines.

You are your brand!

As the owner, founder, designer, face or leader of the business you will be perceived as a key element of the brand. You will need to consider what your own brand story is and how you want to present yourself to your customers.

Every action you take, every word you say and every opinion you express is part of your brand, whether you plan it or not! If you build a strong personal brand it will help your business grow. In the beginning stages as you develop your business people will look at you first of all and decide whether they like you, trust you and want to buy from you. As a founder, the reputation of your start-up label will rest on your shoulders. You will need to invest in and develop your personal brand as soon as possible to boost the credibility of your business. People buy from people, and the customers looking for transparency and authenticity will connect better with brands that have a clear leader.

You cannot opt out of personal branding. It is going to happen to you and around you, no matter what you do. It is, therefore, better to take control, and you decide who you want to be and how you want to be perceived in relation to your business, rather than let other people do it.

From branding to marketing

Developing a strong brand is crucial if you want to build a business that will grow to become a mega brand like Chanel or Gucci, and if you want to license your name to other products to make more money in the future.

A strong brand identity is one that stands out and offers something different to all the other companies in the market. Your brand is reliant on your unique value proposition and the brand storytelling you use to connect with and inspire the consumer. Your brand story will include your product, key words, your ethos and values, design aesthetic, history, designing and making process, how you sell your product and your promotional approach. You need to build a brand that makes an emotional connection with your consumer, so that they feel a consistent emotion about your label, which makes them loyal customers.

The work you have done in this chapter has been about developing your brand and brand storytelling and your promise to the customer. Once you have determined your brand then you will be ready to move on to marketing. Marketing is what you will do to attract customers to your brand through your product, messaging and delivering those branding promises.

What is marketing?

Many people confuse marketing with advertising and promotion. Whilst these are part of marketing, there are many more elements to it. Marketing is the process of creating a business and product that appeals to a target consumer and then persuading that customer to buy your product. Marketing involves market research, analysis, and understanding your ideal customer's interests, needs and wants. Marketing relates to all aspects of your business, including product development, pricing, merchandising, distribution methods, sales, and promotion. The marketing process is fundamental to the business performance because it addresses the most important aspects of the market. It ensures that a business reaches the right consumers with the right product, at the right price, place and time.

In other chapters I have discussed many elements that relate to this chapter, including identifying the customer, developing the right product for them and reviewing your competitors. You may want to review these chapters again in relation to marketing.

Marketing activity can be organised into two broad categories. The first part is identifying your customer and their needs through market research, studying consumer behaviours and then developing an effective marketing strategy. The second part is the implementation of a strategy to meet these consumer needs. The strategy will include your marketing mix, which includes product, price, process, place, promotion, people and physical evidence. I will discuss these elements below in more detail.

Market Research

Every business needs accurate and detailed information in order to be successful. Market research is an integral part of business planning and provides a wealth of information about prospective customers, the competition, and the industry in general.

Good market research will provide you with relevant data, which will help solve the marketing challenges that all businesses have to deal with. From the research, you will determine strategies such as market segmentation to identify your target group within a market, product differentiation and what makes your brand different from your competitors. These are essential elements for your business and would be impossible to develop accurately without market research.

As discussed in Chapter 3, when identifying your customer and competitors you can conduct two kinds of research, primary and secondary but in order to understand the market as a whole there are two business models that can help.

A business needs to assess the internal and external environment and I see many brands that miss these essential elements. If you don't observe what is happening in the wider world and what new things are on the horizon, then your business will have no vision and in time will die. It is essential to keep up-to-date with changes in the fashion industry, consumer behaviours and new technologies.

PESTLE

The PESTLE theoretical model can help you to analyse external factors that may affect your business in the future. These external factors will be things that your company cannot change, but you need to be aware of them and decide how you will react to them. Whilst it may seem like a very dry or laborious chore to conduct a PESTLE analysis, I highly recommend it. I advise all my clients to do them regularly, monthly if possible, as things can move very fast and your business can very quickly be left behind. Once my clients start doing them, then they find them really useful and they get easier to do as you go along. If you regularly do a PESTLE analysis then you will know the types of things to look out for when reading industry journals.

The PESTLE factors are Political, Economic, Social, Technological, Legal and Environment. It is best to lay the PESTLE out in a table format, then you can just jot in the key points for anything that could affect your business in the near future.

Political	Economic
Government changes, laws, global issues, legislations, wars and conflicts, trading policies,	Taxes, interest rates, inflation, stock market, consumer confidence, climate, cotton and oil prices, minimum wages,
Social	**Technological**
Changing consumer buying behaviours, lifestyle changes, media, ethics, advertising, celebrity and role models, fashion trends, social trends	Innovations, smart mirrors, in store technology, VR, AR, AI, automation, global communications, new technologies, manufacturing
Legal	**Environmental**
New legislations, patents and licensing, new laws in each country you trade in	Ethical manufacturing, cotton, over production, sustainability, new ethical fabrics, natural sources, climate change

SWOT

The SWOT analysis is a structured planning tool that looks at the strengths, weaknesses, opportunities and threats and you use it to analyse the potential of your business. I mentioned this tool earlier in the Business Planning section, but we would also use it in marketing. The SWOT will help you understand your business better, assist the decision-making process, address weaknesses, and help you evaluate your business opportunities and threats.

Create the SWOT as a table so that you can easily add in the elements in the different sections, it can be as short or detailed as you want it to be, but the more detailed the better your results will be.

Strengths	Weaknesses
Knowledge, skills, brand story, signature design etc.	Lack of resources, unknown brand name, cash flow, manufacturing etc.
Opportunities	**Threats**
Any area of weakness that could be improved, any opportunities identified in the PESTLE, any of your competitors' weaknesses that you can take advantage of etc.	Any area of weakness that you don't improve, any area addresses in the PESTLE, competitors taking advantage of opportunities identified in the PESTLE or your weakness etc.

The PESTLE analysis looks for hard data and research, whereas the SWOT analysis is more brainstorming. The two business tools though work together, as the information you uncover with the PESTLE analysis will be required to do an effective SWOT analysis. The information you have identified in your PESTLE would be transferred across to the SWOT, as these points could be either an opportunity or a threat to your business in the future. If you only do a SWOT analysis then you are only looking inside your company instead of looking at the opportunities or threats that are coming due to changes in the wider world.

The benefits of these strategic business tools are huge for your brand, they should not be overlooked and you should plan time to regularly conduct the SWOT and PESTLE. The benefits including tapping new opportunities, minimising risks, reflecting on the success and progress of the business, and anticipating what is coming up.

THE MARKETING MIX

The marketing mix is often referred to as the 7 P's of marketing. The marketing mix is a well-known, regularly used business tool to help a business find its unique selling proposition through a combination of seven elements. These 7 elements are product; price; place; promotion; people; process and physical.

- **Product**
  What is unique about the product? Why should the customer purchase it and what benefits, both tangible and intangible, do they get from it?

- **Place**
  Where will you sell your product to make it easily accessible for your customer? This could be in-store, through third parties, on-line, pop up, through parties?

- **Price**
  The product should be seen as good value for money, though not necessarily cheapest. Is the pricing architecture for the product range consistent and appropriate to the market and customer?

- **Promotion**
  Advertising, PR, sales promotions, personal selling and social media are all key communication tools for your business. How will you make sure you promote your business to the correct audiences in a manner that they will hear, will appeal to their emotions and provide results?

- **People**
  All businesses are reliant on the people who run them and having the right people is essential because they are as much a part of your business offering as your products are.

- **Processes**
  What delivery terms will you offer the customer? What are your terms for returns? How easily can you customer see, find and purchase your products?

- **Physical Evidence**
  This refers to your packaging and marketing materials, as well as visual merchandising and displays. All the visual elements of your business need to be coherent and consistent with your branding guidelines.

Once you have looked at the 7P's you should end up with a marketing mix that means you have created the right product, at the right price, in the best place and promoted it perfectly for your customer. It will be a combination of the elements of the 7P's that will make your unique selling proposition (USP). Your brand should not be unique for one only element, such as just product or just price, because this leaves you open to being copied. The unique combination of elements from the marketing mix is what will enable you to stay ahead of the competition.

Creating Your Marketing Plan

Once you have conducted all your research, you are ready to put all the different elements into a marketing plan. The plan will include your customer profile, competitor research, PESTLE, SWOT and 7 P's marketing mix.

Your marketing plan is a working document that should sit on your desk. You should constantly refer to it and evaluate it. A good marketing plan will give your business direction and clarity. The marketing plan ensures your business is proactive, constantly keeping the customer at the front of your brand and makes sure you are creating products and services that meet your customers needs. Having a detailed plan helps you set objectives and measure your progress in a calm and measured way. The plan also ensures you are constantly thinking of the future, building a visionary brand rather than one stuck in the past.

The marketing plan will help you to:

- Concisely summarise your business in the language of your customer.

- Provide a situation analysis of the external environment, market and fashion industry.

- Anticipate changes in the world, the market and the fashion industry.

- Define your customer and competitors.

- Strengthen your product offer and define your brand identity.

- Evaluate your strengths, weaknesses, opportunities and threats.

- Increase your chance of success by setting clear goals and objectives.

- Describe how you add value to your brand through your Unique Selling Proposition and brand storytelling.

- Explore future business growth and new opportunities.

Marketing Plan Template

A marketing plan is part of your business plan, but it is also a working document that stands on its own to help you reach your vision. Developing a marketing plan is essential for a fashion brand to survive and grow when you will be up against so much competition.

An effective marketing plan will set out a detailed consumer profile, competitor analysis, realistic goals, objectives and targets, and the actions needed and budget required, in order to achieve them. The plan should also address how you will: -

- Increase brand awareness.

- Attract more customers.

- Increase the value of sales.

- Increase the number of sales from each customer.

- Encourage customer loyalty.

The plan shouldn't be a long, wordy document. It needs to be clear and concise so that the key information can easily be identified and action taken. Targets are really critical to marketing success, so these should be specific, measurable and realistic.

There is no set formula for a marketing plan, and you will be able to find numerous examples online. Or you can download a template from my website at www.startyourownfashionlabel.com.

Your marketing plan can be as unique as your brand, but below I have given you some general ideas of what you can include. As the marketing plan is personal to you then you can change headings, move things around but it is worth considering having these elements in your plan in some way.

Executive Summary
The Executive Summary always comes first in your marketing plan but is the thing you write last. It summarises each of the sections below to give an overview of the plan.

Background
In this section you would include the history of the brand, where you have come from and the competitive advantage you have.

Situation Analysis

In this section you would include your research and information on
 	
   ☐   *The external environment including the PESTLE analysis.*
 	
   ☐   *The market place – trends, competitors, demographics.*
 	
   ☐   *SWOT analysis.*
 	
   ☐   *The market, how this market is growing and how big it is.*

Competitive Analysis
This is the section where you put all the research you have done into who your competitors are, what they offer and what makes you different to them.

Customer Analysis

This is the section where you put all the research you have done into your customer, including a detailed description of who the customer is.

The Brand

In this section you need to detail your unique selling proposition (USP). You will explain what makes your company different from other brands. In this section you can also include the brand value proposition and explain the brand tone, voice, personality.

The Marketing Mix – 7 P's

In this section you will detail the marketing mix and the 7 P's of product, price, place, promotion, people, process and physical evidence and how you will address each section.

PRODUCT	
PRICE	
PLACE	
PROMOTION	
PROCESS	
PEOPLE	
PHYSICAL EVIDENCE	

Objectives and Goals

This section details what you want to achieve and by what date. The objectives need to be specific, measurable, achievable, and time- related. This section will help you monitor and evaluate your progress and success.

The Implementation Plan
This section will detail the activity you will do to implement your marketing activity to meet your goals. This will include the resources you need including time, people and budget.

The Marketing Budget
In this section you will include details of your marketing budget and a full breakdown of the costs of delivering your marketing activity.

Additional Information
This section is to cover anything else that you have not been able to include in other sections.

Neuro-marketing

It is worth taking some time to look at neuromarketing, which is the study of customer behaviour and how it affects their buying patterns. Neuromarketing is essential when marketing fashion, as consumers mostly purchase fashion product on an emotional basis. Neuromarketing uses emotional triggers to promote a brand based on the psychological traits of the target customer.

To use neuromarketing to increase sales and create emotional triggers in your customers, you can follow some very easy steps:

Tell Stories
Stories trigger emotions and a good story will create positive thoughts. Customers love stories, as they appeal to their decision-making processes in a way that facts and figures don't. Your brand storytelling can include why you started your brand, what makes your brand unique and special, what inspires you, what problems you are solving. Another part of storytelling that is often missed is in the product descriptions. Tell your customers a story about each product, such as how it was made or designed and they will love the piece even more.

Inspire Fear
An unusual approach, but I am talking more of fear of missing out rather than abject terror. The way to increase the fear of missing out, is to create limited edition pieces, or have time limited availability or offers. These types of offers can incentivise the customer to see now

and buy now. A brand needs to provide a strong 'call-to-action' to get the customer to buy now. They don't want the customer to go away and think about it, as they often don't come back.

Altruism

Altruism, or giving back, can be a powerful tool for building customer recognition and loyalty, but it should be used carefully. I often hear brands talk about giving a percentage of their profit to a charity, but they are using it as a marketing tool rather than a genuine passion to support a good cause. As today's consumer is looking for authenticity and transparency, a brand should only use altruism if it is authentic. There needs to be a genuine reason, a clear purpose and an authentic connection between the charity and the brand or product. Genuine altruism can work and will provide a connection and sense of belonging to your social conscious customers.

Use Social Proof

Social proof is where a brand shows that other people have experienced the product and love it. This encourages other customers to buy as well. Social proofing, or as I often term it a '#happycustomer campaign,' on social media will convert more customers to buy. One happy customer always makes another one. It is also worth looking at getting positive reviews on your website, Google and social media, as studies state that 90% of online customers look at the product reviews before making a purchase.

Future Marketing

For your brand to survive and succeed, you will always need to be a step ahead of the competition. Marketing can help your business prepare for a bright future.

Using the marketing tools described in this chapter, you can build a brand with a vision, ensuring you stay ahead of your competitors. Marketing isn't a one-off activity. You need to keep working on your marketing activity, all day, every day. I describe marketing as similar to the circus trick of spinning a plate on a stick, you need to keep the momentum up or it will drop off the stick. To keep all your marketing plates spinning you need to schedule time to regularly review your marketing plan. The regular reviews will ensure your business is still relevant in the current environment and relevant to the customer.

The world is changing and your marketing approach will need to adapt. The customer will change, as will their buying behaviours. Your competitors will change as new ones come in and others change direction. The tools you use to connect with and sell to your customer will also change over time.

There are constantly new challenges in trying to get your brand heard in a crowded market place and you will need to be entrepreneurial in your approach. Use every tool you can in reaching out to and connecting with your customers, including traditional media as well as social media, using Instagram, podcasts, YouTube etc. These methods may change in the future, so you will need to keep ahead of developments.

How you sell to your customer, and the type of product they want, will change as well. We already have more brands using the DROP model rather than seasonal collections, as well as an increasing number of fashion rental brands and labels also trying out new circular economy models.

In this book I speak a lot about changing consumer behaviours and how the customer of today is interested in more authentic, experiential brands that are more transparent in their processes. To meet this demand, marketing activity will move towards creating experiential rewards rather than offering discounts. You will be able to build more of a community around your brand by rewarding your loyal customers with one-of-a-kind experiences that they can't get anywhere else.

This chapter has hopefully enlightened you on the benefits of a strong marketing strategy and the need to have a working marketing plan that becomes your to-do list, rather than a boring document stuck on a shelf.

Recap – Branding and Marketing for Success

In this chapter you have learnt that branding begins within your company, creating your brand values and storytelling, and marketing begins with the consumer. Before you are ready to market your business, you have to develop a clear brand position.

This quick recap will remind you of the key areas to consider in building your brand and developing your market.

Know your customer
Every part of your business relies on you understanding your customer and this is also the case for branding and marketing. Without in-depth knowledge of your customer, you will be unable to create a brand that connects with them, or create and market a product to them.

Know your competitors
You need to identify your competitors, understand their product and brand position in order to ensure that you have a point of difference.

Create a strong brand

To make a strong brand, you need to determine several elements including the key qualities and benefits your brand will offer to the consumer. You will need to decide which words you will use about your business that will act as emotional triggers with your customer. You also need to decide on your brand's personality, tone of voice, logo, image guidelines and brand experience. Strong branding makes selling easier.

Consistency

Consistency is critical and you need to ensure that all elements of your business convey the same brand message. Your brand resides in your customer's mind as a result of all the impressions they make whenever they encounter your name, logo, product, social media and marketing messages.

Be Visionary

You will need to regularly review your marketing activity and adapt to changes. The best way to ensure you are up-to-date, and making the most of opportunities and considering threats, is by conducting regular SWOT and PESTLE analyses. Be entrepreneurial and always look for new opportunities and ways to market your brand to make it heard. You will need to constantly review changing consumer behaviours and adapt to them, taking advantage of any new ways of reaching customers and connecting with them.

Build your marketing mix

Using the 7 P's of marketing you will successfully develop the right product at the right price in the right place, provide the right process and physical environment, and offer the customer the processes they desire. Within the 7 P's is your unique selling proposition, a group of elements that will help you stay ahead of your competition.

Build a community

Put your customer at the front of everything you do and create a brand community. Your brand needs to be authentic and transparent to build a loyal customer base.

Research

Research, research and research! By constantly doing research you will be able to make informed decisions in your business and understand your competitive advantage. Assumptions can lead you down the wrong path.

Resources

Don't forget that on my website www.startyourownfashionlabel.com you can download loads of great resources to help you set up your business, including a Marketing Plan template.

Chapter 7 – Selling your collection to Stores

You may have designed and created the most amazing collection but, if you don't make sales, then you don't have a business, just a very expensive hobby!

The brands that focus on sales are the ones who will stay in business, but selling your collection isn't easy. Every designer and brand who I have worked with during the past 10 years, have asked for advice on how to sell. They usually come to me when they have already tried to sell their collection to stores either by taking part in trade shows or emailing buyers. However, they have failed to attract the buyer's interest or haven't sold anything in one or two seasons. By this point the brands are often running out of money, as they have invested everything into a wholesale strategy that hasn't worked.

In this chapter, I want to look at ways of ensuring this doesn't happen to you and give you the tools to develop a wholesale strategy that is more successful.

There are two main routes to market to sell your collection:

- **Wholesale**, when you sell your collection at wholesale price to store buyers who will place your pieces in their retail shops, or
- **Direct to consumer**, when you sell your collection direct to the customer through your own online store, events or pop up shops.

My advice to start-up designers is always to focus on selling direct to consumer. I talk about this more in the next chapter, but I find that many brands still want to find out how to wholesale. In this chapter I will talk you through a wholesale strategy and the steps you need to take to make it successful, whether you start to wholesale in the beginning or further down the line.

To wholesale your collection successfully you need to develop a strategy. You should be prepared to spend time on research and preparation for it to achieve results. For most brands, it can take several seasons before they get a buyer from their target stores to even look at their collection. Then the likelihood is that the buyer doesn't place an order, instead advising the brand that they will continue to 'watch them,' or will see them again next season. This can be soul destroying for emerging labels who have put everything into this collection, only to have to do it all again in six months' time.

A brand needs to be very focussed if their wholesale strategy is to succeed, making sure they spend time and money in the right areas. You have to make sure that you have prepared and have the right documents to answer all the store buyer's questions, otherwise you will be wasting time for both you and the store.

In the past, start-up fashion brands wanted to wholesale as it was seen as the most beneficial way of growing a label. The major advantage of wholesale was that it was less risky for the brand, as they just had to create a sample of each piece and didn't have to invest in holding stock. Brands only put the collection into production once they had orders from the stores and usually only when the store had paid a deposit, so there was minimal risk. Selling through wholesale gave the start-up labels credibility by being associated with well-known store names. It enabled the new label to have brand alignment next to their potential competitors, increasing their brand awareness, and gave them potential to be in stores around the globe. It is easy to see why brands preferred this method of selling their collection.

However, as I will explain throughout this chapter, many of these advantages are no longer relevant, as the market has changed and selling through wholesale can be very different for new brands entering the market these days. Stores no longer pay deposits and usually don't actually place an order anymore with a young brand, instead asking for pieces on a sale or return basis. This means that the level of risk has now moved from the store to the brand and this can an unfeasible risk for a start-up brand.

Wholesale is still an option for a brand, but it may come later when the business is able to better manage the risk, or when the label has more power to negotiate an actual sale by proving they have a hungry customer base that the store wants to access.

This chapter will take you through the wholesale process from preparing your brand to developing the strategy for selling your collection wholesale. I have split this chapter into two halves to make it easier to follow the steps.

Preparing Your Brand for Wholesale

- What the store buyers want to see
- Look book
- Pricing
- Line sheet
- Terms & Conditions
- Order Form

The Wholesale Strategy

- Researching the stores
- Contacting buyers

- Trade fairs
- The Buyer appointment
- Writing the order
- Consignment / SoR / short orders/ drop shipping
- Working with agents and distributors
- Maintaining the relationship

PREPARING YOUR BRAND FOR WHOLESALE

There are some basic steps that you have to take, and documents you need to prepare, before you are ready to talk to buyers or sell your collection wholesale.

I have already touched on one of these documents, the look book, in Chapter 6 Marketing and Branding, but I will discuss it again here, as it is the primary tool in your selling process. I will also talk you through pricing your collection for wholesale, creating the line sheet, order form and preparing your terms and conditions.

It is essential that you have everything ready before you contact your first store, as you only get one chance to make a great impression. If you get it wrong and don't present your brand to its best advantage, then there is a good chance that the store buyer will never open another email or take another call from the brand. There are thousands of other brands that the store can work with, so the buyer is only interested in working with professional brands that can make the most of the opportunity their store offers.

What the store buyers want to see

It can be really difficult to get a store buyer to look at your collection, answer your email, or visit your stand at a trade show, but when you do finally get in front of them, what are they looking for?

Over the years I have worked very closely with store buyers from the leading department and independent stores around the world. I maintain the relationships with the buyers in order to understand what they are looking for, so that I can make sure the brands I work with can meet the buyer's needs. Here is a list of the things that the buyers tell me they are looking for:

- Product and prices that fit with their store and customer.
- A brand that offers something new, or fills a gap that the store doesn't have at the moment.

- A brand with a collection of unique products with a strong brand signature.

- A brand that has great images, which are appealing, and shows the collection in a way that makes it easy to understand who the customer is, the quality of the pieces and any special design features.

- A brand that has developed great story telling that adds value and connects with the store's customer base

- A brand that has a good Instagram account with a very engaged following. They are not looking at high numbers of followers and likes, but for people talking about the brand and potential customers asking about the product or reviewing it.

- The buyer wants to find a brand that has a buzz about it, with lots of press features and a really engaged following on social media with people talking and asking about the brand.

- The stores are looking for brands that have started to build a customer base, proving that there is interest in the brand and the product. The store would expect the brand to drive this customer base towards their store to buy the product.

- The buyer is looking for products that will have great hanger appeal, look great in store and can be merchandised well.

- The store is looking for commitment from the brand to go above and beyond to ensure sales will be made in store, this can include a marketing and PR campaign, press coverage, in-store event, and a social media campaign to drive in customers.

- The buyer is looking for a brand that has a consistent design aesthetic. The reason the buyers will often watch a brand for several seasons, usually three seasons, is to ensure the brand has a consistent brand signature, quality and style.

- The buyer wants to know that the brand has production sorted and can deliver an order to the size that they require on time.

- Stores often look for exclusive product or ranges, so they seek brands that could provide them with something unique to offer to their customer.

Stores now look for brands to do more than just supply product and even a start-up brand has to prove that they have a customer base. The industry standard of buyers watching brands for several seasons, to see how they develop before they will even consider buying, is very challenging for start-up labels. This means that a start-up would have to have a significant amount of money behind them to keep making collections to show to the buyers, even though you know they won't buy them. As the buyer is also looking for the brand to have started to grow a customer base, then my advice is to put the wholesale strategy second and make selling your collection direct to consumer the priority.

Look books

Your look book is the document you create for each collection, either printed or digital, which features images of your product in a visually appealing way that will encourage sales. The look book can have two purposes; it is a document for wholesale buyers, agents and distributers to view the collection for purchase and also for the press and stylists to see the pieces for PR purposes. The images can also be used for social media and sales on your own website.

The task of the look book is to create an emotional connection with the reader, persuading and inspiring them to buy your collection. A good look book creates brand awareness, speaks to your customer, relates to them, shows your brand personality and reflects the brand values and quality. It is one of the most powerful tools you will have for your brand!

When creating your look book, you need to think about how the buyer or customer sees it, not just how you want it to look. Can the person connect with the images and see themselves or their customer in the pieces? Without an emotional connection, there is no purchase. The look book can also raise the perceived value of the product by presenting it in a high-quality way, or de-value the collection by showing it in a bad light.

The look book can have a combination of editorial style images as well as e-commerce style product images, which clearly show the product pieces in detail. Whilst it is important to show detailed product images so that the person knows exactly what they are buying, you also have to remember that you aren't just selling 'product.' In everything you do you also need to sell the experience of your brand! Therefore, the images need some context so that they allow the person to see the lifestyle they would be buying into if they were to purchase a product. Creating fully styled looks, or shooting the images in a realistic or aspirational location, rather than against a white background, can achieve this.

The wholesale buyer, agent or distributer needs the look book to provide them with an understanding of your collection, both from the style of images as well as the product detail. You can do this by ensuring you use professional high-quality images, so you really need to invest time and money into creating the best look book you can. The buyer needs to be able to see the details of the product as well as the general 'look', so you need to ensure you have captured images that provide both.

If your look book is bad then the buyer will think the brand is unreliable, unappealing and not market ready, therefore refuse all requests for appointments. Even if they see you at a trade show and think the collection looks great but then walk away with a poor look book, they are likely to refuse the brand.

When sending a look book to a wholesale buyer they may ask to see the look books of previous seasons, so that they can see the growth of the brand and the consistency of the style, aesthetic and brand value. Therefore, it is beneficial to create a brand style for all your look books to strengthen this opportunity.

The look book shoot

When you are planning your look book, create a mood board of the style you want for both the final design layout of the book, as well as inspiration for the style of images, styling, hair make-up and location. This will help you translate your vision to the team you hire.

When you are booking the team, you need to tell them exactly how many looks you have so that they can work out their fees and tell you how much time it will take to shoot all the looks with the different changes.

Plan the shoot day by writing up a running order of the looks, so that you stay on plan and don't waste time and money or miss out any looks. On the day, take along print outs of the running order and mood board for all the team, that way everyone can keep to time and the required style.

Costs of creating a look book can vary greatly and it would be impossible for me to give you a guide, however my advice is not to skimp on the cost, as selling your collection relies on these images! I constantly hear buyers saying they are shocked by designers who have spent time and money creating an amazing collection but then totally ruin it by cutting costs when shooting the look book, ending up with horrible pictures that put the buyer off buying the brand. You need to budget for a good quality look book and don't resort to using friends and family to be the model or photographer, or think of doing it all yourself. A low budget look book will damage your brand. The team you need for developing your look book includes:

- Photographer — you will have to confirm usage rights, the number of looks and the deadline date for final images to be delivered.
- Retouching — you will have to check if the photographer's fee covers the final images or is there an additional cost for retouching.
- Model — you will have to confirm your usage rights and time span.

- Stylist.

- Hair / make-up team.

- Location.

- Food and drink for team.

- Graphic designer to create the look book layout.

Picking your team

Having a great team will help you create a fabulous look book, so hire the best team you can afford and carefully negotiate the usage for the final images.

Photographer

You need to hire a professional photographer who is experienced in shooting fashion look books. A good photographer will be as passionate as you are about getting the best pictures. Be very clear when booking them about the number of looks you have and the style you need to achieve. Show them your mood board so that you can be sure that you all have the same idea of what you want to achieve.

You will need to negotiate the terms with the photographer including image rights, date for the finished pictures to be delivered and be sure to check that this includes finished pictures, not ones that still need retouching.

The photographer will always own the pictures and license them to you. You need to negotiate the use of the images for an agreed length of time for the printed look book, website use, social media and in-store use. If you were going to use the images for an advertising campaign then this would add an additional cost. Be very careful in agreeing the terms, as you don't want the photographer to ask you to take the images off your website in six months' time because the license has run out.

The photographer can often help you identify the rest of the team, as they will have relationships with model agencies, hair and make-up teams.

Model

You need to choose a model that is a good fit with your brand and is someone your customer will connect with. If you have a middle-aged customer and they look at your pictures, which have a very young model, they may think the brand is not for them.

An established, professional model will save you time and money in the long term as they know how to pose, can take direction and look natural, which will speed up the process and allow the photographer to get the shot quickly.

You will have to negotiate the usage rights with the model agency. You need to negotiate the use of the images for an agreed length of time for the printed look book, website use, social media and in-store use. If you were going to use the images for an advertising campaign this would add an additional cost. On a model release form, they often allow you to use images up to three years on your website but again check, as agents like to chase for extra fees!

Stylist

A stylist can be a really great addition to your team, as they help put the looks together including sourcing shoes and accessories, will make sure the product looks great, and help with the creative direction. Many designers feel that they can style the shoot themselves, but a good designer understands that the stylist can help them realise their vision in a way that the consumer will perceive it and wear it, not just how the designer sees it.

Hair and Make-up

The hair and make-up team also need to help you create a look that connects with your potential customer. This is not the opportunity for them to create something outlandish, which they can use for their portfolio. So be sure to share your mood board and vision and explain who your target customer is, so that they can create an appropriate look.

The digital and/or print look book

Many designers just create a digital look book due to the expense of printing, but also because most buyers only see the email version or ask for it to be emailed. Even if you only create a digital version, it still needs to be professionally designed to represent your brand.

The look book should include the following:

- A cover page with your logo, brand name, collection name and/ or season date and an editorial style image.
- Inside pages should include the product shots (clear images against a white / plain background showing the product detail) or a mix of product shots and editorial style.
- Back cover should again have an editorial style image, brand name and logo, and contact details including website, email address, contact number.

All pages of the look book should have a footer with the copyright © information and brand name. Don't include an order form, prices, descriptions or brand information, as this will be included in the line sheet.

There are lots of examples of look book formats online, so do some research and find one that is right for your label, one that matches your brand value and aesthetic.

Pricing

Pricing your collection correctly is important to your profit margins, but will also affect where your collection fits in the market. I have met many designers over the years that have made disastrous mistakes with their pricing. Too many of them hadn't worked out their costs properly, which meant that they had sold their product at a loss, often resulting in them going out of business very quickly. I have also met designers who have been selling their collection direct to consumer at wholesale price and only later realised they can't find the margins to sell the collection wholesale to a store. It is then too late to increase their prices to retail level, as they will lose the customer base they have built, as these customers wouldn't have accepted the prices being doubled over night!

I have also met brands that say that they are happy to sell their collection at cost price in the beginning just to get into a store, thinking that they can increase their prices later. This strategy never works, because if the store has bought within a certain price bracket then that is where they have positioned your brand and they won't pay higher prices for future collections. This strategy would also affect the long-term sustainability of your label as your business needs to have some profit margin when selling, in order to give you working capital and the money to help market your brand and take it to the next level.

Therefore, whichever way you look at it, you need to get your pricing correct right from the start.

Industry Pricing Format

There is a set industry accepted formula for working out your prices which works very well:

Cost Price
Cost price = (cost of materials, trims and labour) + (overheads, admin costs and design expenses including pattern cutting and samples divided by the number of items produced in this style)

Wholesale Price per piece
Cost price × 2 (up to 2.5) = wholesale price

Recommended Retail Price (RRP) per piece

Wholesale price × 2.7 (up to 3) + tax / VAT = Recommended Retail Price (RRP)

There is very little flexibility in this format. The store buyer will not reduce their mark-up between the wholesale price and the RRP, as they need this to cover their overheads and make their profit. You would be foolish to reduce your mark-up between the cost price and wholesale price, as you need this profit margin to give you the working capital to grow your business. If your prices are too high then your only option is to look at reducing your costs.

Many start-up designers price their collection against the competitors instead of working out their prices properly and this can be disastrous. Your competitor might have negotiated better costs than you, or be producing in greater volume so that they have lower costs. The only sensible approach is to use the industry formula to work out your prices.

New brands tend to fall into the premium market, as their costs are higher due to the smaller numbers they produce. However, many feel that their prices are too high and think that they must lower them in order to sell, but can never get their prices low enough. Instead of trying to lower their prices, I always recommend that they should look instead at increasing their brand value so that the customer would not balk at the price. If you have a great brand story, a point of difference in your collection and product, a strong design signature, awesome packaging and a great connection with the customer, then the perceived brand value is high and the customer would be willing to pay a more expensive price.

The pricing of your collection, using the industry format noted above, does not include any shipping costs, taxes and insurance for delivery of the collection to the store. The wholesale prices stated would be 'ex-works' which means the store will pay the shipping, import taxes and insurance. For further information on adding shipping costs see the section in this chapter on terms and conditions.

A final point on pricing is to remember that it is not about how many pieces you sell, it is about margin you make and the only way to increase your margin is to reduce your costs and overheads or increase your price. Over time as your brand grows, you will increase the efficiencies in your business, so some costs will go down due to economies of scale, in that you will be able to meet the minimums for cheaper production and fabrics as well being able to reuse patterns.

Line Sheets

The line sheet is a separate document to the look book. The look book showcases the collection through beautiful images and the line sheet gives the facts, figures and details. The line sheet is the selling tool to help the buyer from a retail store understand and place orders for the collection

The line sheet includes the following information: -

Cover Page
Name of brand, logo, collection name and /or season date, website and contact information as well as copyright © information

Product range
You need to include the information about each piece in the collection such as the colours and sizes it is available in, the fabric composition, the wholesale price and recommended retail price.

Name	Image of Product	Colour	Fabric	Sizes	Wholesale Price	RRP
Name of each piece or the stock number	A photo, sketch or outline drawing	All the colours and prints the pieces are available in	Fabric composition	The full size range each piece is available in	Include prices in £, €, $ or the currency of the country you are selling to	

Detail of Packaging
If you offer special packaging, bags, boxes or unique visual merchandising then include the details, Images and costs if appropriate.

Exclusivity
If you can offer any additional styles, fabric or colour options as an exclusive to a store, then include the information in the line sheet.

Terms and Conditions
The line sheet should also detail all your terms and conditions including delivery times, minimum order quantities, shipping and payment terms. Further details on this are below.

Order Form
The final page can be an order form if you don't use a separate order book.

I have a really great line sheet template on my website www. startyourownfashionlabel.com that you can download and easily use or adapt to your needs.

Terms and Conditions

Preparing a set of terms and conditions in advance of making your first wholesale order protects your business and can you save you a lot of time and money in the future. The terms and conditions make it very clear for both sides about what is expected when placing an order. It makes sure you are covered in case of late payments and can protect you from any misunderstandings or queries later on.

You should include a page with all your terms and conditions on your line sheet, as well as standard business terms related to the laws in your country. This section needs to include statements about protecting your copyright and design rights, any details about product inconsistencies if handmade, or any other areas relevant to your brand.

The terms and conditions should include all the details that the buyer from the store needs to consider when placing their order, including:

Minimum Order Quantity
You should set a Minimum Order Quantity (MOQ) that the wholesale buyer would need to place to have your brand in their store. This can be either a minimum total order value, or the minimum number of each piece, such as a minimum order of 5 pieces per style. The number required by your manufacturer may determine the minimum order per style.

Payment terms
As a brand, set payment terms that make the best sense for your business. Often the store has their own payment terms, so you will still have to negotiate, but the best way to start off is by setting your terms on the order form that you need for your business.

There are all kind of payment agreements, for example:

- Prepayment Deposit of 30% and 70% on delivery.

- Full payment prior to shipping the order.

- Net Payment Terms are most common when working with sales agents and/or with repeat wholesale customers. For example, Net 30 would require payment 30 days after deliver but some stores will ask for Net 60, 90 or even Net 120.

You would only want to offer net payment terms to companies that you have a good relationship with and who have previously paid on time. If it was a new store then your preference should be to take a 30% deposit, as a true sign of commitment and this would give you a safety net to cover production costs. If you were offering a new store net payment terms, then you should conduct a credit check on the store to make sure they are able to pay.

Even if you set payment terms and the store agrees to them, it is still likely that you will have late and bad payers. Therefore, I recommend that as part of your terms you should also state that you charge interest on late payments, as well as additional charges for debt recovery. In the UK, there are statutory interest rates set by government for small businesses to claim interest on late payments.

The payment terms should also state the methods of payment you accept such credit card, cheque, PayPal or brank transfer.

In the pricing and the payment terms, you also need to confirm who pays shipping costs, taxes and insurance for deliveries, see the section below on shipping and taxes.

Shipping & taxes

The prices quoted for your collection in the line sheet are 'ex-works' which means it is just the price of the piece and doesn't include shipping, import duties and insurance.

In the terms and conditions, you should state who would be responsible for shipping costs, the brand or the wholesale buyers. This will be an area open for negotiation but your preference should be to sell your products 'ex-works.' You should have decided in advance whether you offer worldwide shipping or only ship to certain countries.

Examples of shipping terms are:

- **Ex-works** — This is the easiest model for a start-up brand as it means you wouldn't need to work out and pay all the additional costs, as the store would take responsibility for it.

- **FOB** — Free on Board, is when the brand will pay the shipping and taxes of the goods to a certain location and then the goods become the property and responsibility of the store and they pay the on-going costs. Some stores have central depots where brands deliver goods to and then the store ships them overseas.

- **Delivered Duty Paid** — This means the brand will deliver the goods directly to the store and cover all the costs including shipping, duties, taxes, and insurance except for local sales tax.

- **Landed prices** — The same as Delivered Duty Paid except the brand also needs to pay the local sales tax.

- **Domestic Orders** — If you are delivering goods to stores in your home country then you still need to decide if you will charge the store the delivery costs or find out if the store has a courier account that they use to collect goods.

- **Drop ship** — Some online stores work on a drop ship model, which means they include your products on their website but they don't hold any stock. If an order is placed, then they advise the brand and you have to pay the costs and ship the product direct to the customer.

For many of these shipping terms you may need to work with a shipping company. They will help you with the process of delivering the goods to the stores and ensuring all the paper work is correct and all duties and taxes are paid.

The store will need to know how long the shipping will take so that they have an estimated time of delivery to their store. Some international stores will ask for a 'shipping window,' this is a date by which the store would need to cancel the order before it is shipped. If they ask for this be wary that they may cancel the order!

Order deadline
You should set a date by which all orders need to be placed by, fixing a date that you will close your books for that season. This is important for the brand as you can then collate several orders together for manufacturing, which can help you meet your manufacturer's minimum order quantity.

Delivery Dates
You need to set a delivery date, or a timeframe, such as three months after confirmed order, or set the actual date according to the buyer's requirements.

Returns and Exchange Policy
Sometimes things do not go as smoothly as hoped and the store returns goods due to poor quality, faulty pieces or an incorrect order is delivered. You should set clear terms on which you will accept returns and what your exchange policy is. Examples of return and exchange terms are:

- Replacement of faulty goods within 7 days.

- The store needs to advise the brand of any incorrectly delivered goods within 3 days of receipt of the goods.

- No returns will be accepted apart from pieces that were faulty or damaged on delivery.

- 30-day money back guarantee.

- Items can be exchanged within one month of delivery.

None of these terms may suit you but you need to consider how you will manage any returns or complaints and having a clear set of terms can help avoid misunderstandings.

Intellectual property
It is also really important to include a section in your terms and conditions to protect your brand identity, designs and images against copying. These terms would state how the store could use the brand name, for what purposes and for how long.

Order Form

Order form
The order form can be included with the line sheet so that the buyer can complete it quickly and easily. It needs to include spaces to fill in the following information:

- The store's address and contact information.

- Purchase order number if necessary.

- Details of the order, including style names and/or numbers, fabric, colours, sizes and quantities.

- Estimated delivery date.

- Shipping details, including who is paying shipping costs, duties, taxes and insurance.

I have a great example of an order form with terms and conditions on my website www.startyourownfashionlabel.com which is easy to download and use or adapt to your needs.

THE WHOLESALE STRATEGY

Selling to stores is not as easy as it may seem, as a lot of designers and start-up brands find out. It can be a very frustrating and slow process. As stated at the beginning of this chapter, you may only have one chance to make a great impression, so this strategy will take you through the steps to ensure you understand what will be required from you if you decide to wholesale. As much as I can advise you on how to set up your strategy, I cannot guarantee you success with getting your collection in the stores straight away. It can take time, sometimes years before a store will take a brand on. With this strategy though I can advise you how to improve your chances of impressing the wholesale buyer.

Researching the stores

As a start-up brand, you need to be realistic when choosing the stores that you will target. Ask yourself these starting questions:

? Does our brand price point and aesthetic match with the store?

? Does the store have the same customer base as the one we want to target?

Too often brands make assumptions about a store's customer without ever actually visiting the physical shop. It is really important to visit the store in person, see who their customer is and what types of brands and pieces they are buying.

Over the years, no matter what country I am in, start-up brands all tell me they want to have their collections in the same list of stores, they just reel off the names such as Harvey Nichols, Harrods, Lane Crawford, Saks, Liberty, Joyce amongst others. Yet all of these stores have very different fashion customers, focus on different types of product and have different price points. Therefore, you need to do a lot more research in order to select and focus on which stores will be best for your brand.

Store buyers get very frustrated with brands that approach them with no knowledge or understanding of the store and its customer. You need to do really careful in store research, looking at the customer, which other brands they stock in each department, what type of product and price points they carry, and what terms and additional services they offer their customers. You can also talk to the sales staff to find out what sells well and what customers are looking for. Make sure you understand the different departments so that you can contact the right buyer, such as International Designer, Contemporary, Ready to Wear, etc. Before you contact any store buyer, it is essential you have all the above information, do not waste your time, or theirs, by hassling the wrong buyer.

There are different kinds of stores that you can sell your brand to including:

- Department Stores can offer credibility, prestige and brand exposure as well as brand alignment, by being placed next to your competitors. However, they can be very demanding as they have high expectations of the returns they can get from each brand.

- Independent retailers and boutiques are often less demanding and they are more willing to try newer brands, as they seek to offer a more unique selection to their customers.

- Overseas stores can offer great opportunities, but the brand needs to understand logistics, export regulations, international pricing.

- Online stores are popping up every day and are always looking for new brands. However, you need to research them to check they are genuine, can offer you the right brand alignment and the prices match yours. Another issue with online stores can be that they request exclusivity and that can be disastrous if you aren't careful, as it could stop you taking on stores in other countries.

To have any success in selling to stores, you really need to understand each one, how they work and who their customers are. Remember to actually visit their store as well as looking at their website, to find out which brands they carry, the product categories they stock and the retail price points so you can show the buyer that you know where your label fits. You will also need to know your brand adjacencies, both the ones they have in store but also in the overall marketplace, as a store buyer will often ask which brands you would sit next to.

Once you have completed your research, you are ready to contact the buyers.

Contacting buyers

I understand that you are desperate to reach out and start selling your collection and see it stocked in stores around the world, but don't rush into contacting any buyer until you have got everything ready.

Are you ready?
If you have been following the previous sections in this chapter then you should now be nearly ready, but to be sure let us have one last check.

The buyer will decide on your brand within the first few seconds, so you really need to make that first impression count! Being ready means that you have the following in place: -

- A really great look book,

- A detailed, well-presented line sheet that includes all the necessary information, including sizing, colours, fabrics, payment terms and pricing in the appropriate currency for the store,

- That you have written terms and conditions that include your delivery times and minimum order value or quantity,

- That you have considered if you have any styles, fabrics or colour options that could offer to a store looking for an exclusive,

- That your social media and website is clear, branded and visually pleasing with a good following and engagement.

- That you have determined your key messaging and brand story.

Who is your customer?
Understanding your customer is an essential part of the selling process, the buyer may ask you to describe them and they will not be interested in short, generic descriptions, such as "24-35 female interested in high-end designer fashion". If you do not have a clear customer profile then you are not ready to talk to the buyer, and if you don't know who your

customer is then you may be contacting the wrong store. Create detailed consumer profiles and consider which stores they shop in, the types of product they buy, the price points they will pay, what competitor brands they purchase, their demographic and shopping behaviours, and what they value and care about. I cover developing customer profiles in more detail in chapter 3.

Finding Your Contacts

It can be really difficult to find the contact details for buyers, as their email addresses can be really elusive. It can also be really difficult to get hold of buyers by phone, so you will mainly have to try a combination of emails, but you can also send them a letter by post.

For department stores, you need to find the right buyer for your type of product, there is no point just emailing any buyer you can find. The fashion director can be a good point of contact, as they are the person in the store who looks for the next new thing. For independent stores and small boutiques, the owner is usually the main buyer as well.

For small independent stores then the generic email address such as 'info@ thestore.com' is usually managed by the owner/buyer. However, steer clear of generic email addresses for the big buying groups or department stores, as there is very little chance that your email will reach a buyer. Make it your mission to gather the name, telephone number and email addresses of the buyers who will be useful to you.

One easy way to connect with the store buyers is through Linked In, as they all seem to keep their profiles updated on this platform. On the app, you can type in a search term such as 'buyer Harrods' and then sort through to find the correct department buyer for your brand. Also follow the buyer on Instagram, as many buyers say they now research for brands and products on this platform.

What the buyer needs

When you are speaking to the buyer, do you have everything to hand that they want? You need to be sure that you have everything ready in a folder, such as a Dropbox file, so that you can send over the link within an email, or as you are talking to them, or as soon as you hang up. In the Dropbox folder include your look book, line sheet and a killer brand profile. It is a good idea to include some examples of press that the brand has been featured in, as this shows them that there is interest in your brand, as well as evidence that you are actively promoting your label. Also ensure that you have samples ready to send to them if requested.

When to contact

The main buying seasons for high-end fashion brands around the world are predominantly based around the traditional fashion calendar:

- Spring Summer — August to October

- Autumn Winter — December to February

Although these dates are when the buyers are out and about attending sales appointments, they have often apportioned their budgets ahead of these times. This can mean that there isn't any money left for start-up brands by the time the buying season starts. Ahead of the buying season, the stores decide which brands they will have in store, either because they are already selling well or because they fill a gap that isn't covered. The buyers then apportion their budget to buy from the collections of these brands and they go off to see their shows, visit their studios and showrooms to place an order. It is now very rare for a buyer to wander around a trade show looking for a new brand, or trawl through their inbox looking for an exciting new brand.

Money for new brands is very limited, so the earlier you contact them and get your collection ready to show them the better. During the main season, the buyer's in-boxes are jammed packed with look books and line sheets from brands around the world. Therefore, to improve your chances, it can be advantageous to build a relationship with a buyer outside of the buying season. You can do this by introducing the brand, rather than a specific collection, and ask to show your previous collection to the buyer to ask their opinion on whether your brand would be right for the store. You can ask for their feedback on your pieces, so that you don't waste their time when they are busy.

I still meet many brands at fashion weeks that take part as their first step in meeting buyers and obviously fail to achieve sales. Fashion weeks are now predominantly at the end of the buying process, so you need to have contacted the buyer months before to introduce your brand, invite them to view the collection and make an appointment for them to visit your trade stand. Do not wait until fashion week to contact the buyer, as it is too late.

Once you are sure that you are armed and ready to contact the buyer, you need to decide what it is that you will email or send to them. You also have to consider how many times to approach them.

Making contact

Once you reach out and make contact with a buyer, whether by phone, email or in person you need to quickly communicate your brand's unique selling proposition (USP) and convince them why the store will benefit from stocking your brand.

You will need to be brief and concise, not giving too much information before they ask for it. I recommend sending a carefully written email that is concise, introduces your collection and asks for an appointment to show the pieces. Be wary of attaching look books and line sheets, as some buyers do not open emails with attachments from addresses they don't know. It is therefore better to include a Dropbox link within the body of the email.

It is likely that you will have to contact the buyer numerous times before you get a response and each contact needs to be fresh and exciting. You will need to plan different emails with different content. You can send them emails that introduce the brand, show the new collection, feature a piece of the month, tell them about a new piece of press coverage, or invite them to your studio, trade fair or event.

Always be succinct, do not call them more than once a week and don't take it personally if you get no reply or they are curt or unfriendly on the phone. Remember all the buyers are very busy and are being hassled by thousands of brands.

Building the relationship
It would be really beneficial to your brand to build a relationship with the buyer outside of the key buying periods, so that they are aware of your brand when you are ready to send them the look book and line sheet.

If you have followed the suggestions above, you will already have followed this person on social media and commented on their page, researched their store, and know the types of brands they are interested in. If you haven't, go back and do these things first. One of the best ways to build a relationship with a buyer is to get into their mind-set and know what you can offer them to meet their needs.

Remember to always be polite, gracious, and certainly don't be pushy, condescending or rude. Don't go straight into the pitch, as this could be seen to be rude, but also don't waste their time with idle chitchat if you don't know them. Quickly introduce yourself, say you would like to introduce your brand to them and remember to ask them if they are free to talk for a couple of minutes. Then keep to that time!

Pitching your brand
Pitching to a buyer can be really difficult and most of the time it can feel like you are working in a call centre making cold-calls to them. You may also feel disheartened when you send emails that don't generate any

response. You are not alone, as every start-up brand feels the same. You just need to understand that this is the way the industry works and not take it personally and you can't give up, as persistence pays off.

Store buyers receive hundreds of emails a day from brands all over the world, what you pitch to them has to be exciting and grab their attention. When emailing, be sure to put an interesting subject line and keep the body of your email short and to the point. Do not send lots of attachments, instead put all your images and documents into a Dropbox link so that they can download if they want to.

Remember if you are calling, when you get hold of the buyer not to go straight into your pitch but ask them if it is a good time to talk. If they say yes then carry on but if they say no, ask when is a good time to call back? You need to practice your pitch in advance, as there is nothing more boring and annoying than someone reading it from the page. Practice it to make it sound natural, interesting and show your passion for your brand. Talk about the product and not just the inspiration behind the collection.

Whichever way you pitch, by email or call, give the buyer the information they need about the range, the customer, the price and why they should choose your brand. Make it exciting and make it relevant to them!

Follow up
After you have spoken to the buyer, or if they didn't respond to your first email, then send them a polite follow up a few days later. Don't pester them too much, if they want to find out more about your brand then they will let you know. You can check that they received all the information they needed from you, or offer to send them further information or images. It is also OK to call again to see if they received the additional information you sent through and what they thought of it. Remember still to be really polite and patient, they may not buy your brand this season, but you need to keep the relationship friendly for future opportunities.

Go above and beyond
If a buyer does show interest in you and your brand then make sure you go above and beyond in any follow up. Answer their questions quickly, provide the images straight away, arrange an appointment to show the collection promptly. If you do not respond quickly or meet their timelines, then they will not trust you to deliver the product on time.

Also consider what else you can offer the buyer to help increase sales of your product in store, such as press coverage, window display, merchandising or even an in-store event. This is a great way to show your commitment to the store.

Keep in touch
If you didn't get a response from the buyer, or they didn't buy this season, don't be disheartened. Stay in touch with them on social media and keep them up to date with your news. If you keep in touch with them, then in a few months' time or next season, they will remember how interesting your brand was, how friendly and polite you were and get in touch with you!

If you need more help researching the stores or contacting buyers then consider booking a mentoring session through my website www. startyourownfashionlabel.com when I can help with the more specific needs of your brand. I have also created templates for both cold calls and emails to buyers to make it easier for brands to have an example of what to say.

Trade Fairs

A trade fair brings a whole range of brands together under one roof and then the brand and the organisers invite the buyers to see the collections. There are lots of different trade fairs, shows and exhibitions all around the world and many brands choose fairs as a way of reaching out to buyers. They see the trade fairs as a way to find out about and meet stores that perhaps they don't know exist, or meet the buyers that they haven't been able to get a response from by email or phone.

You need to really research the trade fairs before deciding to take part. I recommend that you always visit the fair first. You need to know what the exhibition looks like and the layout, the brands that participate and how they merchandise their stands, as well as which buyers attend and how busy the fair are.

Taking part in a trade fair can be very expensive so you need to make sure you don't waste money by participating in the wrong one. Even the smallest space, such as a 3ft rail, could cost you over £6000 depending on the show, then there are the additional expenses of creating promotional materials, décor for your display, transportation, staffing, travel and accommodation if overseas.

Each trade fair attracts buyers from different countries and they look for brands from particular countries such as Italy or UK. Some shows attract more buyers from the Middle or Far East, whereas others will have mainly European store buyers. If you have the chance to talk to buyers as part of your research, ask which shows they attend, or talk to other designers to find out how successful they were in particular fairs. You can also ask your Embassy or your Government International Trade Department if they have any advice about which trade fairs work best.

As I mentioned earlier in this chapter, buyers no longer wander around trade fairs looking to discover new brands, most attend the shows with set appointments already arranged. They have a clear idea of who they will buy from, and how much budget they have. If you are lucky and a buyer does stop to look, then they may just put you on their 'review' list to watch for the next two or three seasons.

To make the most of taking part in a trade show, I recommend that you make a clear action plan and consider all these questions before you sign up to have a stand.

? Have you done enough research on the trade fair and visited it to see it in action?

? How will you make the most of being there? How can you make your display more appealing so that it stands out more than your competitors? You need to plan the layout of the stand and make sure it showcases the product in the best way, such as not blocking the product by having a table in front of it.

? Are you prepared to talk to everyone? You will need to speak to everyone that looks in your direction, so you can't be sitting there reading a book or fiddling on your phone.

? You need to consider who you will give look books and line sheets to? Often there are manufacturers, students or other exhibitors walking around who you wouldn't want to share all your information with. You need to work out how you will work, so that only buyers get your information.

? Where do you want your stand within the trade show? You need to be on the main footfall path and not be blocked by people queuing for coffee, food or toilets or tucked in a corner. It would also be advantageous to be near your competitors, so that their buyers may also see your collection.

? Do you have a coherent collection that would look great on a rail in the exhibition and appeal to the buyers? You need to consider how many pieces to show and how to merchandise them. It can be unappealing to have rails packed with pieces and you need space to showcase the collection to its best advantage.

? Are you sure you are ready to take part in a big trade fair? Have you organised production? Are you sure about your minimum order quantities and have accurate costings for every item? Have you worked out when your books will close and what your delivery dates are?

? How are you going to staff the show for all the hours it is open every day? Your stand has to have someone on it at all times, as often buyers call in when the fair first opens or right at the end of the day.

? Are you sure that you can export your product overseas? Have you worked out the costs for this and do you know how to manage the logistics?

? Are you ready to start taking part in trade fairs every season? Many of the show organisers will ask you to commit to every show and the buyers will expect to see you every season, so you would need to be developing seasonal collections that the stores can buy into.

? Do you know enough buyers to invite? Will you be able to set up appointments to see the right buyers at the fairs?

If you are unsure on how to answer any of the questions or haven't attended the show to check it out first, then don't pay for a stand. It is too risky to lose a large amount of money on a trade fair that may give you no return on investment.

The buyer appointment

When you finally get in front of the buyer, don't waste the opportunity or their time. If you are prepared and have covered all the areas discussed above, then you will be ready to make a great impression.

First of all, give the buyer the chance to look at and touch the product before asking them if they would like you to talk them through the pieces. Don't just rush into giving them the full background of the brand, why you set it up and waffle on about your inspiration of the collection, if they haven't even looked at it yet. You have to be careful not to 'over talk,' because when the collection is in the store, it has to speak for itself, so let the collection speak to the buyer first.

If the buyer is coming to your showroom or studio, then you can present the collection all beautifully steamed and merchandised. However, if you have to take the collection to the store plan it carefully. First of all, you do not need to take every piece of the collection, pick out the best pieces that you think will be right for that particular store and their customer. If they wanted to see the whole collection they would have booked to visit your studio or showroom, so they probably just want to see a sample of your collection to get a feel for the brand. Have the pieces hung up ready in suit carriers rather than in a suitcase, that way you can present them more effectively showing the hanger appeal and they will look better presented, less creased.

When you start the appointment, have the line sheet, look book and pricing all out ready so that you can refer to them to answer any questions. Having the look book open in front of the buyer also shows them what the pieces look like on a model, as well as on the hanger. If you are able to offer pieces in alternative colours and fabrics, also have fabric samples to hand to show them, as this could help you offer the store an exclusive. If you offer unique packaging or branded packaging, also have this to hand to show the buyer, as well as your press book open so they can see the coverage you have received. I would recommend investing in some nice portfolio folders, which are easy to get out and open to show all this information professionally to the buyer.

Writing the order

If the appointment with the buyer is going well, your next step is to ask for and write the order.

As the buyer starts to select the pieces, you will need to confirm with them the MOQ (minimum order quantity) per piece. If the order isn't big enough to meet the factory MOQ then you may have to advise the store that you can't accept the order. It would be very damaging to the relationship to accept, but then go back to them later and tell them you have to drop a style because you can't meet the MOQ. The buyer will not be happy and may cancel the full order. Your job is to try and persuade the buyer to meet the minimum order number during the appointment.

It can be either the designer or the store that sets the date for deliveries. Larger companies and department stores are much more rigid in delivery terms, sometimes giving not only a day, but a time slot, in which you have to deliver. If the order isn't delivered in time, then they can refuse to accept it. If you have any doubts about delivering on time, advise them you need to confirm delivery date with them once you have spoken to your factory, do not just agree to the order if you are not sure.

The main thing to confirm before any order is written is that they are actually buying and not placing an order on an SoR basis, I discuss this more in the next section. If they are ready to place an order to buy pieces of the collection, then go through the order form with them. Talk them through your terms and conditions (see the beginning of this chapter about setting your terms) and confirm with them the pieces they are ordering, sizes, colours and quantities. Also confirm pricing with them, discuss who is paying the shipping costs, and check any special packing and shipping requests. You should try to ask for a deposit and then confirm the payment terms with them, but be prepared that most stores now don't pay deposits or pay prior to shipping.

There is a downloadable template for an order form available on my website www.startyourownfashionlabel.com

Consignment / SoR / Short Orders/ Drop shipping

One of the biggest changes in the fashion industry for start-up brands is that most stores no longer actually buy emerging brands collections, instead requesting goods on an SOR (sale or return or consignment) basis. This is when the label provides the goods to the store and the brand will only get paid when the store sells the items.

This is very risky for start-up brands, as you have to take all the risk. If the goods don't sell, then the store will return them to you at the end of the season and you then have to try and sell them. Other risks include the pieces being returned to you in poor condition, or the store does not pay you when they sell the pieces. The store may have no incentive to sell your pieces as their first priority will be to sell the product that they had to buy from the more established brands. This means they may just keep your collection in the store room in case they have a gap, or put your collection in the worst sales space on the shop floor.

Another downside of the SoR process can be the payment terms. Stores may still only offer you the wholesale price, which means that you have taken all the risk but with very limited margins. If the store then doesn't pay you promptly, sometimes still paying 120 days from invoice date, then you could end up having huge cash flow problems, which would damage your brand. If possible, you should try and negotiate a better rate, splitting the Recommended Retail Price, so that the brand takes 60% and store 40% would be preferential.

Another change to the ordering process can be a 'short order', where the store buyer looks at the collection but won't make a decision or place an order to buy it months ahead. Buyers like short orders, as they want to go back to the brand when they want the stock, rather than ordering and paying for it months in advance. This makes sense for a store, as they can spread their buying and purchase stock when they need it, meaning they can be more responsive to changing weather conditions or trends. However, for a small brand this may not be an option if they do not have the resources and capacity to turn around orders at short notice, sometimes in two/ three weeks.

The final method could be 'drop shipping,' where an online store doesn't buy product or keep it in stock. Instead the store will include product in their online shop and when an order comes in, the store will send the brand the details and tell them to ship the product direct to the customer within an agreed timescale. This can be difficult for smaller brands that would have to keep product to one side just in case an order came through from the site, which isn't an ideal way of managing your small stock runs.

Working with Sales Agents and Distributers

Many designers struggle with selling. I often compare designers selling their collections like a mother trying to sell her children — it is too personal!

Though it is difficult, I always recommend that a brand starts by trying to sell the collection themselves, as there are several benefits for the brand if they do it at the beginning. If the brand sells the collection, then they can start to build a direct relationship with the store. The buyers like this, as they prefer to meet and know the designers/brand owners that they will be working with. The other benefit is that the brand will directly hear the feedback from the store buyers, which can help them decide how to develop future collections.

If the designer/owner is struggling to manage the sales process due to lack of contacts, or doesn't understand the sales process, then a sales agent or showroom could handle all the negotiations, set the terms and conditions, and manage difficult demands from stores.

Brands can work with either agents or distributers. An agent or showroom will sell your collection in return for fees and commission, whereas a distributor will the buy goods directly from you at a significant discount and then sell on your collection to stores in their territories.

Therefore, if you decide at some time in the future to hand over the sales to an agent, or work with distributers overseas to help you get into more stores, this chapter will give you the basic information you need to take your brand to this next level.

Finding a good sales agent, showroom or distributer

It can be quite difficult to find an agent, or at least a good one. It may take you a while to find one and then you have to build the relationship with them before they will agree to take on your brand. It isn't as simple as deciding on an agent, walking in and handing them the collection to sell. Many new brands find they cannot take on an agent in the first few seasons, as they don't have the margin to pay the commission fees and showroom charges. To take on an agent or showroom they would have to increase their prices significantly to cover the extra costs. It can be as difficult working with distributers, as you would need to heavily discount the product for them and they are looking for brands that have international brand awareness that the stores in their territories would be interested in.

You also need to be very sure that you have found a good agent, showroom or distributer as your business future depends on it. A good agent will not only generate sales for your collection but also build the brands awareness and reputation, however they can also really damage it!

Approaching sales agents and showrooms is the same as contacting buyers. You have to ensure you are ready and have all the tools you need to appeal to the agent, such as a great look book, line sheet, an understanding of the market and your customer, knowing the right stores you want to be in and understand the stores they work with and their price points.

Agents tell me that they prefer working with brands that have already worked with some stores and had experience of producing and delivering a collection to them. The agent's reputation relies on them having brands that can deliver. They wouldn't want to ruin their own relationships with stores because a brand is inexperienced and not able to deliver quality product on time.

When you are looking for an agent or showroom, there are numerous questions that you need to consider:

? Do they have a permanent showroom?

? Do they have showrooms in different countries?

? Do they go out and meet the buyers or only sell in their showroom?

? Do they take part in tradeshows?

? What are the dates of their selling season?

? What other brands do they work with?

? How many seasons have they worked with each brand? An agent that constantly works with new brands should be a red flag.

? How long have they been established?

? How do they promote the brands?

? Which countries or territories do they sell into? Which stores do they work and have relationships with?

? Have they placed the brands they work with in the types of stores you want to be in?

? Do they have personable staff and agents and can you meet the people who will represent your brand?

? Do they manage all the different countries and territories themselves or work with sister / partner agencies?

? What fees and commission do they charge?

? What additional costs will you have to pay for?

? Do they credit check all stores that place orders?

? Do they help with chasing payments?

? What are their terms and conditions?

? How long is the agreement?

? How easy is it to get out of the contract?

? Can you get references?

Some buyers like working with showrooms as they can see several brands at the same time, but also because the showroom team know the sales language and process so the buyer can trust them. For a buyer, an added benefit can be that they can give an honest opinion on the collection to an agent, rather than worry about having to let the designer down gently.

How to get in to an agency or showroom

You need to use exactly the same techniques you use for buyers to get in with an agent or in a showroom. You have to research the company to check that you fit in with their other brands and the stores that they work with. The agent and showroom will need you to have great images, which they can use to attract their buyers, as well as a unique collection that is high quality with great hanger appeal. You need to be able to offer the agent something extra, or have a range that fits in with their current ranges, both in aesthetic and price point.

You have to be sure you can cover the agent's fees and commission rates, which can start at around 10—15% but can go up to 25%. Initially the fee sounds like a small amount but remember if they take a wholesale order of £100,000 then at 15% you are giving them £15,000. Can you afford that? Do you have the margin? Showrooms can also charge you a showroom fee in addition to the commission which can be £2,000 and upwards a month.

Don't rush into signing up to an agent or showroom without checking them out. If they are reluctant to answer your questions or to give references, then be wary. There are some very dishonest agents and showrooms out there and I have seen some amazingly talented designers go out of business because of them. Research them very carefully and look for recommendations of good agents. A good agent may have a waiting list, but it is worth waiting, rather than joining any showroom that has a space. Try and regularly drop into your showroom, or check out how your agent is talking about your brand, as you need to know that they are representing the brand in the best way. There are also all sorts of horror stories of agents who charge for overseas showrooms that they don't have, agents who show the designs to manufacturers who copy them, or discounting products without the brands permission so that they sell products at a loss. The more hands-on you can be with the agent and the selling process, the more chance you have to ensure things are going well.

The agreement with the agent and showroom

Once you have decided that you like each other and are happy to work together, you need to have a very clear written agreement, signed by both parties, which covers numerous areas including:

- how you are going to work together,
- the countries the agency will sell your product in,
- the types and size of orders they will take,
- the currency they will work in,
- that they will conduct credit checks on all stores,
- that there is a clear policy concerning returns,
- the fees and commissions payable,
- the length of the contract,
- the termination process if necessary.

Without a written agreement, there could be in problems later if the relationship with the showroom or agent doesn't work out. They may be protected by Commercial Agency Regulations, which means that you will have to pay compensation to leave and that they can continue to claim commission on all future sales.

Maintaining and developing the relationship

If you engage a sales agent or showroom, they will be a crucial part of your business so you need to choose someone that you feel happy to work with and can trust, as you will need to take their advice. The agent will be helpful in advising you on the stores to approach and what they look for and need, they will help you develop your collection to increase sales, and identify new market opportunities for you.

It is important to maintain the relationship with the agent, and keep in regular touch with them; you cannot just drop your collection off and leave it with them for a season. Ask them if you can attend occasional meetings with buyers, or spend sometime in the showroom or trade show. The more you keep in touch, the easier it is to identify any potential problems, but also means that you can be responsive to feedback and start adapting your collection to meet the needs of the buyers for the next season.

A final concern to highlight about working with agents and showrooms is that the brand may have no relationship with the buyer or the store direct. If at some point in the future you decide to change agents, then you may lose some accounts. Therefore, if you do take on an agent you need to ensure that you also build the relationship with the buyer so that you aren't totally reliant on a third party.

Maintaining the relationship with the stores

Once you have secured orders and delivered the product to the stores, it is not the end of the process. You have to maintain the relationship with the store to make sure the product is selling well and to ensure they buy from you again the following season.

It can be advantageous to the brand to offer the store sales team training about your brand and product, as the more brand information they know, the more they can pass on to the customer. You may also offer to help with merchandising when the product first goes in, or host a small event for press or customers to raise awareness and increase sales. Some stores don't want any assistance, whereas others may be really happy to involve the brand in store activity.

You should also keep an eye on sell through to see what sells well and what doesn't. That can help you with future negotiations with the store. Some brands will also offer 'swap outs', offering to switch product that isn't selling to more popular pieces, sometimes the store request this and you need to anticipate if you are able to do this or not.

Downside to Wholesale

Whilst there are advantages to the wholesale route to market for young brands such as awareness and brand credibility, the changes in the buying process now means that many start-up brands choose to avoid it and focus instead on direct to consumer.

The disadvantages to wholesale that you should be aware of include:

- Rather than less risk, if you have to provide your collection on an SoR basis then you will be taking a higher risk.

- It can be very difficult to make contact with store buyers a

- Some stores are not interested in emerging labels as they see them as too risky.

- The margins for wholesale are not as good as direct to consumer, and many small brands find they don't have enough margin to be able to wholesale, as their recommended retail prices would be too high for most stores,

- There are increasingly fewer opportunities to wholesale, as more independent stores and boutiques close down.

- Finding a reputable sales agent or showroom can be challenging and the fees too high for a start-up brand.

- Poor payment terms from stores, such as Net120, means your cash flow is severely hampered by having to wait long periods for payments to come in.

- It can be difficult to manage the relationships with both manufacturers and buyers around minimum order quantities.

- Sale or return deals can result in greater risk of returned goods and waiting longer periods for your money with very little margins at the end of it.

- Cash flow problems due to long gaps in the selling process, as you are relying on two short sales windows a year when money will come in.

- Problems with stores buying product but then asking for 'swap outs' if products don't sell.

- Charge backs from the store if you don't meet their guidelines on packaging, on time deliver and labelling, or just refusing orders if they don't arrive on time.

- Having to pay the high costs of trade shows to showcase your collection to buyers.

- Having to produce new collections and pay for trade shows every season to appease the store buyers.

Final Recap — Contacting Buyers

Don't rush into contacting store buyers until you are ready and review the sections in this chapter to make sure you have covered everything. Remember you may have only one chance to make a great impression, so you need to make sure you can make the best advantage of the opportunity once you get in front of the buyer.

You need to remember what the buyer is looking for and not just focus on what you want to sell. You need to show the buyer you have a strong signature, a unique product and brand identify, high brand value and all the tools needed to make the buyers job easier.

Here is a final recap to help you when contacting wholesale store buyers:

- **Make sure you are ready** — Before you speak to anyone it is absolutely essential to ensure you have everything ready and perfect, including your look book, line sheet, terms and conditions, pricing, social media, website and brand profile all in a Dropbox folder so that you can send them the link. If anything is missing go back through the process to put everything in place.

- **Your customer** — remember you can't approach a store buyer if you don't know who your customer is, or you might be contacting the wrong store.

- **Research the stores** — only focus on stores that have the same target customer as your brand, that you have the right price points for and that you have visited and understand how the store works, what customers they have and what product they carry.

- **Finding the buyers contact details** — make it your mission to gather the name, email addresses and phone numbers of the buyers who will be useful to send your look book too, find and connect with them on Linked In and Instagram.

- **Build the relationship with the buyer** — work at building the relationship with the buyer outside of the key buying periods. Then they will be aware of your brand when you are ready to send them the look book and line sheet, you can do this through social media as well as emailing them.

- **Practise your pitching** — as the buyers receive hundreds of emails a day from brands all over the world your pitch needs to be perfect, excite them, and grab their attention.

- **Follow Up** — it is OK to follow up with the buyers. Send them polite follow-ups but don't pester them too much, or contact them more than once a month. Even if they don't buy your brand this season, you need to keep the relationship friendly for future opportunities.

- **Go Above and Beyond** — show the buyer that you will go above and beyond, answering their questions quickly, providing images or samples straight away, keep to times and show them that you will do activity to help increase sales of your product in store, such as press coverage, window display, merchandising or even an in-store event.

- **Keep in Touch** — if you didn't get a response from the buyer, or they didn't buy this season, don't be disheartened. Stay in touch with them on social media and keep them up to date with your news.

Finally, please be realistic in your expectations. There are thousands of brands out there all contacting the same buyers and stores. It can take a few seasons to get the buyers to look at your collections in person, but they may still be watching your brand, so keep in contact and keep building the relationship with them. Be persistent, but also keep up the research as stores do change their buying patterns over time. Also continue to be really friendly and you will in time get results.

Happy selling!

If you need more help researching the stores or contacting buyers, then consider booking a mentoring session, as I can then help with the more specific needs of your brand. You can book mentoring sessions through my website www.startyourownfashionlabel.com where you will also find easy to use templates for line sheets, buyer calls and emails, and terms and conditions.

Chapter 8 – Selling direct to the customer

An emerging brand needs to focus on sales if they want to survive and succeed, yet many do not consider how to take advantage of new methods of selling their collections. The fashion industry continues to adjust and adapt to the changes brought about by new technology and social media platforms, which has changed the speed at which a new business can grow, as well as how consumers shop. Brands can take advantage of new retail methods and changing consumer behaviours by developing a social selling sales strategy that connects them directly with their consumer.

Your brand can now build your business, by listening directly to your customers to find out what they want and need. You no longer have to rely on middle men in order to grow your business and sell your product. To build your brand you will need to be entrepreneurial, looking for new ways to build relationships directly with your customer through social media and social networks. You can then create and adapt your product to their needs, and sell to them directly, with the benefit of higher margins leading to greater profit.

In this chapter, I will discuss why social selling is taking over from traditional selling methods, look at identifying if there is a whitespace for your product, and how you can engage your community to build the brand. Then I will take you through the steps of building a social selling strategy.

Why traditional wholesale & e-commerce isn't working?

Traditionally the route to market for emerging designers was to focus on wholesale sales to stores. You developed this market by creating a sample collection, emailing look books to buyers, contacting them for appointments and participating in trade shows to show store buyers your collection. This method of selling was less risky for designers, as they only had to make samples, the stores paid deposits or on delivery for their orders, and the store did all the hard work in selling the collection to the customer.

However, the world has changed, and the wholesale market for emerging designers does not exist in the same way anymore. Firstly, the cost of the pieces from emerging labels can be really high due to them producing in small quantities. This squeezes margins and pushes up retail prices, with the result that their product can be too high for many stores. In addition, the demands of the store buyers have changed and the terms for emerging brands are now often unfeasible. Store buyers predominantly ask emerging labels to provide the collections on an SoR (sale or return or consignment) basis and then also offer appalling payment terms (such as 120 days) that badly damage the brand's cash flow. There is also a chance that the store doesn't sell the collection, so a few months later the brand gets it returned and then have little option but to discount the pieces to try and sell them.

Many independent retailers have closed due to difficult trading conditions over the past few years. Others have dropped their price points to high street levels in order to be able to find customers, which means they are buying less high-end emerging labels. With this decreasing market for higher priced emerging labels, not only is competition intense, it also means that taking part in a trade show no longer makes financial sense. This is especially the case when fewer buyers attend looking for new brands, so there is no return on investment of the high cost of participation. Participation only makes sense if you already have relationships with the store buyers and have made appointments with them in advance, yet newer labels can find it very difficult to get any attention from emailing the store buyers, so find it impossible to make appointments.

If this doesn't put the brand off and they still want to pursue wholesale orders, then they have to consider what they have to offer the store other than product. Many of the big department store buyers tell me that they now look to only take on brands that have already built a good customer base, as they need the brand to promote to and drive these customers towards their store. The store can look for evidence of a good customer base through the brands social media account, looking for high engagement, not just likes or followers. Therefore, the brand has to work on building a direct to consumer business first anyway, to prove to the store buyers that there is interest in their product.

As the traditional wholesale market became harder to master, a lot of young brands turned instead to direct-to–consumer methods by setting up their own online shop, which appealed as it would give them the opportunity to sell with margins three or four times higher than wholesaling, as well as connecting directly with their customer and gathering their data.

The reality has been that most start-up fashion brands find they make no, or very little, sales in the beginning through their own on-line stores. The problem is that due to the high number of brands selling fashion on-line, it can be impossible to even be discovered by potential customers. In order for your product to be found, you would need to pay for a lot of SEO work to ensure you are high up on the search engines, but this is beyond the budget of most start-up brands. Designers have also tried using social media to drive customers towards their online shops, but click through rates are low and usually didn't convert to sales.

Adopting a direct-to-consumer business model is not as easy as many brands anticipated. Larger and more established brands have the resources to build and operate their own sales channels, through a combination of physical brick and mortar stores as well as online and have the hefty marketing budgets needed to attract consumers.

For smaller, start-up labels this model is harder but it isn't impossible. I am going to take you through the steps to build your social selling strategy that I have used many times with the brands I work with, a strategy that has proved to be very successful.

What is Social Selling?

Social selling is a strategy that involves using your contacts and social network to grow your business. This includes engaging friends, family and colleagues, as well as your social media contacts, to find and talk to new customers and make sales. With social selling you will find, connect with, understand, and nurture sales prospects in a genuine way, but also run your business with a cash flow strategy that can increase your survival rate. It is the modern way to develop meaningful relationships with potential customers that keep you and your brand at the front of their minds, making your brand the natural first point of contact when a prospect is ready to buy.

Social Selling is starting to gather a growing fan base with emerging designers who are adopting this method of selling their collections with much more success than through traditional wholesale models. Many designers hate selling their own collections and avoid the sales process, but they find social selling much easier, as the focus is on the social not the selling. If a brand is being social with their customers and building a genuine relationship with them, then the customer learns more about the brand, feels part of it and trusts it, so then the sale becomes a natural part of the process rather than an enforced, hard sell to a stranger.

Your social selling strategy will involve you following your potential customers on social media, meeting them at events, interacting with their posts, encouraging them to sign up to your regular newsletters, asking friends hosting an event or at home party for you to meet new people. Then once you have established a relationship, built trust and maintained contact, you can convert this activity to regular and consistent sales through your e-commerce site.

Benefits of social selling?

There are numerous benefits of building your business through a social selling strategy, which is why so many brands are now adopting this method of growing their businesses.

The benefits include:

- You can build direct consumer relationships, which means you do not need to rely on third parties such as stores and magazines.

- It is easy to start the process and manage it yourself, easily keeping in contact with your customer through social media, networks and newsletters.

- The strategy helps you build a long-term sustainable business, as you can build it through the direct feedback you will get from the customers on what they want and like.

- This strategy gives you the opportunity to grow your business organically. Instead of having to produce large quantities of stock, you can initially make small numbers of pieces to sell to the customer, then put that money back into the business to make more pieces, growing your business bit by bit. This method enables you to grow your business whilst maintaining your cash flow with regular income from sales.

- Social selling will give you better profit margins, as you can sell your pieces at retail rather than wholesale prices.

- The investment in social selling can be lower than wholesale, and you can release the money back quicker. Instead of spending money on expensive trade fairs and waiting for wholesale buyers to pay you, you can release your money much quicker when selling the product direct to the consumer.

Where is your 'white space'?

Finding the 'white space' in the market is about finding market opportunities that your label can meet, or in other words, finding a gap in the market that isn't as crowded. To find the 'white space', you need to review the market and identify key needs for your target customer which are currently not being met by anyone else. You would then work out if your brand can profitably address these needs. This is where your 'white space' lies and is where you should focus for growth.

To identify your 'white space' you need to:

- Develop your unique selling proposition and brand story-telling, so that you are offering brand experience not just product.

- Identify one niche customer group to work on and focus on how to reach this group first, rather than try to develop a brand that appeals to everyone

- Take time to really understand your customer's needs, what they like and dislike, so that you can respond to them.

- Focus on what you do best and consider how you can show or explain that.

- Know your competitors and determine what you can do better than them in order to get competitive advantage.

- Create the wording and brand description that promotes how you are different.

Developing a social selling strategy

Some people may perceive social selling as an unprofessional way of developing a business, with businesses just wasting time hanging out online or on social media platforms. Other company's just dive headfirst into social selling without developing a strategy, so have no idea what they are doing or what they are hoping to achieve. Worse still is when they start heavy selling to everyone they meet, not understanding that the focus should be on the 'social' part.

Social selling is a process, and as with any businesses process it needs a strategic plan to ensure the business stays on track and grows. The brand also needs to continuously reviews the progression to ensure success.

Social selling isn't about hanging out with friends either in person or on Instagram. It refers to the process of researching, connecting and interacting with people to build a relationship with them so that the convert to customers in the future. Through relationship building in person, or commenting on, liking and sharing posts on Instagram, social selling is a process that can be hugely successful when you plan and execute an effective strategy.

Your potential customers are already hanging out online and buying from your competitors. Building a strong social selling strategy will allow you to meet customers where they are and engage with them to introduce your brand and shorten your sales cycle.

The Social Selling Strategy Steps

1. Understand your customer.
2. Design and build a great, easy to navigate, online shop.

3. Create stunning social media pages and set up your Instagram shop.

4. Start social listening and building engagement with your followers and potential customers.

5. Design a great, portable, visual merchandising display which you can use at selling events such as shared pop ups and trunk shows.

6. Take part in social selling events, pop ups and trunk shows, both to sell your product and to gather contacts. These events are the starting process of building a relationship with a customer, not just selling to people.

7. Use the data list gathered to send regular 'interesting' newsletters to give information about the brand and product, as well as other content that would be of interest to the potential customer.

8. SEO (search engine optimisation) and social advertising to drive traffic to your site.

9. Measuring your return on investment to see what activity works.

I will now take you through each of these steps in turn to show you how to develop your strategy.

Understand your customer

To develop a successful social selling strategy, you need to be sure that you have identified your customer and have a good understanding of who they are, what they want and where they hang out. The more you understand your customer the easier it will be to attract them, either to an event, pop up or through your social media and newsletter, engage with them and then sell to them.

The most important element to define is what your ideal customer needs? Remember, the success of any business relies on one thing — customers who are willing to pay money for products that meet their needs. If you are not sure who your customer is, what they need and want, then go back to Chapter 3 to revisit the steps you need to go through to identify your customer.

Your potential customer already uses their own network and social media to discover brands and form opinions on products. They are out there waiting for you! Customers are using their social contacts and following influencers to discover products. Digital savvy brands are 'social listening' and engaging with these people. If your brand isn't doing this then you will miss out on potential sales opportunities.

'Social listening' involves tracking, analysing and responding to conversations about brands, products and topics that could be relevant to your brand and help you connect with potential customers. If you want to build your brand and engagement with your customers then you will be able to gather most of the information you need by social listening. I discuss this in more detail later in this section.

As social selling is about building relationships, then you have to be able to start conversations with your potential customer and to do this you need to know a lot of detail about them to start that conversation. Before you go any further, review again your customer profiles to identify where the conversation can start.

Designing and building a great online shop

To have a successful online shop, it takes more than just buying a domain name, putting up the product on the site and hoping that customers will find it. Customers now shop through multiple channels and whilst they are spending more time online it does not necessarily mean that it is easy to sell through e-commerce. The business of selling fashion online is becoming much more complex. The market is totally saturated with thousands of sites selling fashion product, and social media platforms are now also adding shopping functions, which means brands need to develop a well-planned strategy in order to make e-commerce sales.

The millennial customer is conducting less research on online stores, as they are now more likely to discover new product and brands through other channels, such as in a physical store, on social media or through newsletters. Often the online shop is now the last step in the process, with the customer seeing the product elsewhere and only visiting the e-commerce site once they have made the decision to purchase and want to make a quick checkout.

One of the biggest challenges of online sales for fashion brands is that the customer can not touch the product and this is particularly relevant for start-up brands. How likely is it that the customer will buy from a brand they have never heard of before? Customers are wary of buying from brands they don't know, as they can't trust that the quality will be good, they don't know that the sizes will fit or if they will even get the product delivered at all. These are all considerations that prevent a customer from making a decision to purchase online from a newer brand. Therefore, having an online shop is a key part of your social selling strategy but it is only a step in the process, as you will have to do a lot of work to drive the customer to your online store and make sure it is amazing when they get there.

Designing and building your online shop

An online shop needs a lot of planning, because if you don't get it right then it can cost you a lot of money in lost sales. You will have to do a lot of hard work to even get a customer to your online shop, therefore you need to make sure that the store has everything it needs to engage with the customer once they get there. The shop needs to be aesthetically pleasing, have great content, provide an easy user journey to get your customer through the buying process quickly, offer a secure check out process and gather the data you need to increase your chance of repeat sales.

Before you look at different platforms or talk to web developers, I would recommend you consider a few key questions:

? **Traffic** — Who is your customer? Where will the traffic come from for your site?

? **Point of difference** — Why will the customer shop from your site rather than your competitors?

? **Aesthetic** — Do you have a branding guide or are you clear on the design aesthetic you need for the site to match your other marketing materials?

? **Competitors** — What are your competitor's sites like? Which work well, which don't and which do you prefer and what type of features do they offer?

? **Shipping** — Have you planned your shipping process and worked out all shipping and returns costs? Will you offer the customer free shipping, or free returns?

? **Backend functionality** — How would you like the site to work? How do you want it to process orders and receipts and what CRM (customer relationship management system) do you need? Do you want auto-responders so that you can nurture all contacts?

? **Stock levels** — How much stock will you keep on the site and how often will you be 'dropping' new stock?

? **Photography** — What type of imagery do you need to make the product sell well?

? **Content** — What type of content and features will you have on the site and who will write it? Will you have blogs, fashion film, news pages etc.?

? **Testing** — Who will test the site to make sure it is working and ensure the user journey is right for your customer?

? **Analytics** — Will you want the site to track all data so you can see what is working and what isn't?

? Launch — When do you want to launch the site? Have you set a realistic timeframe for the design, building and testing of the site?

I would advise you to prepare answers to all these questions in advance, so that you can confirm with the web developer or the platform that it can meet your needs. It is possible to design and build an e-commerce shop yourself these days, however as your business is going to rely very heavily on the site for sales, my recommendation is always to find the right partner, employee or agency to help you. A website professional knows all the best tools to use and how to use them, how to make sure the site functions are quick and effective, as well as advising on different automations that can help with increasing sales. If you don't have this kind of knowledge yourself, then look for a website developer who can help or choose a platform that is designed for your kind of business.

Which platform

There are lots of different platforms and website builders out there, and they vary in price and effectiveness. Shopify, Squarespace, Wix, Weebly, Go Daddy and Big Cartel are a few examples of ecommerce website builders that fashion brands use to create their sites. These platforms are all very easy to use and offer a range of benefits including:

1. They host your store.
2. You can buy or connect your domain name to the store.
3. They offer hundreds of design templates which are easy to adapt to your needs.
4. They are more reliable about keeping your site up and running to make sure it doesn't crash.
5. They manage the back-end so you can concentrate on developing great content and marketing the site.
6. They manage the security certificates to ensure that customers details are kept safe when taking their payments or handling their data.

If you are going to use a site such as Word Press, then you need a lot more technical skills, and hiring a developer to do the coding for the site could be a lot more expensive.

Choose your payment service provider

The last part of the purchase process is an important one, taking the payment. You need to ensure that you have chosen the right company to partner with. The web builder platforms offer lots of options for payment service providers, including companies such as PayPal, Stripe, Checkout by Amazon, Square to name a few. Each provider may offer different services and you will need to decide which is the best one for you and offers the most affordable rates. Some web platforms only offer one or two options, so that limits your choice, but this may make the process easier for you to integrate it with your website.

Create great content

Once you have decided on the platform for your site, the next stage is to plan what type of features and content you are going to create to go on it. This content needs to represent your brand personality and meet the customers' needs and interests. As mentioned earlier, one of the hurdles to get over is that the customer can't feel the product when they buy it online, so you need to make sure that you have provided lots of great content that can help them make the decision. You also need to show the brand value and benefits, such as amazing images and videos, great product descriptions, and brand storytelling to increase the customers perceived value of the product.

Your website and online store content needs to be easy and enjoyable to read and quick to understand, otherwise in a few seconds they will have clicked away from your site.

Here are some standard points to consider when planning the content for your website and online store:

- **Create a great homepage**

  Many visitors to websites only take five to six seconds to understand a page, so your homepage needs to deliver an outstanding first impression of your brand. Successful online fashion retailers showcase their best-selling product on the homepage but do not include any prices, preferring to encourage the potential customer to experience the brand before they try to 'sell' to them. Others may place their selling products with prices at the bottom of the home page, that you would scroll down to find.

- **Have a good selection of pages**

  You must make sure that your site has all the pages you need to inspire your customer, sell the product and also provide all the key information they need such as delivery times, returns policies etc.

  - **Contact Us**
    This page is very important on your site, as many customers check on this to see if you are open about the way they can

contact you. Usually if there are no contact details, then there is no way they will purchase from you. It can be great to have a contact form, as this makes it easy for someone to reach out, but make sure you also clearly state your address, email address and phone number.

○ **About Us**
Use the 'about us' page to tell your story and show your customer who is behind the brand, what you care about and your passion for what you do. It is the perfect place to describe why you set up the brand, what inspires the design and any transparency you can offer in the sourcing and manufacturing process. Make the page personal. You do not need to pretend to be a bigger company than you are, as many customers prefer to buy from small brands as it is more personal. Customers also look for genuine brands they can trust, so it's better not to mislead them.

○ **Shop**
Clearly title the page where the customer can go on to shop the product. It is surprising how many small fashion brands miss out on this important word! On the shop page make sure the product is easy to search, find and give full product details and sizing specifications.

○ **FAQ/ Shipping/ Returns Pages**
An FAQ page really helps a customer and can save you a lot of time answering customer's questions. It is also important to be very clear about your shipping details, returns policies, and customisation options for example. These pages also show that you are open about your company policies and this can help build trust by showing you care about the customer's experience.

○ **Security and Privacy Policy**
You have a legal requirement to advise your site visitors how you will protect their security and privacy and ensure them their data is protected.

○ **A blog or news page**
A blog can take a lot of time which many brands say they don't have, however, with a social selling strategy you will have content from your social media and newsletters that you can add to your website too. A blog can be a great part of your marketing strategy as high quality, engaging content can help with raising brand awareness and increasing sales. You can use

your blog or news section to connect and build trust with your customer when you provide interesting, valuable content such as inspiration, tips and brand information.

- **Great Images**

    Excellent images with great photography and styling are needed to sell product online, yet many new online stores fail to create images that meet the standard needed. Beautiful images that really showcase your products and add value to them, will increase sales. Here are a few points that can help:

    - You need to make sure you have chosen a model who will connect with your customer and don't over style them, so that the customer can relate to them.

    - Ensure the garments look their best, which means well lit, with no creases, loose threads or seams showing that shouldn't.

    - Take lots of pictures so that you have options to show the product from all angles as well as showing any details up close.

    - Keep to one background style so that all product images are consistent on the site.

- **The power of the product drop**

    You need to decide how often you will add new product to the website, as more regular drops will encourage the customer to keep returning to your site. Regular, limited edition drops on your website create a buzz and also incentivises the customer to purchase quickly before the product is sold out.

- **Product Presentation**

    Your product selection needs to be beautifully and clearly presented to help the customer make their selection. You will need to determine the brands style of presentation of the product so that it is consistent. It is likely that you will use different models and venues for each collection photoshoot, but not all your product will sell out before the next collection is available, so you could end up with a mixture of images and models, which is difficult to manage on the site. A web shop can quickly look unappealing when a brand adds new images in different formats or with different models, so right from the start you need to decide how you will manage this.

- **Create great product descriptions**

  For each product, you need to give detailed and inspiring descriptions to give character to your product, add value and help the customer understand the benefits of each piece. With more customers looking for brand transparency, you can use the opportunity of the product description to explain how and where it is designed and made. These descriptions can also help with SEO.

- **Site search tool**

  You need to have a great internal search tool for your site so that your customer can easily find their preferred product, size or colour. This needs to be designed and your product categorised to make the purchase process very simple for the customer.

- **Have a pop-up subscribe form**

  This pop up subscribe form needs to appear a few seconds after a new visitor has landed on your homepage, to invite them to subscribe to your newsletter. This is an important part of your social selling strategy. It can be worth offering a free give-away, discount code or entry into a competition to incentivise the visitor to register.

- **Sell a full look**

  Help the customer put looks together by having a 'related products' section. Most customers like to see how the product works with other pieces. For the brand this can be a successful way of encouraging the customer to buy more products.

- **Explain your sizing**

  Being unsure of sizing is one of the biggest hurdles for customers buying fashion online, so try to make the process easier for the customer. You can do this by having very specific size, fit and measurement guidelines, such as height, waist, hips etc. or by explaining what size and height the model is and the size they are wearing.

- **Be honest with product reviews**

  Showing product reviews can really help customers decide to purchase. The better the reviews, the more the product will sell. However, it is likely that you could also have negative reviews. Some brands only allow positive reviews on their site, but this is not an honest approach for a transparent brand. It is better to show your response to the good and bad reviews, as how you publicly handle this can help build trust in the brand.

Using cookies on your site

The prime objective of cookies is to enrich the browsing experience of your users by personalizing it according to their behaviour. For example, it enables a user to save their username and password into the browser so that they don't have to remember it. For an e-commerce shop, there are four most commonly used cookies:

- **Website functionality cookies:** which enable a visitor to use features like shopping carts and wish lists.

- **Website analytics cookies:** which online retailers use to measure and analyse how customers use the website, which can help them improve the shopping experience.

- **Customer preference cookies:** these cookies enable the website to remember the customer's preferences such as their name, language or location, which makes the browsing experience of the user simpler, easier and more personal.

- **Targeting cookies:** which are used to deliver targeted content.

When you are designing and building your website and online shop you need to remember that success lies in creating a great experience for your customer so that they come back time and time again. The fashion retail customer is looking for easy to use sites, with high perceived value products, a great personalised shopping experience and a simple, safe checkout.

Setting up your Instagram shop

Instagram is a very important part of the social selling strategy, as it gives you a shop front that potential customers can explore. Instagram is where the fashion world is living, both customers and sellers, and it is the primary platform where you can communicate and maintain the relationship with your customers. Instagram shopping allows you to share featured products through your Feed and Stories and gives your customers a chance to interact with your posts to learn more about products that inspire them.

There are a few steps that you need to take to be able to make your posts and stories shoppable:

Step 1: Make sure you are using the most up-to-date version of the Instagram app and your account is a business profile. You can check this in the settings of the app.

Step 2: Your Instagram business profile needs to be associated with a Facebook catalogue or Facebook Shop Section. On your

Facebook Business page click 'set up shop' and once set up, either add products to your shop, or link your Instagram business account to the Facebook product catalogue. It may take a few days for Instagram to approve the shop.

Step 3: Once approved, when you go on your Instagram account settings you can go to the 'Shopping' button under the 'Business Settings' and select the product catalogue you want to use.

Step 4: On Instagram, you can tag up to 5 products per single image post, or in Instagram Stories you can create one product sticker per story. Product tags in posts or stories will show the name and price of the tagged product. For Instagram feed posts, tap 'Tag Products' from the share screen and for Instagram Stories tap the sticker icon and then select the product sticker option. Select the product you want to tag from the catalogue and put your product tag or sticker on or near the product you are tagging. You will then be able to share your post or story. You are now selling on Instagram!

Once your Instagram page is shoppable, you need to tell your followers that they can buy through the page and also make the most of the captions to describe the product in detail, just as you would on your online shop.

One sales strategy on Instagram that really increases sales are posts of actual customers in the product. Posts of #HappyCustomers in your garments can increase sales by 30%, as one happy customer helps encourage another, so persuade your customers to share their pictures with you.

Social listening and customer engagement

If you are not social listening, then you are missing out on an important part of your marketing strategy. Your potential customers are already online on social media platforms talking about fashion, brands and what they need and want. You need to be listening to them. You can learn an incredible amount through social listening about how to talk to your customer, the language to use and the topics they are interested in.

Here a few tips to help you start and make the most of social listening:

- **Which platform?** At the start, you need to consider social listening across a range of platforms including Facebook, Twitter, Pinterest and Instagram. That you can learn about the different types of people and conversations on each platform, as they do vary and your customer and potential customer might be on some platforms and not on others. From this research, you will be able to develop a strategy to join the conversation on certain platforms more effectively.

- **What to listen for?** You have to decide what you want to listen for including keywords and topics; these may evolve over time, as you learn more about the kinds of words your potential customers are using when they talk about products and brands similar to yours.

- **Listen to your competitors.** You can gain a lot of information from listening to your competitors and what people say about them. Through social listening you can learn what works and what doesn't, what people think and say about them, and this can inform your strategy. You can learn what your competitors are up to, the type of product they are launching, what people think of their brand, and identify opportunities and threats for your brand.

- **Listen out for changing trends or movements.** When you are social listening you should be able to identify changing consumer behaviours, interests and sentiments. This will enable you to develop the right language to engage with your customers and also be ahead of the curve, adapting your strategy to take advantage of social changes.

- **Take action.** You can't just social listen and not take action, as this would be a waste of time. Through social listening you will gain real insight into what your customer and potential customers want from you – so you need to take action and address those needs.

Social Media Engagement

The best way to ensure you have a good level of engagement on social media is to have great content. Exciting, strong content can build a connection with your audience, such as behind the scenes of your brand, styling tips, transparency in the making process and industry information. You are looking to provide the type of content that your customer will find interesting, valuable and engaging. This needs to be more than just telling them you have product for sale.

When creating your content for social media make sure it is relevant for each platform. You need to plan your content to ensure it is consistent and visually pleasing, not a hotchpotch of styles, colours and sizes. The images need to communicate as much information about your product and brand as possible, so that the customer understands the brand's quality and values. You should design content that creates a bond or connection with your audience and it needs to tell a story. Engagement will increase if you develop genuine content that connects with your ethics and brand values and highlights why someone should buy your product. On social media, you need to tell your brand story through the images, as well as through the captions, ensuring that someone landing on your page can quickly understand your brand.

If you really understand your customer, then you will know exactly what type of content to create that your customer will engage with. Your social media platforms are the place to start the conversation with your potential customer and build communities. Create content that they can comment on, ask questions or have polls. Responding to all comments and questions, reposting, engaging with other people's content and sharing customer feedback are all ways that help strengthen connections with your community.

One way that you can start to build engagement and find potential new customers and followers is to hang out on other people's accounts. You can also join groups, take part in discussions, participate in question and answer posts, and share other people's posts.

If you have posts that get a lot of positive engagement then look for the reason behind it – is it the style of picture, the topic or the hashtags? If you are not getting much engagement at all, then you need to do more social listening to help you adjust the type of post you are creating.

An element of social media that is always a topic of conversation is whether influencers and celebrities help sell product. Working with fashion influencers and bloggers can be difficult and very costly, often with little, if any, return on investment. For an influencer to have an impact on sales, then they need to have influence over a potential customer who would like your product, be in a position to buy it and afford it. In reality, many influencers have little influence on sales for higher priced, start-up fashion brand products. However, if you partner with the right person and agree a favourable deal that doesn't cost a ridiculous amount, and that person acts as a brand ambassador wearing pieces several times rather than just once, then it might work. My recommendation is to be very wary and remember a bigger number of followers doesn't mean more sales, as it might not be a genuine account, or they might not have genuine influence over your potential customer.

I should also point out that you shouldn't confuse the number of followers you have on your own social media account with customers. Just having more followers doesn't mean more customers. Followers are not sales leads, or at least not yet. A person only becomes a sales lead when they have shown interest in buying a product, so the purpose of the social media activity in our social selling strategy is to turn your followers into leads. The way you do this is by providing great content and building genuine engagement and relationships through your page.

Developing your visual merchandising display

Before you are ready to go out and meet potential customers at pop-up shops and events, you need to consider how you will display your product. A great display dramatically increases the impact of your product and increases sales.

Customers have high expectations. Whether shopping at a department store, a beautiful concept store, a pop up or trunk show, the customer expects to have a great experience. Therefore, you need to consider how you will manage your display in a temporary store or space. A challenge is to also create a consistent display that is mobile, easy and quick to put up, as you will need to travel with it and use it over and again in different spaces.

Your display needs to incorporate and communicate your brand identify and values. Every time a customer comes into contact with your brand, whether through your social media, online shop or in a physical store, the experience has to evoke the same emotion and make the same connection. At events, you need to do more than 'sell product,' you are looking to communicate a lifestyle and create a connection with the consumer, starting to build a relationship with them. Just hanging product on a rail won't do that. In all events and pop ups, you need to bring that identify into the shopping experience and create a lasting impression. If the display is Instagram worthy it will increase your profile, as people share the images across their accounts, and if people don't take a picture then consider how you can improve the display to make it more appealing.

You need scalable elements of your display, so that it remains consistent whether you have a small corner at a trunk show, a space in a shared pop-up, or your own pop up shop. When creating a solo pop-up shop, you will also need to consider the visual merchandising elements of the total space, including use of the floor space, window displays, lighting, music, scent, staffing, colour scheme and décor, making sure it all stays on brand message.

Social selling events, trunk shows and pop-ups

As mentioned earlier, one of the biggest challenges for start-up fashion brands that just sell online is the lack of customer interaction and barriers to purchase including being able to touch the product and see the quality. E-commerce rarely works on its own for start-up brands, so I have always advised new businesses to make sure they get in front of customers as part of their sales strategy. Your social selling strategy will only be successful if you spend some time at events building direct customer interactions and connections.

There are different types of selling events that a brand can participate in to get in front of potential customers. My recommendation is to always try going to where your customer already is, rather than relying on a solo pop up shop and having to get customers to come to you.

- Types of pop-up and trunk show events:
- Trunk shows at private members clubs, corporate companies, hotels, gyms, or school and church groups where you can take a selection of your products to their venue for a few hours to sell.
- Trunk shows within another store, boutique or gallery which doesn't sell the same kind of merchandise as you.
- Private parties, host in the studio or at home events, or ask friends to host events for you.
- Shared pop-up spaces with other designers and brands.
- Pop-up or concession within a department store.
- Solo pop up shop.

Small events and trunk shows in places where there is already a captive group of customers, such as corporate offices, can be of great value to your business. These enable you to get in front of customers and talk about your brand to small groups without incurring huge costs, so this is a great way of starting to build your profile.

A shared or solo pop-up shop gives you the opportunity to test a local market and get in front of your customer, without having to commit to a long-term rent or expensive shop fit. There are now more options than ever before of hiring shop spaces for a short period, with platforms such as Appear Here and Storefront making finding and hiring spaces much easier. Taking an instore concession or shop-in-shop can offer the benefits of showcasing your brand to the store's customer base. Being in the right store can help build brand credibility but the costs can often be ridiculously high.

I am also seeing an increase in brands being entrepreneurial, finding unique ways to get in front of their customers, such as creating mobile spaces in revamped school buses and food trucks, then taking their retail businesses on the road to find even more customers and connect with them in their own communities.

Benefits of direct-to-consumer events

There are very clear benefits in taking part in direct to consumer events and it is a sensible approach to building your business. The benefits of this short-term flexible approach include testing the market, attracting new customers, instant feedback and data collection. Events are a good opportunity to be creative and test new products and ideas, and get quick feedback to help you grow your business with less risk.

Events are the opportunity to build relationships, not just sell. At an event, you have the opportunity to build the relationship with your customer by really talking to them and finding out what they want, need, like and hate. You can show them that you care about them and this can turn them into long term loyal shoppers and promoters of your brand.

At pop-up shops and events, you create a sense of urgency, in that the consumer has only a limited time to buy from you in person and this can incentivise the sale. The customer can feel that they have access to a unique shopping experience, as well being able to access limited-edition products which makes them feel special. This helps build long lasting consumer relationships and brand loyalty. It can be hard to build this type of experience when selling on-line, so the event needs to meet the experiential needs that the consumer craves.

An added benefit is that it helps you build your brand organically, by producing small quantities of stock, selling them and releasing the money back into the business to make and sell more. This can be useful to start-up brands with limited cash flow.

If done right these events will create a lasting impression with customers and help drive repeat business beyond the event, but you need to do them right! The event is as much about increasing brand awareness as it is about selling. It should be seen as part of your marketing plan, so that you also encourage visitors to follow your social media accounts, post pictures, tag you and start the conversation so that you increase your social engagement.

Planning your pop-up shop, trunk show or event

There are numerous questions you should ask yourself when planning your events:

? Is it in the right location?

Will you be in the right place to meet your target customer and will you have the right amount of space that you need to showcase your collection in the way that meets your needs.

? Does the site have the right resources?

Does the space have good light, Wi-Fi, electricity points, a changing room space, bathroom, kitchen facilities etc.

? Does the space fit with your brand identify and aesthetic?

You need the space to have a connection with your brand aesthetic, for example if you are a high-end luxury women's wear evening brand, you do not want to be in a space with an edgy, industrial feel. Consider whether the space reflects the brand values and quality.

? Have you considered the shop fit?

Will the space work with your shop design, merchandising displays and will you be able to visually merchandise the space within your budget?

? How will you create an experience?

How can you use the space to create a unique experience for your consumer and make buying your collection pleasurable?

? Will you have a power spot?

Retail researchers have found that 90 % of customers turn right when they enter a store, so this is the 'power spot' and whatever product is in this space needs to be the most exciting and enticing, otherwise the customer is likely to turn around and leave. You need to make most impact in this space and if you are going into a shared space, then you should always try to get this space to the right of the door on entry.

? Consider the pathway round the store or event?

Will it be easy for the customer to walk round the store and not miss any product? If you are going into a shared space then consider how the customer / visitor will walk around the space and make sure you aren't tucked into a corner or behind a wall where people may miss you.

? Where will you take the money and wrap the sale product?

You need to make sure you consider how you will take the money and wrap the goods. This needs to be part of the experience to make sure the customer feels valued. Consider how you will take the money and offer credit card facilities to increase the likelihood of sales.

? How will you staff the event?

As the owner of the brand or the designer then you are an important element of the social selling event, as the customer wants to meet you. When planning events ensure that you are personally there for as much time as possible. If you have other staff or helpers then ensure you brief them well about the brand story and identity as well as the details about the product, to ensure they give the visitors the right experience.

? How will you market your event?

You will need to consider how you will market your event to capture customer attention and drive footfall to your space. The benefit of a shared pop-up space is cross promotion, where you can all work together to drive footfall to the event. If you are running an event within a company or private members club, you may be restricted in marketing the event to people outside of their membership, however you should still consider how you will market your brand during and post event. If you are able to promote the event to attract customers, then consider reaching out to local media and online event listing sites, as well as promoting the event regularly through your own social networks and social media platforms. At the event don't just sell to visitors, instead focus on building the relationship with them first. You need to talk to them, ask them questions, explain about your brand, invite them to touch the product, take a picture, follow you on social media or sign up to your newsletter (perhaps offer an incentive to do this by entering them in to a prize draw) and find some common ground to connect with them.

? Is it possible to host events?

If you have time whilst you are in the space, then consider hosting a range of events from meet the designer, making workshops, talks and launch parties.

? How will you stay in touch?

During the event, you have hopefully encouraged the visitors to sign up to your newsletter and social media. It is to your advantage to gather their email address if possible, as this helps you control the relationship more. If you have an email address you can send a thank you email, encourage them to sign up to the newsletter and reach out at different times to offer a unique discount code or advise them of new product drops.

? How will you evaluate the success of the event?

There are several ways you can evaluate the success of your social selling event and you need to do this to make sure you know which ones to repeat and which ones to not do again. The obvious evaluation comes from the actual sales you made during the event itself, however the event may have achieved a lot more than this. Brands often find that they make more sales post event as a result of customers attending a pop-up or trunk show, therefor this should also be monitored. Monitoring can be made easier if you have given out a special discount code at the event. You can also evaluate the increase in subscribers to your newsletter, followers on your social media or an increase in engagement on social media with more posts, likes and comments. You can also evaluate how you felt the event went, this might be more of a gut feeling but still valuable. Judge what you got from the event through customer feedback, reactions, response to displays, or how the shop layout worked and think about what you would change next time.

Whatever the event, the purpose is to keep it exciting, engaging and creative, it is really important to have fun with it! If you are having fun then your customers are more likely to as well. Creating some real buzz and excitement around your brand you will generate great customer relationships and more sales both at the event and online in the future.

Developing your newsletter strategy

The social selling strategy is about building and maintaining relationships with customers so that you can drive consistent sales through your online shop. The prompt or stimulus for these sales is usually a newsletter/email campaign that prompts the customer to visit the site. Therefore, creating email marketing campaigns, or a newsletter process, is the next important step in the social selling strategy.

Fashion brands are using intelligent email marketing campaigns to not only prompt sales, but to build relationships with their customers. By collecting their customers email addresses and information when they subscribe or at events, they can then send them targeted content, product information and special deals, giving their customers a personalised shopping experience.

The key to success is the content. It has to be more than just information on product and prices, you need to provide your audience with content that adds value. This can be content that is entertaining, informing or solves their problems, it doesn't matter which as long as you are giving them something they want or need. Before you start sending out any newsletters or start building any email campaigns, consider what would be unique about your content and style that will engage with your customer and build the relationship with them.

Some examples of content from brands who have created successful newsletter campaigns, includes creating content on different parts of the ethical manufacturing process, or have a pod cast or film of the month, or they conduct interviews with influencers or their customers, or include features on their favourite hotels or restaurants. You can give some detail about your product but it shouldn't be the primary purpose of the newsletter. One clever way is to have a regular feature that includes a #HappyCustomer or brand ambassador who is wearing the product, as one happy customer always makes another. The benefits of featuring other people or brands on your newsletter, is that people love reading about other people and you can also do some cross marketing here for mutual benefit.

You will also need to consider how often you send the newsletter, it is better not to bombard the customer, but a regular monthly newsletter with valuable content will bring about better results and increase sales. A regular email hopefully ensures the customer doesn't forget your brand and make a purchase elsewhere.

There are various platforms that you can use to automate your email campaigns and newsletters, such as MailChimp, Constant Contact, AWeber, Active Campaign and Campaigner to name a few. These platforms make the whole process easier and they ensure that your emails and newsletters are professional, consistent and make the process seamless. They also give you the opportunity to monitor open and click through rates.

SEO and Social Advertising

Many start up brands find SEO and social media advertising confusing with lots of sites giving conflicting advice and information. I am not going to go into the fine detail as it is an area that needs a training course and/ or a book just on this section alone. What I want to do is highlight to you that this is an area you need to consider to increase your sales success on line.

Search Engine Optimisation

SEO (Search Engine Optimisation) needs to be part of your long-term marketing strategy to make sure your site is highly visible to search engines such as Google. Having a good presence on Search Engine Results Pages (SERPs) increases the chance of customers discovering you and increases the traffic to your site. However, for small businesses it would be impossible to compete financially on SEO to get to the top of the listings above companies like Net-A-Porter, Amazon, and ASOS etc. That said you do need to do the best you can.

The basics behind SEO is the need to include keywords in your content that are the phrases that your customer may be searching for. All the search engines have strict guidelines, so it is worth finding an expert who can help you with the technical aspects of your site that you need to improve your site visibility, such as keyword optimisation, meta descriptions, link building, site speed and crawl rate optimisation.

Pay Per Click

Pay per click or PPC is the paid form of digital marketing advertising and with this you can be featured at the very top of the Search Engine Results Pages and many users instinctively click on the paid links at the top of Google. With Pay Per Click you can set your own budget and monitor the results you are getting, monitoring the amount it costs you to get a user to click on your advert. It is easy to set up your own Google AdWords or Big Ads account and create an account but you could easily find that you spend a lot of money with little results. It is recommended that you seek advice on how to make PPC work for your business.

Social Media Advertising

It is possible to advertise on all the different social media channels including Facebook, Twitter, Instagram, LinkedIn and Pinterest. Social media is saturated with brands. You will need to find ways to stand out and connect with your potential customers. With careful targeting, you can build brand awareness, increase engagement, make sales or drive traffic to your website.

With social media advertising, it is worth focussing your efforts on one channel to make sure you haven't spread your efforts too thinly to have any effect.

All the social media channels constantly change their algorithms which effect how you can advertise and what works and what doesn't, therefore you will need to research carefully before spending any money. The Facebook and Instagram business pages both have very clear guides on how to create adverts and sponsored posts on their platforms, so these are a great starting point. I would also recommend getting some independent advice from a specialist to make sure you are doing what is best for your business.

Search engine optimisation and social media advertising could be just what you need to jump-start the marketing process quickly and affordably. However, you need to be clear on your objectives and set a budget to ensure you don't waste money or fail to increase engagement and sales.

Measuring ROI

You should measure the success rate of your social selling strategy and evaluate what is working for your brand and what isn't, making sure you are getting an ROI (return on investment). You need to set up the evaluation process before you start the strategy, so that you have already determined what you are going to measure.

To measure the activity, I would recommend following these simple steps:

Have clear objectives

You need to decide what you are going to measure such as:

o   Brand awareness

o   Increased Sales

o   Increased revenue

o   Customer satisfaction

o   Increased followers

o   Increased engagements

Set Smart goals and objectives

You need to specify what you are hoping to achieve by using social media, what are the actual numbers you are hoping to reach and by when. Simple examples include:

o   10 new Instagram followers per week.

o   Drive 20 new subscribers to the newsletter per month.

o   Increase comments per post to 10 comments by the end of first quarter.

o   Increase sales through e-commerce by 20% by end of January.

Measure the right things

While making sales is an easy metric to measure, sometimes 'vanity' metrics such as likes and comments have value as well. You also need to look at all aspects of your activity including website traffic, leads generated, open rate on newsletters and increased reach.

Monitor your Spend

It can be very easy to start spending a lot of time and money on social media that doesn't bring a return on investment. I recommend keeping a careful track of all expenses including paid adverts, costs of tools and platforms, cost of any content creation as well as time spent on the activity.

Final Recap – how to use social selling to increase customer engagement and sales

The benefit of the direct to consumer model is that it will offer you far better margins than wholesale. It will also give you the opportunity to own and manage the relationship with your customer, capturing their feedback to help you build your brand. Here is a quick reminder of the steps you need to take for the strategy to work for you:

- Start small — taking part in shared pop up spaces and small trunk shows to test the water.

- Focus on storytelling build your brand's culture and concentrate on being entrepreneurial and creative with your story telling to cut through all the noise from other brands.

- Keep the customer in your mind – don't just sell them a dream, show them the benefits of buying your product.

- Take all the steps of the strategy in order, as you need to have the foundations of the online shop, social media accounts and newsletters in place for it to work.

- Manage your online advertising budget — it can be tempting to spend money on advertising online but it is easy to spend a lot of money in a very short time, so make sure all spend has an effect on the bottom line.

- Raise money to create stock — one of the challenges of moving into a direct to consumer model is the need to produce stock to sell. I recommend that brands only produce small quantities initially which they can quickly sell and then invest that money back in to business to make a slightly bigger range, enabling you to scale your business organically.

- For the social selling strategy to work and be successful, you need to remain focused, schedule the activity and keep to it, and remain consistent in the content you create.

If you establish your social selling strategy with a strong digital foundation and a customer focussed mentality, then you will be able to break through all the noise and increase your visibility, build customer engagement and increase your revenue streams. Happy selling!

On my website www.startyourownfashionlabel.com you can connect with other brands to share pop-up shops and events through our membership programme. This also provides access to our closed Facebook group,

where members of the group are able to post questions, share ideas and opportunities for events and find other brands to work with to share the costs of pop ups etc.

Chapter 9 – Public Relations

Do you dream of seeing your brand featured in glossy magazines? Would you like to see your name trending on social media? or see a top celebrity wearing your dress on the red carpet?

If the answer to these questions is yes, then you need to develop an effective PR strategy to compete with the thousands of other brands out there trying to get their companies noticed too.

It can be really hard for a start-up brand to stand out in a saturated market; competition is tough. The glossy fashion magazines are packed with advertising and articles on the big-name brands. How, as a small designer, can you compete?

In this chapter, I will cover all the tools you need to develop your PR strategy and achieve success for your brand. We will start with the basics, including what PR is and why you need it, before looking at the elements of how to contact the press and build relationships with them.

There are lots of tips in the chapter for you to start the PR process yourself, and from these tips you will see that there is no need to take on a PR agency straight away. Many emerging fashion brands take on a PR agency too early and then become disillusioned as they don't achieve the results they are expecting. I want to talk you through the process of building the PR for your brand yourself initially and then you will be ready to take on an agency later and achieve a greater return on investment.

Section One – The Basics

What is Public Relations/PR

Public Relations (PR) is about reputation - what you do, what you say, and what others say about you. The aim of public relations is to achieve understanding, earn support, and influence opinion and behaviour. It is the planned and sustained effort you take to establish and maintain goodwill and mutual understanding between your brand and your public.

A good reputation is not earned overnight. It takes time, has to be carefully managed and has to be undertaken with integrity and honesty. Your reputation is very fragile and can be quickly lost if you don't get it right from the start, or fail to manage the process.

Many brands state they will start PR when they can afford it, but the reality is you can't afford not to do PR. Whether you like it or not you are actually already doing PR every day in the way you present yourself and your company. You may just be doing it badly! Nor can you do PR for a while and then stop, as PR has to be on-going, and is a core element of your day to day business planning. PR is about building and maintaining relationships; you need to be doing this every day, therefore PR is a core function you need to embrace in your business.

Why is PR important

PR is crucial to your business growth because it is about building, managing and maintaining relationships with your public. Your public includes your current and potential future customer, suppliers, partners, sponsors, in fact everyone your brand comes into contact with. In every business, you have to work to maintain the relationships you have with suppliers and customers, so PR is a very important part of your business.

Changes in Fashion PR

The fashion trade press is full of stories about the broken fashion system and an industry in crisis. We constantly see the impact that the changing industry has on our fashion brands. There are too many new, independent designers entering an already saturated market and fewer wholesale opportunities for emerging brands, so they need to find new ways of selling. There are changes in consumer demand, as well as a decreasing number of print publications, and an increasing cost of on-line coverage with bloggers and influencers. Then there are the many column inches given to the relevance of fashion week events and catwalk shows for buyers and print media, and the debates about the shows only being attended by a 'rent a mob' crowd of irrelevant influencers.

There is a growing demand for more transparency in the PR process. A growing number of brands are taking their PR back in house to manage, as they discover that the majority of their online activity and spend is reaching bots, rather than potential human customers.

There has always been an 'elusiveness' of the PR function, that secret formula that only the PR agencies know, or those magazine contacts that will only speak to PR professionals. This has been a lie promoted by PRs desperate to keep their jobs. Many start-up and emerging designers have, over the past couple of decades, been the victims of some very unethical working practises by fashion PR agencies, who have taken advantage of their naivety.

In the current fashion PR world, there are the daily frustrations of trying to place features for emerging brands in ever decreasing print publications. Added to this is an ever-growing list of contacts who have 'gone freelance' and the endless bloggers and influencers who request gifts and ridiculously high fees in return for posts. Whilst many in the industry are arguing that the digital age has killed PR, actually the value of PR is even more significant in this saturated and overwhelmed market.

For more established labels the conventional fashion PR approach is still appropriate to an extent. Recruiting a PR agency with a proven network can help the brand focus on building and maintaining relationships with publications and stylists. The agency can write and send out press releases, generate press coverage, product placement, and social media mentions. However, this approach needs long-term, high-cost investment, due to it taking considerable time to build relationships, create momentum and generate editorial coverage. This approach however is usually unrealistic, very expensive and inefficient for most start-up brands.

For smaller, independent brands, the focus has to now be on you delivering genuine public relations yourself, communicating directly with your public, the consumer, rather than through a third party, such as a magazine. This means going beyond traditional communications methods and no longer worshiping at the shrine of the press release. The phrase 'content is king' is true, but brands need to put out content and tell stories direct to their consumers in the way the customer wants to see and hear it. The consumer is reading less and purchasing fewer magazines and they are not interested in being talked at or sold to. Instead they want a genuine conversation with the brand. They are looking for authenticity in the content, and brand story-telling in bite size formats that captures their imagination and engages them. The consumer is now much more astute and won't waste time reading meaningless bumf, sales pitches or deceptive hype.

Designers and brands need to take the time to understand how PR works and its value, and consider whether they need or are ready for a PR agency. Unfortunately, if brands don't understand the process and what results they want, then there will still be lazy PRs out there who will offer 'cookie-cutter' services. These include product placement services and ambiguous retainer contracts, using their 'network' (read 'rent a crowd' or mates!) to deliver untargeted posts, tweets and Instagram stories or fill your fashion week event. If the activity then generates little result, both the brand and PR are at fault for not specifying the expected results and agreeing the outcomes.

As the market is constantly changing, brands need to regularly review their PR tactics to ensure they are targeting their activity to someone who is listening and not just adding to all the 'noise' that everyone else is busy making. Later on I will look at Social PR programmes, which can help brands differentiate themselves and create customised, proactive communication programmes focussing on social media and social selling.

Core elements of PR

There are some core elements of PR that cross all sectors and these are: -

- PR involves planned and sustained relationship building activity, so it is a core part of managing your brand and can never be left to chance.

- PR is about the relationships you build between you and your suppliers and customers.

- Good PR produces positive changes in awareness and attitudes about your brand, it takes account of opinions & attitudes both inside and outside your brand.

- PR always involves two-way communication. PR is small talk, it is about conversation between two people not just you telling your story.

- PR is about building new and maintaining current relationships.

Types of PR Activity

In fashion, there are numerous types of PR activity that brands can get involved with to raise awareness of their brand and generate positive opinions. The main types of activity include: -

- Building relationships with print and on-line publications and broadcast media. This involves the brand contacting editors and writers to feature the brand; creating and placing exclusive stories and features in magazines; product placement in shopping pages and being interviewed by publications.

- Building relationships with stylists, so that they feature your brand in their editorial shoots or select your brand for their celebrity clients.

- Building relationships with influencers, celebrities and celebrity agents, to ensure product placement at red carpet events and in press features.

- Creating PR events such as catwalk shows, presentations, installations, press days and trade shows.

- Social Media, managing activity on all social media channels, website, blogs and with influencers.

Do It Yourself Public Relations

Journalists and publications are genuinely interested in hearing about smaller labels as much as big brands, and the silver lining is that YOU are the most authentic spokesperson for your business. You can champion your brand like no one else and journalists love to hear real-life stories from designers about how they have built their businesses. You can start to develop your own PR and then consider taking on an agency later, when you have the budget, or are no longer able to manage the hundreds of requests you get!

Are You Ready for PR?

Before you rush in, you need to be sure you have everything ready and all the resources you need to make your PR campaign successful. So, can you answer the following questions...

? Do you know who you are? Do you have a really clear brand story, with key messages and unique phrasing?

? Do you have amazing images? – you will need an image bank that includes high and low-res images, look book pictures, editorial pictures and flat product shots.

? Do you know what you want to achieve and will you know when you've been successful? Have you set some objectives of what you want to achieve through your PR activity?

? What unique PR stories do you have? Do you have exclusive story angles that you could offer to different publications?

? Who is your competition? Journalists will often ask you about your competitors and brand alignments.

? Who is your customer? You need to really understand your customer in order to target the right publications, celebrities and influencers that they connect with.

? Are you media friendly? Are you confident in the brand messaging, able to speak clearly, concisely and with passion about your brand, can you provide profile images or be confident to have a photo shoot?

? What time do you have? You need to plan time as PR activity has to be constant and consistent, so have you planned time in your schedule.

If you can answer positively to all the questions above then you are ready to go. Start doing your PR now!

If not, then let's go over some of the elements you need to move forward with your PR!

Section Two – The Key Components of a PR Strategy

Schedule

For PR to be successful it needs to be consistent and on-going. Your first priority is to block time into your diary each week to focus on PR. This could be just 1 – 2 hours but this regularly scheduled time could achieve a lot.

This regular time can be used to plan your social media for the following week, reach out to someone new to start building a relationship with them, time to brainstorm new PR story angles, plan your next PR event, follow up with journalists, or check if you are included in a publication, and research new publications and journalists to contact.

Brand Storytelling

Storytelling is a powerful technique that you can use to connect with your customer and communicate how you brand is different. If you don't have a story to tell, then you are just selling product, and that really limits your chance of success. The brand story is important to make sure people care about your brand, want to support it and buy into it. Your brand story is not just a tag line but the very foundations of your business. The brand story is more than your "About Us' statement from your website, it's goal is to connect with your customer and it should tell your customer how you relate to them.

Your Brand Storytelling includes key messages and Images: -

Key Messages

Before you start to communicate with anyone outside of your business, and definitely before you start a PR campaign, you have to develop the key messages for the brand. Key messages need to be clear, concise and easily understood. The point is to create phrases that you use regularly and consistently across all your platforms and releases, which your customers, as well as everyone else, will then repeat when they talk about your brand. For example, Gucci brand proposition states "Influential, innovative and progressive, Gucci is reinventing a wholly modern approach to fashion."

To develop your key message, you can: -

- o   Revisit the goals of your business.

- o   Consider the signature of your brand.

- o   Research how your customer speaks and what language and words they connect with.

o Create your own brand vocabulary and develop your own set of words and phrases such as quintessentially, disruptive, disciplined, subversive.

o Compare your words and phrases with your competitors, as you don't want them to be too similar or your business will lose out on SEO, search engine optimisation.

Images

In an increasingly visual world, the need for powerful, impactful images has never been more important. Too often designers are only focussed on the product and the images are an after-thought and subject to limited budget. This is a disastrous approach, because the brand's success rate with PR and Sales is totally reliant on good images. One of the first things a journalist will ask you is "what images do you have." Great images will dramatically improve your chances of getting the publication to feature you.

The images for your brand need to tell a story and relate to your customer and speak to them. The images bring your brand to life, gives the brand a personality and adds value. With so much focus on social marketing, you need a library of images to use across all your social media platforms, including both still and moving imagery.

The types of images you need for your brand include: -

o Look book – clearly showing the product attributes.

o Product shots – cut out, flat pictures on a white background that can be used on shopping pages.

o Lifestyle – imagery that shows the brand story-telling, the value and quality of the product and helps your customer imagine themselves with or in the product.

o Bio photo – a picture of the designer that can be used for interview features.

o Flat lays – a combination between product and lifestyle images that is predominantly used on Instagram, these are composition pictures which can include brand alignment with other luxury products for example.

Building Relationships - Do your homework

You know your customer better than anyone else, so figure out where they spend their free time. Are they reading fashion blogs, glued to the news channels, fans of reality TV shows or watching the morning chat shows? Once you figure that out, develop a list of your media targets (magazines, TV shows, celebrities, influencers, blogs, etc.). You need to create a long list because this process isn't easy and it is a numbers game, the more people you contact the more chance of results!

The next step is to research the publications in depth to find the right fashion contacts at each one that matches your brand. Then read their articles, follow their tweets and Instagram posts, or watch their show regularly. You need to know what they feature, what interests them and how they work. The other points you need to consider for each publication or broadcaster is who is their end reader/ viewer or listener and are they the same as your customer. Another consideration is the price point bracket that the publication features, as they will often have price limit or restriction around either high street or high-end pricing.

Track down contact information

This will most likely be your toughest challenge. The benefit of working with a PR firm is that they have a big black book and established relationships with journalists, stylists and publications. But don't despair because there are ways to find someone's contact information.

Many publications list contact details for journalists in their masthead or on the editor's page and email addresses are sometimes included. If the publication doesn't include the email addresses, then you should be able to work out the format by looking at addresses of those that are listed, as they usually include contact details for their advertising sales or subscription teams. If in doubt then ring the main reception and ask to be connected to the Fashion Cupboard or fashion assistant and ask them who the best contact is for you to speak to. Don't take it personally if people are a bit short on the phone, as press rooms are always busy. If they won't give you the address, it can be because they have a policy to not release the information under new data protection laws. But the way around this is to tell them you have sent an email but it is bouncing back and give them the format you tried (just guess the format for this), they are then more likely to give you the correction, rather than just hand over the address.

You can look on the company website for contacts, but steer clear of generic email addresses such as info@condenast.com, these are usually not checked regularly or emails don't get passed on. Make it your mission to gather the name and email addresses of the contacts who will be useful to send your story to.

It is great to have the contact's telephone number too, then you can call and pitch your story to them before sending an unsolicited press release. It is really difficult to get hold of editors and features writers, but make the fashion and features assistants your friends, as they can help you get your story through to the right people, or call in your collection for an editorial shoot, so gather the fashion assistants contact details too.

Another easy way to connect with the fashion team is through social media. Follow them on Facebook, LinkedIn and Instagram then comment occasionally on a few of their photos; do it naturally over time, don't like 50 of their pictures all in one go, as that is just creepy. If you comment occasionally with a full proper comment rather than two words or an emoji, then they will start to recognise your name, which will help when you send through emails, as they may then pick you out of the thousands of emails they receive.

Finally find networking events where you can meet potential contacts, or ask friends and colleagues who they can introduce you to. A note of caution here though – networking is different to partying! Lots of fashion events revolve around alcohol and parties, so just make sure you are making business contacts not drinking buddies.

Manage your contact lists

Don't put all your contacts in the same list as this will create problems later down the line. Separate your lists for different areas of your public, as you may need to target different emails to them, as you won't necessarily send the same thing to everyone. Here are some examples of the types of lists to have:

Customers

Potential customers

Employees

Investors

Sponsors, partners

Suppliers – fabric, manufacturing etc

Fashion editors and writers

Bloggers, influencers

Features editors and writers

Editorial Stylists

Celebrity Stylists

Shopping Page editors

Celebrity management

Friends and family

Exclusive Story Angles

Exclusive features are a really great way of your label getting the attention of potential customers, as a feature offers a larger article with significant imagery. In order to secure a feature, you need to develop a story angle that will be of interest to the publication's readers.

Most of the time, brands only consider what they want to tell the world, rather than what the reader of the magazine wants to read about. It is really important to work out what stories the publication wants for their reader and then for you to angle your story to that. For example, if I own a company that makes backpacks and I want the publication to write about the new collection but MagazineX is looking for features about 'back to school' – then I would give them a story about how our backpack helps kids keep their schoolbooks better organised. For MagazineZ which writes about health and fitness, then I would angle my story about the special straps on our backpacks which help prevent back problems.

Journalists are bombarded with hundreds of emails and releases on a daily basis, so it is essential that your story stands out. Press releases are not the best way to contact a publication. If you have an exclusive story angle then pick up the telephone and discuss your story with the journalists you want to target. Don't lose heart if you get an indifferent response. Think of the discussion as an opportunity to gain a better understanding of the type of story angle that will impress that publication.

Are you ready to pitch your story?

Would you walk up to a total stranger and ask them to do you a favour? Of course not! However, if you had to ask a friend for a favour you wouldn't feel so bad? Probably not, as you would already have some idea about how your friend would react. Pitching to a journalist is the same thing, you are asking them a favour to write about your brand, so first of all you need to start to build the relationship. If you have followed the suggestions above you will already have followed this person on social media and commented on their page; researched what they write about; know what they are interested in; and read their articles. If you haven't, go back and do these things first.

One of the best ways to build a relationship with a journalist or editor is to get into their mind-set and know what you can offer which will help them. Don't call them when they are on a deadline and don't waste their time calling them at the wrong times. Some examples of getting timing right include: Christmas editions in glossy magazines are put together in July so don't contact them in November; don't contact the fashion team during fashion weeks, holiday seasons or weekends; if it is a daily newspaper their deadlines for the next day edition are usually around 2pm.

As the journalist or editor is doing you a favour, remember to be gracious, and certainly don't be pushy, condescending or rude. Don't go straight into the pitch as this could be seen to be rude, but also don't waste their time with idle chit-chat if you don't know them. Quickly introduce yourself, say you have a story idea you would like to talk to them about and remember to ask them if they are free to talk for one minute. Then keep to one minute!

Here is an example of an opening sentence to a journalist "Good morning Jessica, I am calling you from new womenswear brand XX and was hoping for just a minute of your time, as I am a big fan of your shopping page in Elle and would love to put my brand forward if its suitable?"

Online Press Pack

Make sure you have everything ready to send to a journalist as soon as you have spoken to them. The best way to do this is to create a press pack file online on a site such as Dropbox. This is a better way to share information with journalists, as an email has more chance of reaching them if it doesn't have any attachments and they also don't need to download everything to find the one image they need. You need to make it as easy for them as possible to access the information they need, otherwise they will ignore your request and go to another brand who does provide the information in the correct way.

The type of information to include in your on-line press pack is: -

- Look Book
- High Res Images
- Low res images
- Brand profile Including detail of stockists and celebrity dressing
- Image of the designer
- Pricing
- Press release

Selling in your story and brand

It is now time to pitch your story, which you can do by either by email or phone. First of all, remember that fashion writers and editors all receive hundreds of emails a day! Therefore, what you are pitching has to be exciting to them. Don't just send a blanket press release, as it will be ignored along with the rest of the junk mail they receive. Instead target your contact with a personal email or call, the press release will become useful later. The best way to establish a relationship with a journalist is to consistently provide them with stories they can use. In other words, you must create stories not just send out press releases.

Consider what you are asking the journalist for, as there are different types of content and different contacts for each, so be clear about what you are hoping to achieve. Which of the following are you looking for? –

- An interview – which person on the fashion team conducts the interviews and prepare the reasons why they would want to interview you.

- Product placement on a shopping page – who writes or edits the shopping pages and have your flat product shots ready to send them- they won't want any other format of image, so don't waste their time with model / lookbook pictures.

- If you have a particular story angle or feature, then plan your story angle to that particular journalist and their readers and connect it to the appropriate feature they run in the publication.

- Product placement in an editorial shoot, then ensure you have all the samples ready to send to them straight away if they request them.

Everything you have to say about your brand is exciting, because, truthfully - to you it is! But your news, might not be so exciting to the journalist you are pitching your story to, or their reader who has bought the publication. It is really important to look at your news story from the media's perspective and ask yourself if the story will be as exciting to them. Try to imagine if the headline to your story would make someone read the article or buy the publication.

Be sure to put a catchy subject line on your email and keep the body of your email short and to the point, stating which regular feature they write that you think your product would be perfect for, identifying a particular trend your collection fits or the briefest detail of your news, event or feature idea.

Remember if you are calling, when you get hold of the journalist do not go straight into your pitch but ask them if it is a good time to talk about the story idea you have. If they say yes then carry on but if they say no - ask when is a good time to call back? When you do pitch your story, always practice it first, there is nothing more boring and annoying than someone reading it from the page. Make your pitch sound natural, interesting and show your passion for your brand.

Whichever way you pitch, by email or call, it has to be a story not an advertisement. The journalist's job is to provide interesting stories for their readers not give brands free publicity. Refer to the journalist's interests, features they have previously written, a current news story or event and use these angles as a way to introduce your idea. Make it exciting and make it relevant to them!

How often to contact them?

After you have spoken to the journalist, or if they didn't respond to your first email, then send them a polite follow up a few days later. Don't pester them too much, as they will let you know if they want to feature your brand. You can check that they received all the information they needed from you, or offer to send them further information or images. It is also OK to call again to see if they received the additional information you sent through and whether it is suitable for the publication. Remember still to be really polite and patient. They may not use your information or story this time, but you need to keep the relationship friendly for future opportunities.

Online Magazines and Blogs

Although we all love to see our name in print and having hardcopy magazines featuring our brand, evidence shows that online magazines and blogs are more likely to create a drive to action and can generate instant sales. The immediacy of online content is that it results in instant coverage rather than waiting the longer lead times that are required by print publications. You can drive significant traffic and awareness for your brand through blogs and online magazines and use social media to push this content out to even greater numbers.

The downside can be that some online magazines and blogs are badly written and this could be detrimental to the value position of your brand. Also, many online sites and blogs charge for inclusion either by fee or gifting of product for reviews. It is important to ensure that there is synergy with the publication, they have an appropriate readership who would buy your product and consider if you want to spend money on being included.

Success

Your pitch has been successful and the publication responds positively agreeing to feature your brand, include your story or call in your collection ….. so, what should you do now?

First of all, it is essential that you respond quickly to any request from a publication, as journalists and editors usually work to very tight deadlines. So, if they want something – they want it now!

If the fashion team or stylist requests pieces of your collection, pack up the pieces quickly to send to them. Create a contract that states the details of the pieces you are sending, their retail value, which publication or celebrity you are lending the pieces for, the date you expect the pieces to be returned on, and a section about who will be responsible for returning the pieces or paying if they are damaged or lost.

If the editor of the shopping page has requested an image of a specific piece to be included in a feature, then send them that cut out flat product picture, don't make them search through files to find it and don't send other images such as model or editorial pictures.

If the publication has agreed to interview you and sends you email questions, answer them quickly and send them straight back, or ask the editor what the deadline is. Usually they want the answers back within a very short time.

After the feature or call in of the collection is completed, thank the journalist and ask them for the possible publication date. You will then know when to look out for it and won't keep hassling them about publication. If a stylist has dressed a celebrity in your collection then ask them for an image or where you can get a copy from.

Always, always, always go back afterwards and say thank you!

Section Three – The Press Release

What is a press release?

A press release is a written and visual communication that tells your latest news story. Carefully targeted, well-written press releases save reporters time and trouble by creating newsworthy stories that they can cut and paste from. The types of content for a release can include:

- New product launch
- Contests and promotions
- Awards or industry recognition
- New staff hires and promotions
- Grand store openings or pop up shops
- New stockists
- Collaborations and partnerships
- Involvement in events

What to include in the press release?

There are some generic elements that should be included in all press releases

1. The first paragraph needs to excite and should be a summary of the entire story you are promoting. The first paragraph has to grab attention and cover the key points you need to get across to the journalist – remember the reader may not go any further than this first paragraph.

2. The headline should always include the name of the brand.

3. Make the reader want to read more. Make it exciting but keep it concise and don't waffle or give too much information, they will contact you if they need more information.

4. Make sure the story is newsworthy. The press release has to be of interest to the reader of the publication and cannot be a straight sales pitch.

5. Always make sure you have included the main information including the who, what, when, where, why.

6. If the release is about a new collection include details about the shapes, fabrics, design inspiration, colours, prices, silhouette and unique features.

7. Use hooks to get straight to the point - what is happening, when, why, who is involved. Target this to the publication and the interests of their readers.

8. Include a quote from the designer as a way of supporting the story and providing a personal angle to the release.

9. Include all of the brand information including name, email address, contact person, website.

Visual Characteristics of a Good Press release?

Journalists and editors receive hundreds of press releases every day, so if you want the press release to stand out from your competitors, it must be well designed and professionally formatted, in a font that is easy to read, and put it into pdf format so that it opens correctly on the readers email. Keep the press release to one side of A4, then at the end of the page offer to send additional information and images if required. Use great images to improve your chances of getting the press release published and when emailing images, make sure the picture is in a low-resolution format (approx. 1mb) so that it doesn't block their email systems. If the publication requires larger format images such as 2mb, 300dpi they will request them and then you can send a link to your on-line press file which includes these images.

Section Four – The Media Interview

As a brand owner you need to always be ready to answer questions about your brand to the press and ensure that you have a concise description of your label. Be poised with a 45-second elevator pitch about your brand that includes your key messages and buzz words and practice it and be ready to adapt it to any circumstance or audience.

You need to become a promoter who can always speak about your brand with a degree of boldness and confidence, and a tremendous amount of energy! Make sure that you really believe in what you are promoting, as an audience will always be able to detect insincerity. However, be wary that there is a fine line between being a self-promoter and arrogance. It is acceptable to self-promote if you do it with honesty and integrity, however arrogance will not provide the results you desire or build the relationships you need.

It is very rare to find someone who is comfortable being interviewed and even big artists and celebrities usually receive some media training to make sure they are prepared for interviews. Here are a few basic media training tips to help you with interviews. These tips work for magazine, radio and TV interviews....

Research

In advance of the interview, you need to research the journalist or interviewer, the magazine or broadcast company and research their reader, listener or viewer. Don't presume you know who they are and who they reach, as you will need to adapt your language accordingly, so do your research. It also helps if you know something about the person interviewing you, so that you can greet them in the right way and also have small talk with them if you are waiting for the interview to start. This will put you and the interviewer at ease!

Your personal brand

Consider yourself as a brand as well as your label and be ready to present yourself, your company and collection. The journalist needs an interesting, engaging person to interview as that helps them create a great feature, this is even more important if you are appearing on TV or radio.

You need to prepare yourself so that you create the right impression, in both the way you are dressed and the way you speak. When dressing for an interview it is preferable that you wear pieces from your own collection, but if this isn't possible then wear something smart but not too identifiable with another brand, as you don't want to be blatantly promoting another label.

Practise your speech to make sure you speak slowly and carefully, keeping the right tone of voice. It is a good idea to practise and record yourself to have an idea of how you speak. You don't want to speak too slowly or change your tone so that you lose your unique character, instead you are looking to find the balance between being enthusiastic and passionate and calm and collected! Practise, practise and practise a 45 second elevator pitch to the point where you don't have to think about it. With a good elevator pitch it gets much easier to introduce yourself and your brand.

What Journalists Want to Know

Journalists and interviewers are not hostile. They want to like you and they want to write or record a really positive story that will excite, inspire or interest their readers. You need to consider what could be the likely questions they will ask and what you can answer, and you need to give full answers not one or two words. If possible ask them for the list of questions they want to cover in advance so that you can prepare, but often they do not have these, or do not want to send them in advance so you may have to wing it.

EXAMPLES OF JOURNALISTS QUESTIONS; -

? How old are you

? Where did you study

? What inspires your designs

? Where were you born and how does this place inspire your designs

? Why womenswear/ shoes/ menswear

? Do you have any family connections in the fashion industry?

? Do you have any other passions or hobbies that have influenced your designs?

? Can you describe your design aesthetic?

? Where do you want the label to go next?

? What makes your brand unique

? What is the signature of your brand

? Which other designers do you admire

? Who is the customer for your brand?

? Which celebrities inspire you

? What other brands would you like to work or collaborate with

? What types of fabrics inspire your designs

? What is the most important thing you have learnt since you started your label

? What is your opinion of ethical fashion

? Who is the best fashion designer in the UK?

? Which fashion trends influence your designs

? Do you think being based in New York/ London/ Tokyo will benefit you as a designer

Do not panic if you are asked anything that you don't know how to answer, just say "Let me come back to you on that" and then turn it around to say something positive or turn it around to cover a point you want to tell them.

General Preparation

Interviews can be scary but they get easier the more you do them and you will be much more confident if you are prepared.

- Be aware the press interview starts from the moment you or they walk in the room or you answer the phone or the camera is on. Remember a camera and microphone picks up everything you say, even before and after the interview is finished, so be careful what you say or do. There is also no such thing as "off the record," if you said it, they can use it!

- Decide on your key messages and prepare in advance the points you want to get across depending on what you want to achieve from the interview.

- Remember to consider who the audience is and prepare your answers to the people reading the magazine or listening to the interview. Each magazine or programme will have a unique audience that you need to consider. Think about what they would understand and perhaps simplify your answers so that they could be understood by someone not in the industry.

- Stay composed and remember to keep eye-contact with the person interviewing you. The only time this doesn't work, is on a TV interview if they ask you to speak directly to the camera.

- If it is a magazine interview then take along an A4 portfolio book that includes images of your collection, line sheet and anything else you may cover in the interview.

- Take a few deep breaths before starting and try to talk more slowly and clearly.

- But talk with PASSION - Inject enthusiasm in your answers and think of it as a performance.

- Get your message across early. Don't be polite and wait to be asked, drop your key messages in early in the interview.

- Don't be scared to simplify your language – it won't compromise your message.

- If you are sitting when the journalist approaches stand up and greet them.

- If you are doing an interview on the telephone, then try standing up to give you more energy as this improves your tone of voice.

- Take every opportunity to get over your message and mention your brand name at every opportunity, particularly important if on radio or TV as the person may not catch it first time.

- Help the interviewer by giving them full answers not one or two words. Don't waffle but keep the conversation flowing, as the more easily you talk the more content the interviewer has, or the more engaging you will appear to the viewers or listeners.

- After a magazine or newspaper interview offer to send the journalist your press release with key points and a quote, as well as a selection of high resolution, great quality images suitable for their publication.

After all these points, you probably think I am crazy to say "enjoy the experience!" If you enjoy the interview then it will come across well, but if you feel uncomfortable and don't enjoy it, then that will come across too. As I said earlier, treat it like a performance and recognise that it is a fantastic opportunity for your brand and use it to reflect on how far you have come!

Section Five – Catwalk Shows and Events

PR Events

There are numerous types of PR events that the fashion industry use, including: -

- Catwalk / Runway Shows – either during fashion weeks or independent shows.

- Presentations – events to showcase your collection on live models but not on a traditional white runway. Presentations often happen in hotels, galleries, clubs or other beautiful venues.

- Installations - similar to presentations but using static mannequins rather than live models.

- Press Days – an event in your offices when you invite the press in to view the collection on the racks.

- Launch events for a new collection, fashion film, popup shop etc.

In the fashion industry, there are numerous events every day that the media and buyers can attend, often up to 30 press days or open showrooms in any one day in the main fashion capitals. If you participate in a big trade show then there are hundreds of brands that they can stop and look at or buy. If you want someone to attend your event, tradeshow, pop up etc. then you have to go above and beyond to create something that will stand out. This means your event must be exciting, different, engaging and memorable.

Points to consider when planning any event include: -

- Designing an overall theme for the event/stand and create a 'branded' event.

- Developing a budget.

- Selecting a venue if you are planning an independent event.

- Finding sponsors and negotiate contracts.

- Planning food and drink.

- Planning entertainment/ experience or activity/ social media/ engagement.

- Developing invitations and schedule regular reminders.

- Planning your publicity drive including pre-and post-event press releases and social media.

- Determining your outcomes, what are your measurements for success including the number of people who attend, or the number of social posts etc.

Many PR events fail to achieve any results other than succeeding in allowing a large number of press, influencers and bloggers to get drunk! These poor PR events fail to impart even the most basic information about the purpose of the event, why it is being held and what the person attending needs to take away from it. Event management is a crucial part of the PR event process and should not be left to chance. You should consider these points: -

- Put your guest first by giving them the key information they need to know including the date, time, location, format and what to expect.

- Invite your guests with as much notice as possible and then schedule more reminders than you think you will need.

- Welcome them personally and make them feel comfortable by explaining what is happening at the event.

- Manage the guest list carefully so that your guest can enter smoothly and don't delay guests by gathering unnecessary data at the door.

- Manage the room, talk to all your guests, don't let the PR team just stand at the door.

- Manage the PR activity during the event ensuring guests have the key messages, social media, hashtags.

- Follow up all your guests the next day to thank them and ask if they want more information or images.

Catwalk / Runway Shows

Fashion Shows are extremely powerful, exciting and are often the central focus of the industry as the pictures are circulated around the world. This leads many designers to feel their own show would be a sign of their ultimate success. However, there is the harsh reality that for many young fashion brands, showcasing their collection on the catwalk only leads to financial ruin.

The big brands spend millions on producing a catwalk show, but as an emerging designer with limited budget can you afford to do this and how can you make an impact? Fashion shows are extremely expensive to produce due to the high cost of the venue space needed; the technical build including the catwalk, lights and sound; the models; the large PR team needed; and all the other costs such as hair, make-up, photographer, stylist, show producer, celebrity fees for attending ... and on and on and on!!

Catwalk shows used to mainly happen during fashion weeks, but many brands now consider hosting catwalk shows outside of the main fashion calendar, as they can then make more impact without competing with the packed schedule. If your show is during fashion week, then the costs maybe slightly lower if you use a shared event space where the catwalk is already built, but if you decide to host an independent show then you have to cover all the technical build costs alone.

To host a catwalk show and be on the main schedule during the four fashion weeks in New York, London, Milan and Paris, then you have to apply to the fashion week organisers. There is a lot of competition and it can be difficult to get a place. However, as more big brands move off the fashion schedules then there are more opportunities for emerging designers. I would however, recommend you really review why these big brands no longer participate and if you would get a return on investment or achieve your aims. There are also numerous fashion weeks other than the main four now around the world and they can also offer amazing opportunities to emerging labels, as the industry turns to these weeks to seek out new, exciting brands.

It is every fashion designers dream to have a catwalk show and if you feel that the opportunity to take part in a runway is right for your brand, then here are some key points to consider in planning a successful show.

Purpose

What do you want to achieve in hosting your own catwalk show and how will you measure success? You need to make sure you get a return on investment and that there are benefits of showing, so be realistic on what you can achieve. Many shows end up being vanity projects for the designer, boosting the designer's ego but having a dire result on the brands bottom line.

If your event is going to be during fashion week, but isn't on the main schedule, then it can be very difficult for an emerging brand to attract the right people to the show. The shows on the main schedule attract all the top editors, influencers, buyers and celebrities and with packed schedules from morning to night, the guests that you want may not be able to attend your event. Would it still be worth paying for a show that is filled with friends, family, small independent magazines with limited readership, fashion students and Z-list celebrities and influencers?

Remember the show organisers are keen to take your money and will tell you that they are offering you an amazing opportunity, but their objective in doing this might be due to them needing to keep their jobs rather than caring about the success of your brand. Ask other brands who have shown previously, or ask advice from other industry advisors or buyers.

Are You Ready to Show?

Young designer brands often rush in to having a catwalk show too early and before they are ready to make the most of the opportunity. It is better to wait until you have your product in stores and developed strong relationships with press, buyers, stylists and influencers, as then you know you will have the right people at your show. There is no point showing your collection if you don't have retail stores, as the magazines will not cover brands that their readers can't access. For a catwalk show you need a larger collection, as a show would need a minimum of 24 looks. That size of collection does not make sense for most emerging labels unless they have sales channels set up and working. You are also not ready to show if you don't have manufacturing and production sorted.

Producing the show

You need to set a very clear budget for your show that you will stick to, as during the production planning process it is very easy to get carried away with the excitement and end up spending much more than you planned.

Venue

If you participate in an on-schedule fashion week event then the main runway space would already have all the production in place, which could save costs but often the show organisers still charge a very high fee for using these spaces.

If you decide to look for an independent venue, then you have to consider some key points: -

- The location is really important. Your guests need to be able to get to it quickly and easily. The fashion crowd will not travel far between fashion week shows, particularly if it is for a young designer's show.

- Is the space suitable for the event? There are various considerations such as, is the space big enough to have a catwalk, is there enough capacity and space for seating the number of guests you want to attend and a space for a photographer's pen at the end of the catwalk? Will you have to build a raised catwalk or raised seating so that everyone can see? Is the light good? Will there be space for the guests to queue, be easily seated and somewhere for celebrities to wait? Will there be space for a drinks reception if you want one? Is there enough space to have an organised backstage area for hair, make up and dressing? Does the venue have enough power outlets and can steamers, hair dryers etc be used? Trying to fit your event into the wrong space can be disastrous and not create the right atmosphere or experience.

Guests

- Your guest numbers may depend on the capacity of your venue or on the realistic number of people you know will attend. Showing your collection to more people doesn't necessarily bring you greater results if they are not the right people. Many designers get carried away by the numbers and pay a lot of money to show their collection to hundreds of people, when actually only 5 -10 were the right people who could provide a benefit to the brand, such as the right buyer, editor or influencer. Would you spend £35,000 showing your collection to 5 people? Yet often that is exactly what designers do each fashion week.

- You need to create the right list of people you want to attend your show. Do not just leave this to the fashion week organisers or a PR agency. If you don't ask for a specific list of guests then many PRs and organisers will be lazy and just invite 'rent a mob' of their friends, industry contacts and influencers who may not be right for your brand. Create a very targeted list of your guests, be realistic in who will attend and remember you need to invite more people than there are seats, as 70% of people won't respond and from those that do, on average only a third of confirmed guests will actually attend.

- A lot of the coverage of catwalk shows now focuses on the celebrities and influencers sitting on the front row and the right celebrity can increase the press coverage for your show. The problem with getting celebrities / influencers to your show is that they charge high fees to attend and to wear pieces of your collection, so most are out of the budget range of emerging brands. Hence a lot of start-up brands end up with D or even Z list celebrities or reality TV people who do not match the brand profile nor connect with your brands consumer. It is better to have no celebrities than have a few bad ones. In order to get good celebrities to your show, then you will rely on your PR agency having good contacts and favours to call in. As a brand you should also be trying to build relationships direct with a celebrity months prior to the show, so that you can ask them as a 'friend' rather than booking them for an appearance.

Invitation

The invitation to the show needs to really stand out, as this creates a first impression of your brand or the event. Make sure you include all the key information of who, what, where and when, because every fashion week there are invites circulated with the venue or time missing.

Invitations can be expensive to design, print and post, however priority guests still prefer to have a printed invitation and don't add events on their schedule that only have e-mail invites. They are concerned that they would have to queue or may not be able to access the show swiftly, or at all. For your high priority and VIP guests then it is worth having hard copy invitations. Design these carefully, considering the increased postage costs of sending unusual sizes and remember that a 'posh' or 'unusual' envelop is a great start to making the invitation stand out.

Photography

You need to book a really good catwalk photographer for your show, as great show images are one of the major benefits of doing a catwalk show. The photographer needs to be experienced in catwalk, as this is a very different skill to editorial shoots. You need to book them early as good catwalk photographers get booked up very quickly. Some catwalk photographers work with magazines and can directly upload the images on to the publisher's site, such as Vogue.com. Your photographer will then have the 'house' spot in the photographer's pen to ensure they get the best central shots of the show.

It is also beneficial to capture backstage images including hair and make-up and guest images. This maybe a necessary part of your sponsorship agreements, but also provides extra content that you can use on social media.

Many designers book a videographer as well to cover the show to capture footage for social media content, but also as a way for them to see how the show was received, as being backstage the designer often has no idea what the show looked like from front of house.

Production – lighting, sound, music

In order to create a professional show, you need to book a production company that can deliver the event you desire. The production company can build the catwalk, provide lighting, sound system and seating. Many will also offer production managers and show callers so that you can concentrate on the models and collection.

Good lighting is crucial, as your guests need to see the collection and the photographer needs to get great images. One of the problems with many venues is the poor light and the lack of space and budget to build a full lighting gantry. Before deciding to book a venue, if possible get your production manager and photographer to visit and check the lighting, to make sure it will be adequate or cost out the extra lighting you will need.

You also need a great sound system and a music producer to make a sound track that creates the impact, energy and tempo that makes a successful show. The music needs to be carefully managed to ensure that it lasts for the length of the show and is paced properly to switch tracks at the same time as you change stories in the model walks. The worse thing that can happen (and often does) is the music running out and having models walk the runway in silence.

Models

You need to choose models that will represent your brand in the best way possible, and consider how people will react and respond to your model choices. During fashion week models are really busy, and it can be very difficult for emerging brands to get top quality models, as they are all booked by the bigger labels, so you need to start casting early.

To cast models, contact model agencies and start to build relationships with the bookers and get them to send over cards for their models. For emerging labels, the recommendation is to work with agencies that have newer models on their books. They are more likely to work with you and also be more affordable, as the top girls charge higher fees for shows. Be honest with the booker about what you can afford to pay, as you would be wasting everyone's time if you have limited or no budget. Occasionally newer models who are building their books, will walk in return for pieces of the collection but not very often. You also need to decide on the number of models you need according to the number of looks for your show and how many changes each model will make.

When you are casting, it is important to make sure all the models can walk properly. Ask them to walk in suitable shoes or heels and walk a significant length, so that you can really watch them and see them do a turn, it is amazing how many fabulous models are great in pictures but just can't walk.

We have all heard the press stories about size zero models walking the shows but today there is more focus on choosing healthy models. There is a changing desire for creating greater diversity on the catwalk with more inclusivity, as more designers now choose a range of models who represent their customer base.

In planning your show, you also need to provide a relaxed space backstage for the models (and the rest of your show team) to hangout and provide adequate drinks and food for them. The better the atmosphere you create back stage then the better results you will get for your show, a hungry and thirsty model will not act or look her best!

Styling

Styling of your show is important and every element of the show from the collection to the hair, make up, shoes and accessories need to give a cohesive message. A stylist can help a designer style the show to be attractive to press and customers, and bring in the accessories needed. They can also provide the team of dressers, who will help with the models. Many designers feel that they can save costs by doing the styling themselves but it is not worth the cost saving and can have an impact on how professional your show appears; never mind the increased stress the designer will have in trying to do this job too!

Be wary of over-styling the show and losing the focus on your collection, or adding in elements that distract the eye such as crazy hats or shoes. You have paid for the show so it needs to be about your brand first and foremost.

Hair and Make-Up

Many shows attract sponsorship from hair and make-up companies, who provide professional teams for the show free of charge to the designer. You need to provide a mood board to the hair and make-up team leader to show the style you are looking for and they can advise if they can provide this. It is recommended to have a hair and make-up test before the show, so that there is no debate or need for changes on the day. The hair looks will also affect the models you choose, as they need the right kind of hair to achieve the agreed look. The teams will need models backstage three to four hours before the show time in order to start preparing them, so you need to schedule this call time into your schedule.

Run through

On the day of the show it is essential to have a run through (rehearsal), with the models, lights and music to make sure everything is perfect. At the run through, the show producer and caller will need to make sure the running order has the right models in the right place, in the right pieces at the right time. This is the time to give the models a briefing on how you want them to walk and the attitude they should project. It also gives them a chance to practise walking in the shoes for the show.

Many designers leave the run through until just before the show, but if something goes wrong and they have to reset and do it again, then the show will be late starting or panic sets in as something can't be corrected. It is recommended to get the run through done as early as possible with a quick reminder to everyone just before the show starts.

Start Time of Show

It is well known that fashion week shows run late, as it takes time for people to move from one show to the next and then get several hundred people in and sat ready for the show. If one show runs late first thing in the morning, then there will be impact on every other show for the rest of the day. It used to be that shows ran very late but now the industry is less tolerant of late shows and particularly if it is a newer brand. Sometimes if a show runs really late, then the priority guests get up and leave so that they don't miss another show, this is disaster for any designer.

Gift Bags

Gift bags at catwalk shows used to be amazing, filled with designer goodies, beauty products, cosmetics, food and drink. These days however, many brands have realised that the time and energy it takes them to get the bags and find the sponsors to fill them, that they don't get the value back from it. Although the press loves a free gift, you don't have to provide a gift bag. Some brands now just provide a drink or snack, or a quirky little gift on the seat that is Instagram worthy, such as a fun lollipop or badge.

Press Release and Credit Sheet

At the event, you will need to provide a copy of the press release describing the collection and background of the brand. You will also need to include a credit sheet, a printed document that lists the sponsors, models, hair and make-up teams, styling, production company, accessories brands, PR, showroom and everyone else who has been involved in the event that you want/need to say thank you to.

PR Team

To manage your show, you will need a PR team, whether this is an external agency you employ or an in-house team you recruit. Someone will need to manage all the public relations tasks such as the invitations, responses, celebrities, seating the show and follow up. Your team needs to be professional, have good relationships with the press and ensure that you have the right guests attend. The PR should start before the event to generate a pre-show buzz in the media and then after the show, manage the follow ups to ensure press coverage is fulfilled.

The PR team need to have experience of show seating and manage the complicated process of prioritising guests in where they will sit. Getting the seating wrong can create a bad atmosphere at the event; lead to VIPs being insulted by having seats behind lower-ranked writers and damage the long-term relationship between the publication and the brand. Seating is challenging and should not be left to interns or novices. You will not know exactly who will turn up until the day as they walk through the door, so your team need to be able to think on their feet, make quick decisions, and be knowledgeable about who people are.

Sponsorship

Most brands need to attract sponsors to help finance their catwalk shows and most need hard cash rather than products. It can take a long time to generate sponsorship and it takes a lot of hard work, so you need to start the process really early. There are lots of companies who are attracted by the brand alignment of a fashion week event, but there are also many brands after their money.

In order to attract sponsorship, you need to consider the benefits you offer to a sponsor, rather than the benefits you receive, and be prepared to write professional and exciting marketing decks and sponsorship proposals in order to attract money. You will need to really target particular companies rather than use a scattergun approach, as this will be more successful and you will be sure that you are partnering with the right kind of brand.

It gets harder and harder to find companies that will provide cash, as more want to supply product for gift bags, but sometimes this can be a lot of work without any real benefits. It is better to build a strong, mutually beneficial relationship with one or two larger company sponsors than stretch yourself trying to work with lots of little ones.

The types of benefits that you can offer in return for cash can include tickets to the show for their VIPs, their company logo included on the invitation and press releases, use of the images of the show and images of their product at the event, copies of press coverage etc.

There can be problems with sponsorship if there is clash in the brand messaging or the sponsor is too demanding, wanting greater results or more profile than they have paid for. The most important priority for you as a brand is to make sure you don't give out mixed messages and the main focus of the event is your collection.

Remember you have to fulfil the sponsorship agreements, so you will need to plan time after the show to supply all the information to the sponsor and also build the relationship with them, so that you can work together again the following season.

Section Six – Newsletters and email marketing

One of the most underused elements of PR by emerging brands looking to increase sales through their e-commerce site or web-shop is the email newsletter. Yet it is one of the most powerful ways of connecting with your customer on a regular basis. Often when you meet someone at an event or a pop-up, they may not be ready to buy that day, or may not have the money, but when they receive your newsletter a few weeks later they are ready or just got paid. The newsletter helps you extend the sales opportunity from every event. The other benefits are that it is low-cost, easy to implement and you can control it yourself.

The problem with many email newsletters are that they are often sent out like unsolicited spam, filling peoples inboxes with boring product focused advertising promotions and offers. The reader is not inspired to open it and they put it straight in the trash with the rest of the advertising junk they receive. This problem can be fixed with a little planning, initiative and attention to detail to create content that your customer or potential customer will look forward to receiving each month.

For the brand to start using newsletters to drive sales, they need to start gathering email addresses at every opportunity, so that you have a list of customers or potential customers to send the newsletter too. Under new GDPR regulations in Europe (see chapter two for details) you need customers to agree to receive a newsletter but there are easy ways to do this. You can ask people to sign up to your newsletter and gather their email addresses at events, pop up shops, trunk shows, sales events and through a 'subscribe here' pop-up box on your website. One way to encourage people to sign up to your newsletter is to tell them they will be the first to know about upcoming events and promotions. Or you can incentivise them to give their email address by entering them into a competition to win a piece of your collection. This doesn't mean you need to run lots of competitions, you can run one every six months and say they will be entered in to the draw of the next one.

Once you have started to get a list of customers and potential customers, then you are ready to start sending newsletters. You don't have to wait until you get lots of people to sign up you can have just 5 people, just start as soon as you can. The easiest way to manage your email marketing and newsletters is through an email marketing automation platform such as Mail Chimp, Active Campaign or Constant Contact – there are lots of platforms out there so find the one that is right for you. On the platform, you can then segment your lists to send different newsletters too, such as separate lists for customers, buyers and press.

Ideally, you don't want to commit to sending out newsletters too often. I would advise that once a month is the perfect amount. However, if this is too much of a commitment, then consider sending one out every two months. Leaving it longer than that may not increase your sales. Once a month near payday weekend is best as you want to get hold of the customers when they are most likely to have money and remind them of the amazing collections you have before they spend their money somewhere else.

On an email automation platform such as Mail Chimp, you can design a format or use a template that will make your newsletters cohesive and impactful. Spend time designing the first one, as then each one after that will just be a case of filling in the boxes. Use a format with space for great images as well as small text boxes and make sure it works on laptops and mobile phones. Make sure the images are really inspiring as this will encourage click through to sales.

260 How To Start Your Own Fashion Label

Content of the newsletter is the crucial element, it needs to be simple, relevant to your reader with a concise call to action, or link to buy. Without great content your newsletter will just end up in the junk folder. You need to put yourself in the place of the customer and think what would they want to see and read about, do not just think about what you want to tell them. Evidence shows that great content increases the open rate of newsletters and helps build brand loyalty. Your content needs to create awareness around your brand not just your product and also give the customer something to read that is of interest to them not just about your brand. Depending on who your customer is, then the type of things to include in a newsletter can be: -

- Behind the scenes of the brand
- Showing how the product is made
- The transparency process of the brand
- Interesting articles on sustainability or fashion trends
- Profile pieces on customers or brand ambassadors work really well
- Interesting features on travel, health, mindfulness
- Reviews on films, hotels and dining out
- New music or book features
- Social change, charity projects, campaigns

With the email automation platforms, you can personalise the newsletter/email to each recipient, if you send an email to a named person it always improves the open rate. The subject line also has a great effect on the open rate, it needs to be short, sweet and interesting. There are various blogs and posts with lists of great subject lines so google for ideas if you are stuck.

One of the greatest benefits from the email platforms such as Mail Chimp is that they provide monitoring to enable you to evaluate your success, by checking who opened your email, what they clicked on and you will be able to learn what works best for future emails.

Section Seven – Website

Having a website with e-commerce is an absolute imperative for every business. It seems obvious, but is a relatively recent phenomenon and there are still businesses who believe that a website is an expensive optional extra. It need not be expensive, is not optional, nor is it an extra. It is a critical part of any business's external image. Websites are not only the 21st century business directory, but are also the validators and authenticators of a business's credibility. Not just a phone number, but a complete pitch for the business too.

Before a business is launched, the website must be built and be live. There are two ways to approach this. It can either be outsourced, or the business can do it themselves using one of the online modular tools that are now freely available and inexpensive, such as Shopify, WordPress or Square Space. The more you spend on website development the more you get, but a perfectly credible website can be built by anyone, with very little investment.

But building the site is not the end of the story. You must ensure that the site is 'active'. The vast majority of small business websites have not been touched since they were first built, and at best are merely a 'book cover' or at worst, they are out of date. Many websites also have no connection with the brand story telling or social media profiles. It is essential that your messages, style, aesthetic and story-telling is cohesive across all platforms. A business should see its website as its shop window, so it needs to be fresh and up-to-date. It is a key part of any PR strategy.

It is fine to celebrate how many hits a website gets, but what is more important is how long the visitor is enticed to stay. That applies both to prospective customers, buyers and to journalists. Generally speaking, any journalist looking to pick up on a story in a press release, or deciding which brands editorial request to respond to, will look at the label's website for further background and contact details. On your site, every visitor needs to be able to easily find further background, your latest news and business updates as well as easily find the product. If not, the journalist will see the business as 'uninteresting'. The same applies to wholesale store buyers, they will use the company's website as part of their research into the brand.

This all sounds like a lot of work, but it is perfectly feasible to have everything automated and run at a minimal cost. It is important to make sure your e-commerce or web shop is integrated into the website from the outset.

Section Eight – Celebrities and Influencers

Brands want to work with celebrities and influential people so that they can endorse the brand, give it credibility which will then generate sales. However, the sad reality is that this approach doesn't work for most brands. Brands do not take enough time to fully research the influencer or celebrity and consider whether working with them will be successful. The only point of an influencer is that in the end they 'influence' a sale!

In the fashion industry, there has been a huge increase in the number of fake people, accounts, comments, following and likes but people are still obsessed by the numbers! It seems that many designers are still unaware about how easy and very cheap it is to buy followers, likes and comments.

On a daily basis hundreds of brands are gifting products or worse still paying 'influencers' to promote their product because they have a large following, but you need to look behind the numbers to see if someone is a genuine influencer! Building a genuine Instagram following takes time and effort and so you can understand why people want to bypass this, which is why thousands of websites and apps have sprung up using an automated process to follow, comment/like Instagram posts for you. On these platforms, you simply give them your account details and they'll post comments and/or likes on anything from dozens to hundreds of photos a day from fake accounts.

The blogger or influencer may seem extremely attractive with their high follower number but it may turn out to be no more than a facade without any value at all. Spending money to gift your product or pay an influencer to promote your brand on their account with a large number of fake followers is money wasted - something a small or start up brand can't afford to do. Also, research now shows that micro-influencers, those with less than 100,000 followers, tend to have more influence and engagement within their social circle than big celebrities such as Kim Kardashian or Taylor Swift.

If you want to work with top celebrities for dressing opportunities on the red carpet, then you need to start at the top with A-listers, as you cannot work up to them. Many brands rush into dressing any celebrity in the beginning, but then find later down the line that none of the A list celebrities will wear the brand as it is associated with a lower level celeb. Hold out to dress the level of celebrity that is appropriate for your brand.

You need to match the celebrity / influencer to your potential customer – are they the right person, right age, have the right attitudes and personality? If their following is really young, then they may not be able to afford your £500 dress; or if your customer is older they won't want to connect with a brand that dresses a grime music artist. There has to be a synergy between the customer and the celebrity or influencer for there to be true influence.

Building a relationship with a Brand Ambassador can be more beneficial than working with an influencer. The relationship with the Brand Ambassador is longer term as they become one of the faces of the brand and will have a much deeper knowledge or connection with the brand. This is then perceived as a more authentic relationship to your followers rather than the influencer who wears your piece once and then changes two hours later!

Section Nine – Evaluation

Evaluation is essential to ensure that you are achieving results from all your activity. You need to plan ongoing monitoring to evaluate each activity, because if it doesn't work you need to change your approach rather than just carry on regardless. Sometimes you need to make small changes such as how you are emailing, the images you are sending, the type of show or event you are running and it is easy to try something different and be more successful.

Rather than using a scatter gun approach to try and sell your story to everyone at the same time, break the activity down into manageable groups and try a group at a time, then monitor your success rate. The evaluation is vital to discover which parts of the campaign were successful and which were not.

Part of the evaluation process is monitoring what happens after you have received some press coverage or hosted an event. Did you generate sales, more hits on your website, more social media followers? Also ensure you have set up google analytics on your website and track your social media accounts, as it can be enlightening to find out which type of publications are better for your brand.

People always presume that the big glossy publications get them the most results but often this is not true, as these days there is little drive to action from even the biggest International fashion magazines. You also need to monitor and evaluate your work with celebrities and influencers, checking which ones actually have the most influence on your potential customers. You cannot continue to work with them just because they have a big following, as their followers might not be your customer target.

Section Ten – When to take on a PR Agency

Most brands rush into taking on a PR agency too quickly, instead of waiting until they have seen the response to their collection and understood the PR process themselves. If you manage the PR yourself in the early days, then you will find the time comes naturally when you are ready to hand over, as the brand has started to grow and you have developed it enough to get the value from a PR agency.

You are ready to take on a PR agency for a full showroom contract when:

- You can commit the budget to on-going long-term PR activity for a minimum of 12 months.

- You have all the resources ready including samples, great images including flat product shots, a clear brand story and key messages.

- You have identified the specific market that is right for your brand identity.

- You have a detailed customer profile based on evidence not presumption.

- You have a reasonable number of stockists in the country you are planning the PR in - as many big publications will only feature brands that are available to purchase in large well-known retailers.

- You have a realistic understanding of what the PR agency can achieve for your brand.

Final Recap - 12 steps to successful PR

1. Contacting the Press

   Getting press coverage is a numbers game, meaning the more people you contact the more chance you have of getting results, however this doesn't mean you should just rush into contacting every magazine, journalist or writer you can find. Research and target only a small group of publications at any one time

2. Are you ready?

   Before you speak to anyone it is absolutely essential to ensure you have everything ready, as the press will make a decision on your brand within the first few seconds, so you really need to make the first impression count! Have your really great images in high and low resolution, your release and brand profile etc. in a file ready to send; that your social media is clear, branded and visually pleasing; your website is in full working order; you have determined your key messaging and brand story; and you have a newsworthy story to offer.

3. Who is your customer?

   You are not ready to talk to the press if you don't know who your customer is, as how will you know which publication to approach. Carefully review who your customer is and which print or online publication they read. Think about what is important to them and what they want to read about, and think about the type of articles they read and the type of language and wording they connect with.

4. Research the publication

   Be realistic when choosing the publications to target. Think about your price point and aesthetic and does this match with the publications features and who their readers are.

5. Find Your Contacts

   Steer clear of generic email addresses and make it your mission to gather the name and email addresses of the contacts who will be useful to send your story to. Ring and talk to the team in the Fashion Cupboard and the fashion assistants to help you target the right contact and ask them to confirm you have the right address.

6. Armed and ready

   Do you have everything to hand that the journalist might want once you have spoken to them? You need to be sure that you have everything ready and in an up-to-date online folder, such as a Dropbox file, so that you can send them the link as you are talking to them or as soon as you hang up. Ensure that you have samples to send in if requested, high-res cut out images, great lifestyle / model imagery and a killer brand profile and press release.

7. Build the relationship

   One of the best ways to build a relationship with a journalist or editor is to get into their mind-set and know what you can offer which will help them. Remember the journalist or editor will be doing you a favour if they feature your brand, so be gracious and build the relationship, both through social media and in person if possible. Keep in touch, listen to them and start small talk with them so that you build the relationship over time,

8. Pitch Your Story

   Remember that fashion writers, editors etc. all receive hundreds of emails a day, so your pitch has to be really exciting. Be sure to put a catchy subject line and keep the body of your email short and to the point, stating which regular feature they write that you think your product would be perfect for, identifying a particular trend your collection fits or the briefest detail of your news, event or feature idea.

   Remember if you are calling, when you get hold of the journalist not to go straight into your pitch but ask them if it is a good time to talk about the story idea you have.

   Practise your pitch so that it sounds natural, interesting and shows your passion for your brand.

9. Follow Up

If the journalist didn't respond to your first email, then send them a polite follow up a few days later. You can check that they received all the information they needed from you, or offer to send them further information or images. It is also OK to call again to see if they received the additional information you sent through and what they thought of it. Remember still to be really polite and patient – they may not use your information or story this time, but you need to keep the relationship friendly for future opportunities.

10. Go Above and Beyond

If you get a positive response and interest in your pitch, then make sure you respond quickly to all requests so that the journalist doesn't miss their deadline. Go out of your way and be really helpful to make their job easier. Remember that they are doing you a favour, not the other way around.

11. Keep in Touch

If you don't get a positive this time then don't be disheartened. Stay in touch with the journalist on social media and keep them up to date with your news – you may be more lucky next time.

12. Be realistic

Finally, please be realistic in your expectations. There are thousands of brands out there all pitching to the same journalists, editors, writers and stylists. Building your presence in the press can take months even years, so don't be disappointed if you are not successful straight away. Just keep going, be persistent, keep up the research, be really friendly and you will in time get results.

Getting any press coverage can take a long time. But if you're willing to be persistent and patient then PR can truly pay off!

Chapter 10 – Social PR and Social Media

There have been a lot of changes in the public relations process over the past few years, making many of the traditional approaches no longer relevant for start-up brands.

Firstly, many of the traditional print magazines and newspaper titles that you could pitch a story to are closing, as they struggle to compete for consumer attention in a digital world. This has happened as a result of marketing agencies and big brands moving to social media ads rather than traditional print advertising, resulting in the magazines battling to find advertisers to keep their publications alive.

Marketing agencies have recognised that advertising in print press is one-way communication, because it doesn't connect and engage with the reader, it just tells them the facts. Print advertising is expensive and return on investment is difficult to measure. Whereas social media can provide two-way communication direct with the current and potential customer, data can be gathered through feedback and engagement, there is the opportunity for increased exposure, and it is more cost-efficient. Therefore, we can expect that more of the traditional print magazines and newspapers will disappear, unless they can find a new way of working or connecting with consumers.

The introduction and growth of social media has had a huge impact on and totally changed the fashion industry, influencing how brands now sell and promote their collections. Fashion houses used to build their businesses around the fashion week seasons, in order to introduce their brands to both store buyers and the press. This business model is no longer necessary when the brand can talk to the customer direct.

Social media has given fashion brands the opportunity to have a direct connection with consumers. The brand and its customers can now engage on a frequent basis, enabling the brand to gain exposure and build a fan base in a unique way. Rather than waiting months for a product to appear in a magazine or a store, the customer can now watch the latest catwalk shows from their couch, shop some collections direct from the catwalk, or buy the dress direct from a blogger or influencer post on Instagram. Changes to technology has meant that customer interactions with a brand can be much more effective and agile, and they no longer need to participate in traditional purchasing methods.

These changes have led to the introduction of a process called Social PR, which is still about building relationships but doing it on a bigger scale through social media. Using the power of your social networks and social media, your brand can connect with new audiences, build better relationships with current customers and get more people talking about your label.

Therefore, love it or hate, social media will be a primary business tool for your label and you will need to learn how to use the platforms to your best advantage. You will also need to keep your knowledge up-to-date as the platforms make constant changes to their algorithms. As a start-up label, you now need to look at integrating Social PR into your strategic organisational plan to ensure you are constantly talking directly to your current and potential customer. In order to build online influence and engagement, you need to learn how to create a page and amazing content that connects with your current and target customer.

Social PR and social media will help you to establish your identity and credibility in the industry, share your story and position your brand as a leader to customers. You need to dedicate time to directly engage with your followers, answer questions, share information and include them in the conversation. The rest of this chapter looks at the tools you need to manage your social media and make the best use of Social PR.

Section One – The Key Components of a Social PR Strategy

What is Social PR

Smaller, independent brands you can now deliver a genuine public relations campaign yourself, communicating with your public (the consumer) directly rather than through a third party such as a magazine. You can also talk directly to store buyers, stylists and journalists through social media, without needing a sales or press agent to connect you.

Due to changes in both technology and the industry, a brand needs to go beyond traditional communication methods and not worship at the shrine of the press release. The most successful brands will now communicate through social media and their social networks.

The phrase 'content is king' is true. Brands need to put out content and tell stories direct to their consumers in the way the customer wants to see and hear it. The consumer is reading less and purchasing fewer magazines. They are not interested in being talked at or sold to. Instead they want genuine conversation with the brand. They are looking for authenticity in the content and brand story-telling in bite size formats that captures their imagination and engages them. The consumer is now much more astute and won't waste time reading meaningless bumf, sales pitches or disingenuous hype.

As the market is constantly changing, your brand will need to regularly review your PR tactics to ensure you are targeting your activity to someone who is listening and not just adding to all the 'noise' that everyone else is busy making.

You need to develop a Social PR programme which will help differentiate your brand and create a customised, proactive communication programme through social media and social selling.

Section Two – Which Platform?

Each platform has different benefits, so decide which ones you want to focus on – you don't have to use all of them! Here is a quick guide to some of the platforms, but there is more detail later on this chapter about the type of content to use on the primary ones to make them more successful.

Instagram

Essential for a fashion business, Instagram is the creative platform where the fashion industry lives, networks and does business. Currently, Instagram has the greatest influence on sales. Your Instagram page is your fashion business card or portfolio, connecting you with your customers and drawing them into your world.

Instagram is the place to build a genuine relationship with your customer, not as is often wrongly perceived, a place to gather worthless numbers or likes. It is a social network in the true sense of the phrase, a place to be social, to talk with your following by engaging them in two-way communication. Instagram was not meant to be about likes and emojis but about 'small talk' – sharing ideas and conversations with friends and family.

Instagram rewards accounts that have good engagement so that it appears higher in the feeds so that more people see it, and it can punish accounts that try to beat the algorithms by buying comments, likes and followers.

LinkedIn

LinkedIn is a social network designed for career and business professionals to connect with others. This is the place to present your profile like a resume, so that your network can see your experience, skills etc.

Many creatives avoid LinkedIn as it is less visual, but it is a great platform for starting to build contacts, showcase your brand through posts and share images of your work and products. You can also get some great recommendations and endorsements from clients and customers.

LinkedIn can be a great place to connect with wholesale store buyers, who all regularly update their profiles. It also allows you to showcase your product to a wider and perhaps new potential direct customer base. Many fashion brands also use LinkedIn to connect with businesses outside of their network in order to find collaboration and sponsorship opportunities, looking for companies that want to create more exciting content, entertain their clients or move into new markets.

Groups on LinkedIn are a great way to share your expertise or show your passion for a particular subject, such as sustainability or new technology. This would then position you and your brand as a spokesperson, thought leader or influencer in that subject.

Facebook

Facebook is still a powerful platform for designers to present their work to a huge worldwide network, and whilst Instagram has a greater under 30 demographics, Facebook has a broader age group. Interestingly, statistics show that if you gather followers on Facebook they are more likely to stay loyal and not unfollow than they are on Instagram, where there is much less loyalty.

Facebook offers some highly targetable features that make it a relevant platform still. You need to have a Facebook shop if you also want to sell direct through Instagram, as it pulls the content from Facebook.

Facebook works on algorithms which change over time but it is currently ranking posts from your friends and family higher in your feed. If you aren't engaging with people then they will never see your content when you do post it, as it will be right at the bottom of their news feed.

One of the strengths of Facebook for digital marketers is retargeting, which can offer the highest return on advertising spend. Retargeting is an effective marketing tool that targets your adverts on Facebook to people who have already expressed interest in your site. Retargeting will remind people who have already looked at your product, but perhaps weren't ready to buy last time, that it is still available and direct them back to your website.

Twitter

I feel that Twitter was phenomenally successful in its early years, but in more recent times it has fallen behind other channels with a flat user growth. It was known as the platform for breaking news and was all about creating intrigue and enticing your audience in 140 characters or less.

Although there are still a significant number of users in the fashion industry on Twitter, interest in the platform is waning. For many fashion brands it has become the platform for championing customer service, with many larger brands now having a dedicated customer service Twitter account as customers are tending to use the platform to complain or ask questions.

If your brand is going to have a Twitter account then you need to respond quickly to consumer questions, otherwise you are creating a very negative public awareness about your approach to customer interaction.

Twitter isn't going away yet, but it is not the leading platform we would recommend for start- up fashion brands. You can gain more by focussing on other platforms which suit your more visual brand storytelling. If you do use it, then be conscious of response times and look at using all the tools such as popular hashtags to widen your audience, or use Twitter Chat to create two-way engagement through hosting discussions or Twitter parties.

Pinterest

For visual brands, Pinterest can be a great channel to use as a tool for creating an online community. You can create unique boards to showcase your collections, design inspiration, and brand storytelling in a way that fits your brand identity. There are millions of Pinterest users, so you need to create a page that has a cohesive design to make it stand out, with well-planned names, themes and cover images for each board.

Like other platforms Pinterest is now encouraging meaningful connections rather than high numbers of followers and has added a shopping feature that links pins directly to product pages on a brands website.

Snapchat

While Snapchat has seen a decline in numbers over recent years, for some brands it is still their go to platform to talk to their consumers and Snapchat is updating the platform with new tools, such as selling direct, in a bid to revitalise it.

There is still an audience on Snapchat waiting to be engaged with, but the key is whether it is your brand's audience. Currently it is the Millennial and Gen Z generations who are most active on the site, so it would only be worth you focusing time and energy on Snapchat if you are looking for this younger or more teenage customer base.

Section Three - Scheduling

For social media and social PR to work you need to be consistent, need to schedule regular time in your diary and commit to this time.

The regular time you schedule in your diary can be used to plan your social media for the following week, reach out to someone new to start building a relationship with them, connect with customers, time to brainstorm new story angles, plan your next online event, catch up with followers and also research publications and journalists to contact. You will also need a large library of images and videos to use, so you need to schedule time to generate an image bank ready to use.

Many start up brands begin with all good intentions but then other things come along and they use the social media activity time for other jobs. Social media is crucial, as you need to be constantly in contact with your customers, this is not a job to treat lightly. The best way to manage your social media and social PR is to block out regular time in your diary and keep to it.

There are various tools and apps that you can use to help you schedule your social media to ensure that your content is consistent and cohesive, such as Hootsuite, Buffer, Preview, and many, many more. There are lots of benefits from using a social scheduling tool including:

- It saves time and stress – by taking time to plan numerous posts in one go, then you won't need to panic every day wondering what to post next, or when you are busy on other tasks you have already scheduled the images and captions so can easily post them.

- You can optimise your posts for better engagement, meaning you can ensure you post content at the right time to get more likes, comments and shares.

- Your content will be more consistent – meaning your page will look more aesthetically pleasing and coherent and make more sense to your followers – giving out a much better branded message.

Section Four - Brand Storytelling

Brand storytelling includes your key messages, words and the style of images you use. Storytelling is a powerful technique that you can use to connect with your customer and communicate how your brand is different from your competitors. If you don't have a story to tell then you are just selling product, and that can really limit your chance of success.

The brand story is important to make sure people care about your brand, want to support it and buy into it. Your brand story is not just a tag line but the very foundations of your business. The brand story is also more than a statement, such as saying for example, you make luxury womenswear, it has to have depth, connect with your customer, be in their language and it should tell your customer how you relate to them or why they should be interested in you.

Consistency is a key part of recognition and success, so you need to be very clear on the consistent messages you will use. The brand storytelling can include the heritage and inspiration of the brand, the making process, the designer's story, the way the collection is designed, or the unique way you sell or price your collection. If you don't have a brand story then you need to create one – but it needs to be authentic and truthful.

Before you start to communicate with anyone outside of your business, and definitely before you start a Social PR campaign, you have to develop the key messages for the brand. Key messages need to be clear, concise and easily understood by your customer. You need to create phrases using a unique collection of descriptive words for your brand that you use regularly and consistently across all your platforms. These phrases will then be repeated by your customers when they talk about your brand.

To develop your key message, you can: -

- Revisit the goals of your business.

- Include wording about the signature of your brand.

- Research how your customer speaks, what language and words they connect with.

- Create your own brand vocabulary and develop your own set of key words and phrases such as quintessentially, disruptive, disciplined, subversive. The smallest word change can affect what your customers thinks, or how they feel about your brand.

- Compare your words and phrases with your competitors, as you don't want them to be too similar or your business will lose out on SEO (search engine optimisation).

Section Five - Brand Storytelling 'Images'

Having decided on the key words and phrases for your brand storytelling you also need to consider the style and aesthetic of your images. In an increasingly visual world, the need for powerful, impactful images has never been more important. Too often designers are only focussed on the product and the images are an after-thought and subject to limited budget. This is a disastrous approach, because the brand's success rate with PR and sales is totally reliant on good images. Great images will dramatically improve your chances of getting a publication to feature you, a buyer to book an appointment and a customer to buy your product.

The images for your brand need to tell a story, relate to your customer and speak to them. The images bring your brand to life, give the brand a personality and adds value. With so much focus on social marketing, you will need a library of images to use across all your social media platforms, including both still and moving imagery. The images shouldn't all be product pictures on a white background, instead show the pieces how the customer would wear them, show how they were made and include images that promote the lifestyle you want your customer to associate with your brand.

Research states that 90% of information transmitted to the brain is visual, so your customers will respond more favourably to great design and images. If the images don't create an impact, then they are unlikely to read the words. Every image needs to create an impact and tell your story, so don't rely on explanatory captions, as someone may not read the caption if the image doesn't wow them.

On your social media platforms, you have freedom with the creativity and composition of your images, but this doesn't mean that anything goes. Be creative but make sure there is a consistent style, image size and colour palette, as a brands reputation can be ruined by out of focus, badly lit and random images. Create a visual branding guidelines document, or design some templates to make sure you stay on plan. This is particularly useful if you have assistants or interns working on your social media as well.

Think about what you want each image to achieve. Does it evoke an emotion, does it inspire, does it tell a story, does it have a drive to action?

Also remember that different pictures will work better on each platform, such as Snapchat with its younger following would find brighter, louder pictures more appealing than followers on Facebook who are older and find more classic pictures appealing.

Section Six - Content

It isn't just about the product you make but also the story you are telling and the engagement with your customer! Really good, consistent visual storytelling will cut through all the mediocre content that is posted online. The best brand storytelling involves regular posts that reflect your brand's values, mission and purpose. If you want to grab people's attention and build your following, then you need to get creative with how you share your ideas and tell your story. Every picture and video should connect, tell a story about your brand and add brand value.

Creating valuable content that will be of interest to your target audience will increase your following and engagement. Your content could include product (pieces they can buy), passion (showing your brands personality) and purpose (what makes you different).

Your followers want to hear about what's going on in your world, and not just what's going on with you or your brand. You can talk about latest events happening in your industry or in the media, or talk about subjects that will attract others who have the same common interest, such as music, sustainability, books, places.

Although originally it was thought to be a cardinal sin to overly attempt to sell product, as social media is now a major place to shop, consumers are embracing the change and happy to see more product posts. There is still a fine balance to be struck, of course, and your platforms should not be used solely to sell. You need to develop a strong brand presence that represents what you are passionate about in life, but also not lose the message that you have product to sell. Often brands spend so much time explaining their personality they forget to tell the reader that they are SELLING things. An element that can increase sales is showing 'real' customers in, or with the product. Create a hashtag for your customers to use, encourage them to use it and then you can re-post the best posts and pictures from your clients on your page.

Your brand needs to develop lots of content in advance to ensure that you don't run out of things to talk about. Also break down larger brand stories into small bite-size chunks, to give you more use out of any content created. Offer followers a behind-the-scenes look at your photoshoot, or in the studio, or show the different elements of the design process. This really personalises the content and shows the customer your brand story from a different angle and provides loads of added value.

Here are a few ideas for content

- **Video** — is no longer a trend but the future. These days you don't need a big budget to make a great video. Whether it is posting videos to your feed, creating stories or using IGTV and Instagram Live, there are lots of ways to connect with your customer and sell your product through video.

- **Jump on the back of a popular hashtag** — is an easy and fun way to hijack the buzz that is happening such as the Oscars, or a popular TV programme.

- **Behind the scenes** — image and video content helps build trust as you are showing how something is designed and made. You have an endless source of unique content from behind the scenes of your business.

- **Collaboration** — collaboration can help with cross marketing. Joining forces with another brand or an influencer helps by sharing content to a wider audience group and gives a stronger brand image.

- **Comment baiting** — asking questions can help to build engagement and starts conversations with your following.

- **Reposting popular content** — reposting popular motivational phrases, jokes and memes or latest news can open up new groups of followers

- **Teasers** — build excitement by giving teasers to what is coming up, with sneak peeks of new collections or events etc.

All content needs to stay 'on message.' Before you post anything on social media ask yourself "does this connect with my brand; will my customer understand it and will it excite them." If the answer isn't yes to all these questions, then don' post it!

Section Seven – Instagram Content

For the fashion industry, Instagram is the place to be and the platform is now much more than just style inspiration, as it now has a huge influence on what customers buy. Fashion brands who understand that Instagram is about starting conversations and building genuine engagement are thriving on Instagram.

Instagram uses algorithms to manage the platform which brings forward the best and most relevant content for you to see on your feed. It would be impossible in a book to advise you of the specific tools to beat the algorithm, as Instagram may have changed it before the book is even published. They are likely to continue to change the algorithms to make sure the platform stays relevant, therefore you need to keep up to date with what the platform is changing, such as the new tools they launch and adapt these in your social media strategy. If you don't constantly update your strategy, you could be left behind and your followers may not even see your posts.

Instagram is a social networking platform and this description tells you exactly what you should be doing on it – networking socially! It is not a platform for you to just advertise your product. It is essential that you network with your followers, having genuine conversations not just liking, following and posting emojis. Instagram reward the accounts that interact more with people on both their own account and on other people's accounts. If you start to have genuine conversations then you are more likely to appear on your follower's feeds. Treat Instagram more like small talk and ask questions, have conversations, and start discussions on it.

Here are some specific tips to help you build your Instagram following and engagement.

Tell a Story

Instagram allows you to use your images to tell stories through a series of photos – remember a picture is worth a thousand words. You can make your brand feel more human, really engage your audience and evoke feelings and emotions with planned, curated and unique images.

Style and Quality

Instagram followers love fashion and lifestyle pictures and particularly ones that show real people in real situations, which is why influencer marketing has been so successful. They don't necessarily have to be highly art directed images, but they do have to be impactful and offer something different. Consider different types of images including sketches and illustrations that showcase your brand. If you show your brand's true personality in an unbiased and eye-catching way, your images can help build a following and sell product.

Consistency

Consistent images make a really impactful page, so make sure you consider the whole "insta grid' to create impact, rather than each individual picture. Use filters, camera angles, colours and lifestyle images that are in line with your brand's core image for maximum impact.

Minimalism

Simple, colour-saturated images that evoke an emotion can work better for some brands rather than complicated compositions. Minimalist still life, where your product is not the centre of attention but casually dropped in, can also work well.

Collages

Use close-ups or fragments of the whole picture, to put together collages to engage your audience. Use the Rule of Thirds, a photography technique that splits the images into nine segments, for collages or individual images to produce interesting and engaging results.

Research Your Hashtags

Another way to increase your presence and reach new followers is to use appropriate #hashtags, but first you need to determine which hashtags are best for your audience. The more specific the hashtag the better engagement it will generate, so it is better to avoid the top-ranking hashtags such as #fashion which has millions of posts. The most popular hashtags will not bring you any benefits, as the chances are you will be lost in the vast number of posts and no one will search through the millions of posts to find you. It is better to look for 'longer tail' hashtags that have fewer associated posts, for example going for #fashiondesignerlife (19k posts) rather than #fashiondesigner (10m posts). You need to do your research in the same way you would look for keywords for SEO, to make sure you are using the hashtags that your target audience are looking for.

Engage, Engage, Engage

The only way to make your Instagram account work is through engagement. This means that you have to like, comment and engage with people who could be your potential customers or have an influence on your business. Instagram is exactly the same as building personal relationships in real life, you have to put in some of the effort, show people gratitude and appreciation and have conversations with them. Don't be fooled by thinking it is about the numbers, as the Instagram algorithms reward brands that have genuine engagement not big followings.

Influencers and Customer content

Today most brands don't question whether they should work with an influencer, but rather what type of influencer and how to work with them is more important. Influencers don't have to be someone with a huge following, it is someone who can actually 'influence' sales. Therefore, it is important to build a relationship with an influencer who has genuine engagement with your potential customer. A brand can also encourage their customers to create content and then share it on the brands page, which shows they value their customer, as well as connect with new people.

Make your feed shoppable

Now that you are able to sell direct through Instagram you need to make your feed appealing and shoppable. This means that you need to create 'Calls to Action' for your customer so that they are clear which products are available and click on them to buy.

Instagram Stories and Highlights

Instagram stories are a good way of telling the behind the scenes story of your brand and these stories can be highlighted so that they remain on your feed.

Instagram is an extremely powerful element in growing a fashion brand and is about to get even more so, as consumers grow comfortable with buying directly from the site. Therefore, building your account is an important part of your brand development and shouldn't be left to chance.

Section Eight - Facebook Content

A few years ago, there was an assumption that Facebook would decline due to Instagram taking over as the social media platform of choice, however the platform remains stable with over 2 billion active monthly users. Therefore, it is still a viable platform for you to use to communicate with some customers. Research states that over 40% of Facebook users say they find fashion inspiration on the platform and many brands continue to sell well through the site.

Facebook is where older millennials and slightly older generations hangout and the platform constantly evolves to accommodate the changing needs of their users. This includes helping brands to reach their customer more effectively with visual content through tools such as Facebook retargeting, which is one of the most powerful tools for marketers out there.

Many brands now focus more of their time on Instagram and there is a tendency to abandon Facebook to just reposts of content from other platforms, but there are benefits of managing your Facebook account in order to engage with customers and make sales. You still need to post strong images that are consistent and match the brand aesthetic, create valuable content for your followers, make sure all links work and use consumer generated content to also help with engagement.

Here are a few tips to help you run a successful Facebook account: -

Facebook Retargeting

Retargeting (or remarketing) is using the data your store generates about your customers to better advertise to them somewhere else, in this case, on Facebook. An example is if a customer visits your on-line store and sees a dress they like, but they can't afford it or they get distracted, close the page and forget about it, then after a few days the dress pops back up in their Facebook feed with a Buy button, - then that is retargeting.

Creating Impact

There are a lot of people and brands on Facebook and a lot of noise, so people tend to scroll through their feed quite speedily, therefore it is essential to keep your Facebook content and images simple and impactful. If the imagery is consistent then it will help your brand be recognised quicker.

Keep up to date

Facebook constantly changes its algorithms and tools, so it is really important to keep an eye out for any changes and adopt the new tools, as this could give your brand a boost and keep it ahead of the crowd by using tools first.

Go Live

Video definitely increases engagement, so increase interest in your brand by going live. The same as with Instagram, you can use Facebook Live to show your brand storytelling, behind the scenes of shoots, shows, designing and making the collection and also styling of the collection. You could also live stream from events rather than just posting pictures afterwards to make your customers feel more involved.

Make it Shoppable

Use all the Facebook tools available to make your content shoppable including influencer activity, imagery and videos.

Time to Chat

You can add a chatbot to messenger to handle all kinds of enquiries from customer service to personalised outfit selection to booking appointments. In your feed ask questions or start discussions as a way to start the chat with your customers and to encourage engagement.

Call to Action

Most of the time you can put out posts with no idea if anyone has even seen them. Ask people to like if they agree, or invite them to comment, make suggestions or click to find out more. A call to action will nudge them in the right direction.

Section Nine - Snapchat Content

Snapchat is perceived to be the social network where brands can connect with teens and generation z. At one point Snapchat was considered to be the way forward before Instagram pulled the followers over to their platform, so for many brands the question now is whether there is any point in having a presence there.

The answer is yes if you are targeting a young audience, as they are waiting over there to be discovered and to hear about your brand. They want to connect through the types of raw content and visual stories that resonate with them, as younger followers prefer brighter, louder content packed with text, emojis, and symbols.

Snapchat is the most casual of all social media platforms, so not the place for corporate formalness or complex story telling. Brief and catchy content is key and you can still use influencers and storytelling, but you have to make them snappier.

The tips to make Snapchat work for you include: -

Know your audience

If your audience isn't using Snapchat then neither should you, so first of all make sure your target audience is on the platform. You still need to build engagement, know what to talk about, how to talk about it, and who to connect with.

Be Discovered

Snapchat Story allows you to put video and image content on a single feed for friends to scan through and the app is perfect for giving your followers access to exclusive content such as new collections before they hit the shelves.

Stay on Brand

Although it is a more casual platform, you still need to be consistent and stay on brand message. You can share brand storytelling and behind the scenes content but in a format that is more suitable for this audience.

Run competitions

In order to drive engagement, competitions work well on Snapchat as well as asking for input from fellow snapchat users.

Section Ten - Pinterest Content

Pinterest appeals to a more mature audience and to stand out you have to produce consistently good, high quality images and informative content that offers the follower value or insight into your brand. Well-polished inspirational and lifestyle images work well with some clean-cut photos of popular items mixed in.

Pinterest followers often search for products, or follow brands on the social network in order to be part of the lifestyle, and to understand the back story of the brand before making a purchase.

If you want your Pins to stand out and look their best, then you have to spend time sizing them correctly and ensure they are appealing in the vertical Pinterest format, so that you maximize their impact. Your Pinterest followers will most likely love simple, easy to digest content that is really inspiring.

Here are a few tips to make the most of Pinterest: -

Promote a lifestyle

Pinterest is not about blasting out pictures of your product, instead you need to pin images that capture the lifestyle of the brand or the essence of it.

Curated Boards

Create boards that represent the lifestyle around your brand or include areas that will be of interest to your followers including home, travel, styling tips, latest trends, fashion illustrations, sustainability tips etc.

Know your customer

You can use Pinterest for research into your customer by tracking to see what else they love, who they are following and what they care about. This will help you plan more effective marketing and product development according to their desires, needs and wants.

Engagement

You can ask fans to pin pictures of themselves in your product and tag you in it so that you can re-pin these pictures. This gives you the opportunity to say thank you and show your appreciation to your customers. You can run competitions and ask your followers to curate their favourite products into their own board and share it.

Optimise your Pins

Pinterest can really help with SEO so optimise your posts with relevant keywords and hashtags so that your boards and pins pop up on Google.

The Hard Sell

With the option now to sell through Pinterest too - don't be shy – be clear that you have product to sell and make sure it is all clearly tagged and displayed.

Section Eleven – How to get more followers

Building a genuine following on your social media accounts is of upmost importance, but don't try and skip the process by buying followers. The whole point of using social media is to have a following of potential customers who you can talk with and influence them to buy your product. Just having thousands of followers will not increase sales if they are not the right people.

Firstly, you will only be able to build a genuine customer following on a platform if that is where your customer lives. Don't waste time on platforms that are not used by your customer. The best way to gain new followers is to start following others and engage with them. Or engage in existing and interesting discussions that are relevant to your industry as then your profile will show up in more news feeds, which can increase your following.

If you follow all the tips earlier in this chapter about generating great content then that will increase your likelihood of achieving more followers. If your followers can count on you to deliver their daily dose of inspiration, then your following will start to rise. You will be able to deliver great content if you really understand your customer and know what they are interested in, what they want to see and read about, and the type of content they follow. If your following isn't growing then review the type of content you are putting out and see if it can be improved so that it connects better with your potential customer.

My recommendation to start-up brands is always to analyse your competitors accounts and see what they are doing correctly and well, as you can learn from their accounts on how to run a successful campaign.

Then the next step is to engage with their active followers. If people have shown an interest in your competitor's product, then they could be interested in yours. Therefore, don't just look at the followers or the people who like posts, instead look at who is commenting on their account and talking about their product. Learn from their good examples, such as the types of posts that they get more likes on, which hashtags they are using and what type of content are they sharing.

Remember as well that people like to know who is behind the account and put a face to the name. People buy from people, so you are an important part of the process. Take advantage of using images and video to show you are human, the creator or maker behind the product and show that you are a small brand rather than a robot or some huge factory or company just churning out product. Brands often think that they have to pretend to be a big company, but the authenticity of showing you are a small business, one who cares about your product and customer, generates more followers and more sales.

In addition to looking for potential customers to be followers, it is important to follow accounts that you would like to be associated with professionally. It is good practise to follow relevant accounts that will add value to your feed. An easy way to connect with the fashion team of a newspaper or magazine is through social media. Follow them on Facebook, LinkedIn and Instagram then comment occasionally on a few of their photos; do it naturally over time, don't like 50 of their pictures all in one go, as that is just creepy. If you comment occasionally with a full proper comment rather than two words or an emoji, then they will start to recognise your name, which will help when you send through emails, as they may then pick you out of the thousands of emails they receive.

Another effective way to gain a massive social media following is by connecting with influencers you follow and admire. Try to build a genuine relationship with them rather than think of paying them, you can do this by commenting with full sentences on their posts, rather than just two words and emoji, to engage them in conversation.

Many people ask what the ratio of followers to following should be. To get a balance on the numbers, you don't want to be following more people than follow you. However, you do need to be following some people, otherwise your followers will think that you are not interested in engagement, only in gathering numbers.

In the haste to always find new followers, don't forget the followers you already have. Many people concentrate only on chasing new followers and forget to remain engaged with those that are already following you, which can result in a pattern of losing followers for every new customer you gain.

Here are our tips to increasing your following: -

- Be consistent
- Have great content
- Use the right hashtags
- Post at the right time
- Engage with your competitors engaged following
- Write proper sentences on other people's posts, not just an emoji, to make sure you stand out
- Pay for sponsored posts
- Use geotags to boost local discovery
- Use Stories to tell the story of the brand and organise them into Highlights
- Ask new users who engage to follow you
- Hop on to trends
- Run a competition
- Use all the tools on the platform

Section Twelve - Ignore the Numbers and Avoid the Fakes

In the fashion industry, there has been a huge increase in the number of fake people, accounts, comments, following and likes, but people are still obsessed by the numbers! It seems that many designers are still unaware how easy and very cheap it is to buy followers, likes and comments.

On a daily basis hundreds of brands are gifting products, or worse still paying 'influencers' to promote their product because they have a large following, but you need to look behind the numbers to see if someone is a genuine influencer!

Building an Instagram following takes time and effort and so you can understand why people want to bypass this, which is why thousands of websites and apps have sprung up offering to do it all for you – for a price, of course. These sites use an automated process to follow, comment/like Instagram posts for you: you simply give them your account details, and they'll post comments and/or likes on anything from dozens to hundreds of photos a day from fake accounts.

If you think that a particular blogger or influencer seems extremely attractive with their high follower count remember that the account may turn out to be no more than a facade without any value at all. Spending money to gift your product or pay the influencer to promote your brand on their account which has a large number of fake followers is money wasted – something a small or start up brand can't afford to do.

There are now some apps being developed to help you find the fakes such as Socialblade, on which you can track Instagram accounts and see their daily gain or loss of followers and following. You also need to go on an account and look beyond the numbers and look for these elements which could indicate an account to avoid –

- If the account has a high number of followers but low engagement then it is likely that the account has fake followers.

- Instagram accounts with lots of followers but only a few photos on its page is not a real one.

- If the account has big jumps in the number of followers then it is likely that they have just bought them – unless they made it into all the major news channels that day!

- If the account has lots of "Private Accounts' following it, they are fake accounts.

- If the account has lots of unusual usernames (such as the spam ones which use random letters and numbers) and accounts in different languages to that of the account holder – then they have bought them.

Section Thirteen – Evaluation

Evaluation is essential to ensure that you are achieving results from all your activity. You need to plan ongoing monitoring to evaluate each platform, because if it isn't working you need to change your approach rather than just carry on regardless. If your account lacks engagement or is not gaining new followers then you may need to make a change such as trying new kinds of posts or style of images, try new hashtags, check your customers are still on the platform, or try something completely different in order to be more successful.

Final Recap –Tips on how to use social media to promote your brand

For any start-up business, it is crucial to get your name out there and social media is an easy and manageable way to start this process. There is an ever-growing importance for brands to use social media for promotional and branding benefits but more essentially – SALES!

Here are my final tips to using social media for your emerging fashion label, which can work across all your platforms: -

Don't Rush In

Do not rush into social media, it is too easy to set up lots of different accounts on different platforms which can later become a problem for you. Managing social media takes a lot of time and effort. First of all, think about what you want to achieve, what your goals are, who your customer is and what platforms they use.

Start to Build Your Following

Once you have decided on the right platforms for your brand, then don't wait to launch your business before starting your account. Having your social media account active before launch means you can start to build a buzz and excitement for the brand and start to grow your following.

Your Profile Bio

Your profile bio is the bit of information you can put at the top of your account. Make sure it is consistent across all platforms you use. Keep it short and snappy but clearly stating who you are and what you offer. Link back to your website for more information and also add an amazing brand cover image

Your Network

Follow the right people who can help you build your network. Follow people who are relevant to your brand, who are genuine and post real content not just sponsored posts, and follow accounts where you can get information that keeps you up-to-date with industry news.

Building Your Following

The best way to build followers is to do it organically. Don't buy followers if you want to end up with a following that you will have influence over, because bought followers are not potential customers. Also avoid other people who have bought their following as you will gain little from their accounts. The organic method to growing followers includes: -

- Follow brands similar to yours and begin to follow and engage with their followers;
- Use the same hashtags as your competitors (put them in the comments section to make the content look cleaner);
- Find other people through hashtags and engage with them by liking and adding genuine comments on their posts;
- Reach out to like-minded people and brands about account take-overs or joint promotions;

- Make genuine, full sentence comments on people's accounts, not just two words and an emoji, as then you will stand out more on their page;

- Make sure that you are following everyone you already know. Go through your contact lists and check you are following everyone;

Follow the buyers of the stores you want to be in and the editors and fashion team from the publications you want to be featured in.

Keep Up to Date

All the platforms regularly update their algorithms so make sure you stay up-to-date with any changes and new tools so that your social media accounts stay current and remain effective.

Running your social media accounts may seem like a chore, but try to enjoy the process, have fun and build genuine relationships, then in time you will enjoy the results it can bring you.

Chapter 11 – Finance

I hope that your work on developing your fashion label has progressed well so far? You should now have a fabulous concept, great designs, and a fantastic brand story. You will now be ready to take the next step to make it all become a reality. The problem now is where is the money coming from?

The comment I hear time and time again from start-up fashion brands is that it cost them a lot more money than they ever anticipated getting their brands off the ground. Even after they have managed to raise all the money, they then needed even more to keep it going. Many say that if they had known before they started how much it was going to cost, then they might have reconsidered, or waited a while until they had more savings behind them.

The reason so many start-up fashion labels fail is that they quickly run out of money, because they didn't have an accurate financial plan. I regularly deliver master-classes to graduate fashion students to show them how to cost their business and develop a cash flow forecast for their business concept. These students all think they are going to walk straight out of school and start their own labels, but after writing their cash flow forecasts, they realise the issues they will face. The response is often "Wow, I hadn't thought about all the things that I would have to pay for."

In this chapter I will cover some of the financial challenges and areas that fashion brands should consider. Whilst you need to learn how the financial elements of your business work, my advice is, that unless you are trained and knowledgeable about financial accounting, find yourself a great accountant or financial advisor to help you build a strong financial foundation for your label.

The financial challenges for start-up fashion labels

Many start-up labels think that they will be able to attract an investor or raise finance through a bank loan. The reality is that investors for start-up fashion businesses are the exception not the rule. Banks consider that start-up fashion brands are too risky, so they are unlikely to offer loans to the business,

It is challenging to raise money to start your label, but the challenges won't stop, as fashion businesses face cash flow problems continually. Many labels have to self-fund in the beginning, which means they will stay quite small and only be able to grow their brands slowly. With a lack of financial backing it can be impossible to take on a large wholesale order, as the brand would need the cash flow to be able to produce the inventory and pay the suppliers up front.

If a brand chooses to go the direct-to-consumer model, then they have the challenge of also raising money to produce inventory to sell, as well as the costs of marketing, events and promotion to drive consumers to their online store.

Mention the word 'accounts' and most people cringe, as most of us don't like doing our accounts. For a creative, the word accounts can bring either fear or lack of interest. However, every business owner has to be able to understand and manage the accounts of their business to succeed and grow. Even if you have the most amazing designs in the world, you will still need to understand the money side of the business.

Raising money

It is cheap to come up with concepts and ideas to launch a fashion label, but incredibly expensive to make the dreams a reality and start producing and selling collections.

One of the first things you need to do is consider if your brand is financially viable. Your start-up label will be financially vulnerable to external forces, such as the state of the economic environment, the power of suppliers charging higher fees and any competitive brands that have more resources.

Most brands need some money to launch their businesses, but many approach the process in the wrong way. Before looking to raise money, consider whether it is the right thing to do for your business and which option would be best for you. I have had many brands that initially came to me for advice in finding investors, but after reflecting on it, decided to self-fund, raise finance through other means and grow their business in a different way. Investors aren't the only option.

Raising money can be based on equity or debt. Debt involves borrowing money that has to be repaid with interest, whilst equity involves raising money against a stake in your company. So, your first decision is do you want to pay back a loan or give an investor part of your business?

Below are various options for bringing money into your business.

Personal Savings

A lot of designers decide to 'bootstrap' their business, or fund it from their own pocket and savings. The way they do this is by working for other brands first to learn about the business side of the industry, but also save money to start on their own. Others may use an inheritance to fund their business.

Friends and Family

There are designers and entrepreneurs who launch their labels with financial support from friends and family. A lot of the brands I have worked with have been funded by what we lovingly call the 'bank of Mum and Dad'. Sometimes the support from a friend or family is gifted, other times it may be a loan. Ensure that, if it is a loan, that they understand that it may take some time before they'll get paid back.

Bank Loans

Taking out a loan, whether from a family member or a bank, means that you will have a debt that you will need to pay back with interest. Having to make regular loan repayments can be difficult for a start-up brand that doesn't have regular money coming in. Banks usually see start-up fashion brands as far too risky, so will not give loans to new labels and the only option would be for the business owner to take a personal loan secured against their homes. This is not an option for most people.

Factoring

Factoring is a method of financing that gives brands access to working capital. Factoring would help brands that have big wholesale orders, which they have to produce and ship before receiving payment from the retailer. The factoring company or factor, will consider the brands written wholesale orders, credit check the company who has ordered and if acceptable, then buy the invoices from the brand and release around 80 per cent of the order value to them. The factor will then take on the responsibility of collecting the invoice payment from the store. With so many stores getting into financial difficulty, which has meant that many retailers have not been able to pay their bills and invoices, then the factor acts as credit insurance and still has to pay the designer.

Factoring only becomes a relevant finance option for brands with big enough orders. It is not relevant for brands that have a direct-to-consumer business model.

Sideline or licensing

Many designers in the early years of their brands will have jobs or a sideline that helps them finance their labels. They will act as consultants, act as freelance designers or pattern cutters, collaborate with or work for another brand. They will do this behind the scenes, often not putting their name publicly to the other work or designs they do outside of their own label. The problem with a sideline and side jobs is that it can distract you from your own label, and limit the time you have to work on growing your brand.

The dream for many brands is get a licensing deal with another brand such as a beauty or accessories company. Licensing is a lucrative brand extension and a great way for a brand to expand and move into new product categories or markets. If a brand wants to develop licensing deals then they have to have a brand name that is recognised and already successful, so this is only an option much later on.

Crowd funding

Crowd funding is becoming a more popular method of raising finance for a start-up brand. Crowd funding is a way of raising lots of small amounts of money from a large crowd of people. For fashion brands it is a way of pre-selling your collection by offering pieces as a reward for funding. There are numerous platforms for crowding funding including Kick-starter, GoFundMe and Indegogo.

Many brands that I work with have had successful reward-based campaigns on Kick-starter. They have managed to raise money through crowd funding to produce their first collections and start selling direct to consumer.

There are also options to run an equity crowd funding campaign, allowing a large number of people to invest in your fairly small company in exchange for equity. This type of campaign can be done on platforms such as SeedInvest but this is a less popular option. It is always better to try and raise money without giving away equity if possible.

Crowd funding isn't always the easy option that people think. A campaign takes a lot of planning and work to make it successful. It doesn't work if you just put up a campaign and wait for the money to come in. You will have to work on the campaign every day, sharing updates on social media, asking people to fund you or share the campaign, and use all your networks to push the message out there.

Government Grants and Loans

In some countries there are loans and grants from the government to support start-up businesses, export or business growth. In the UK we have Start-Up Loans and access to funding for overseas trade fairs through UKFT (see the links and resources section for details of these organisations). Brands from international countries are sometimes also able to access showcasing funds to take part in trade shows in key markets. Most of the government initiatives are loan based, which means you will have to pay it back, but some offer grants meaning there is no repayment required.

Competitions

There are a number of competitions aimed at fashion businesses that offer cash prizes, such as the CFDA/*Vogue* Fashion Fund and the LVMH Prize. There are also many competitions such as incubator programmes or the British Fashion Councils NEWGEN initiative, where you win support, mentoring and business advice in the aim of putting you on the right path to attract investors. All these competitions can be intense and very time-consuming. They usually need detailed business plans and sales projections and many small brands don't have the capacity or skills to write a successful application.

Sponsorship

Sponsorships are a great way to raise money for specific projects that can increase your access to new markets, attract press coverage and increase social media reach. Sponsorship is about creating projects that have mutual benefits for all involved. Sponsorship can be secured for events, fashion shows, fashion films and installations. It is possible to raise sponsorship from several companies towards one project. For example, for a fashion event you could get sponsorship from a venue and brands for the goody bags, but also cash sponsorship from a corporate partner in return for tickets to the event. In order to attract sponsors, you will need to learn how to develop inspirational marketing decks or proposal documents, as these are often key in opening the initial conversation. The sponsorship deck should outline the opportunity, include lots of inspirational images and detail all of the benefits that the sponsor will receive in return for their financial support.

Business Angels and Investors

Investors can come in the form of Business Angels, wealthy private individuals, or for larger investments through Venture Capital firms. Both types of investor take equity, a percentage of the business, in return for their investment. They are both likely to provide business expertise and management in addition to the cash, to ensure that their investment is wisely spent and that the business grows.

Investors are looking for a business that they believe has long-term growth potential. They are looking to get into the business in the early stages, when they can take a higher percentage of equity in return for their investment and then push the business for rapid growth. They can seek a high percentage of equity, as the business is worth very little in the early stages, so the label has to give a much higher percentage of the brand for the money.

Investors often seek a fast payback on their investment. Many look to invest in a company, see it build rapid growth and then get out with a good profit. Unfortunately for fashion businesses it can take much longer than other industries to provide the growth level an investor wants. The fashion industry standard is that it takes 8 seasons or four years to break even, never mind make a profit. Fashion therefore, needs much longer investment to get the business to the profit stage. It is advisable to find investors who understand the fashion industry or there could be problems further down the road.

Another issue can be that the investor is focussing on the financial bottom line, looking for good margins and volume of sales, so they may not understand a designer seeking to create slow fashion, luxury or sustainable collections which take longer to make a return on investment. Bringing investors into the business can also change the dynamic of the company, as the business owner can no longer make decisions alone and will need to be accountable for every decision they make. Business Angels may be a more suitable option in the beginning, as they are often prepared to support the business over a longer period and not be looking to make a hasty exit.

To find venture capital investors there are numerous online platforms, as well as pitching events run by financial organisations or business centres. You can also apply to business accelerator programmes, use LinkedIn or ask your financial advisors about contacts or networks. The best way to find Business Angels is through word of mouth and asking for advice and recommendations through friends, family and business colleagues.

Preparing for investment

Before you start to seek out investors, you need to prepare your business and write your business plans. You will need to develop numerous elements in order to prepare your pitch including:

- A compelling brand story.

- Identified your aims, objectives and key milestones.

- Determined your resource requirements including staff and suppliers.

- Clearly defined your USP or point of difference in the market.

- Documents that show your financial accounts are up-to-date including statutory accounts.

- Information on your employees and mentors to show the knowledge base of the company.

Your business has to look like a good investment and show that it has great potential, or already holds a position of strength in the market.

As the business owner, you are a crucial part of the process, as people invest in people! You need to be able to present your pitch succinctly, professionally and with passion in order to attract investment. If you have ever watched Dragons Den or Shark Tank on TV, then you will know how prepared you need to be to articulate your brand, have knowledge of the market and also be able to talk through the numbers.

As well as a dynamic leader, investors will look for companies that have a strong management team who have all the knowledge and skills needed to drive the business growth. If you don't have a team yet, you should identify the key positions you need to recruit to strengthen the team.

Make sure you are asking for the correct amount of investment. You need to ensure that you are asking for enough money to deliver the growth and success you have stated. There is only one chance to get the money, you can't go back and ask for a bit more money later because you didn't get it right first time.

The final part of the preparation will be to have an official, independent valuation of your business. This will determine how much equity in the business you will give up in return for the money you are looking to raise. This will just be a benchmark or the starting point of the negotiation with the investor, who is likely to demand more equity in return for their investment.

Your pitch documents, including financial documents and business plan, need to be well presented and clear so that they present a credible and reliable business to the investors.

Pitching for finance

There are lots of places and networks these days where you can learn how to pitch for finance from investors. Pitching for finance is a skill that needs learning and practising, as you only get one opportunity to impress and win over the investor. Pitching for finance isn't something that you can amble into and just think you can charm the investors. You will need to back up everything you say and show detailed business plans and financial projections.

Here are some basic tips to help you pitch, but I recommend also getting one-to-one training to hone your skills.

- Create a pitch deck that tells your story simply. Don't exaggerate or over inflate your plans and results. The deck should cover the background to the label, about the founders, the vision, the opportunity and some key financial information.

- Keep your pitch short and concise. Don't waffle! Make sure you get to the key points quickly.

- Protect your intellectual property by asking for a non-disclosure agreement to be signed prior to the pitch.

- Make your pitch visual, showing your product and concepts. You are a creative business so show off your creative skills in creating a stunning, inspirational deck.

- Show your passion and commitment for your brand, explain what you have already done and what you will do to drive your business to success.

- Tell the investors what they will get in return for their investment and clearly detail the benefits they will receive.

- Own the process. You will need to be calm, confident and show that you are a credible person to invest in. You don't want to come over as desperate for the money, so be assertive in your presentation.

- Practice your pitch over and over again until you are totally confident in it. Do practice pitches with friends and family not just in front of the mirror.

- Don't give up. Your first pitch may not be successful, but keep going.

Allocating the money

If you have been successful in attracting finance, then you need to manage the process carefully and not start adding in additional costs just because you have the money. I have seen many brands be successful in raising money, but then blow it all quickly on other things rather than the areas they said they would on the financial pitch. I recommend that you are very careful in spending your investment:

- Carefully manage your product development costs and don't start increasing the size of your collection too rapidly or start creating more complicated designs with higher production costs.

- It is not a good use of the money to start advertising to raise your profile, as advertising is a cash sink and brings little return on investment.

- You should focus the investment money on growing sales not on just raising your profile. Look for return on investment on every expense.

- Budget carefully and make the money last as long as possible, because there may not be any more coming in for a long time.

Product costing

To manage your finances and grow your business, you will need to control your costs. For a fashion label this includes managing your product costs but more importantly your margins too. In the start-up stages, fashion brands always struggle with costing and pricing their product.

Determining the price of your product can be overwhelming for start-up brands and many businesses make assumptions on their pricing. This can lead to big problems later on. You can only price your product correctly if you have worked out your product costs. On a daily basis I see and hear designers who have made errors in their pricing, these include:

- Talking about wanting to sell their products at a certain price, picking a number out of thin air rather than basing it on their costs. Later, once they have worked out their costs, they are shocked that they are selling at a loss and the true price of their product should be 3 x times more expensive.

- Missing out a key element in their costing such as trims or a labour cost.

- Selling direct to their consumers at wholesale price not retail price.

- Not able to attract a wholesale account because they have not worked out their pricing correctly and they are now unable to offer the store chance to make any profit.

Cost of Goods

The easiest and best way to work out your cost of goods is to create a cost sheet template that you fill in for each item you produce. This is a good way to check that you have covered all the items and services you use to produce the piece and then work out the wholesale and retail cost.

The kinds of things to include in your cost sheet are:

- Fabric, including dying and printing and lining fabric if appropriate.

- Trims such as buttons, zips etc.

- Extra elements such as embroidery or embellishments.

- Labels for the piece including both brand and care labels.

- Factory or labour costs to make the piece.

- Packaging for the piece including bags, tissue paper and hangers.

- Your design time.

- Shipping of supplies of fabrics, trims, the samples and production from the factory.

Here is an example of a Product Cost sheet. There is a downloadable version on my website www.startyourownfashionlabel.com

PRODUCT COST SHEET			
DATE/SEASON		STYLE NUMBER/NAME	
PRODUCT DESCRIPTION			
COSTING:			
MATERIAL COSTS			
FABRIC	**AMOUNT NEEDED**	**COST PER METRE**	**TOTAL**
		TOTAL MATERIAL	
TRIM COSTS			
TRIM	**AMOUNT NEEDED**	**COST PER ITEM**	**TOTAL**
		TOTAL TRIM	

LABOUR COSTS		
ACTION	**DESCRIPTION**	**COST**
CUT		
SEW		
DYE		
PRINT		
EMBROIDERY		
MARKING/GRADING		
	TOTAL LABOUR	

SUNDRY COSTS		
		COST
LABELS		
PACKAGING		
	TOTAL SUNDRY	
	TOTAL OF MATERIAL, TRIM, LABOUR, SUNDRY	
	WHOLESALE PRICE	
	RETAIL MARK-UP	
	RRP	
	DIRECT TO CONSUMER PRICE	

When completing the product cost sheet, there are some points to consider to ensure you make your information accurate, as well as identify where you can cut costs:

Material Costs

- What are the minimum order quantities? You need to ensure you make the most of each fabric for both cost saving and cohesiveness in the collection.

- Are there additional insurance, shipping, tax or import duty costs?

- Have you considered elements such as lining and interfacing?

Trim Costs

- What are the minimum order quantities? You need to ensure you are being cost effective to meet a minimum order, which could include using the same trim across several pieces in the collection.
- Are there additional insurance, shipping, tax, import duty costs?

Labour Costs

- Have you negotiated the best deal you can get from the factory?
- What are the minimum order quantities?
- Have you given the factory a good lay plan or cutting ticket to ensure there is minimum waste, if not zero waste?
- Have you given the factory accurate patterns and specification sheets to minimise wasted production time?
- If your production costs are high, can you simplify patterns to reduce costs such as reducing frills and trims or removing pockets?

Sundry costs

- Consider how you can package your product in a way that looks luxury without the price tag? Packaging is really important for online sales as it adds to the experience of buying the product. Don't skimp on the packaging if you have a more luxurious or high price product, the packaging must reflect the same quality.

Once the costs are worked out for each piece, then you are in a position to price your collection, and ready to sell.

Product Pricing

As stated in the section above it is necessary to work out your costs in order to create pricing. If you get your pricing wrong and sell at a loss or don't make profit, then you can damage the long-term success and sustainability of your business. Incorrect pricing will also limit the option in the future of setting up a wholesale channel. If your initial prices are too low, then there will be no profit margin for the retailer.

For a fashion brand, there are different prices based on whether you are selling wholesale to a store or direct to a consumer. There is a recognised industry format for pricing fashion collections as detailed below. This is often referred to as the Keystone mark- up method, which means you multiply a price in order to get to the next level:

Wholesale pricing

If your brand is selling wholesale to a store, then the diagrams below show how the pricing is worked out.

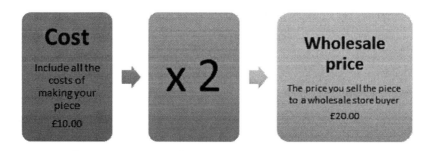

The diagram above shows that if your costs of making a shirt, including material, trims and manufacturing, is £10, you will then multiply this by 2 to get to the wholesale price. So, you will sell the shirt to the store for £20.00.

The store will then take the wholesale price of £20 and multiply it by at least 2.7 – 3 and add tax and that gets them to the recommended retail price or RRP. In this example, if the store multiplies by 3 and then adds 20% VAT, they will sell the shirt in their store for £72.00. It does not matter how much the store sells your product for because you will still only ever get £20.00.

Direct to consumer pricing

Many brands that decide to start selling directly to the customer get confused and will often sell at the wholesale price. This a dangerous precedent that can damage your business in the future and prevent you from ever having the option of selling wholesale to stores. If you sell at wholesale price you will also miss out on making more profit, as you have only a small margin at wholesale price.

My recommendation to all start-up brands is work out your pricing based on the wholesale model to reach the Recommended Retail Price. This ensures you are priced relative to the market so you can compare your pricing, but also enables you in the future to wholesale and offer a store a decent margin.

If you publicly sell your product, or list it on your own e-commerce shop, at a price less than RRP, then you risk store buyers showing no interest in your brand. Your brand can never be seen to sell a product at less than a wholesale store, so you need to be very careful in your pricing strategy.

There is however, a discreet way of selling your product at a more favourable rate without the wholesaler seeing it. You list your product at the recommended retail price on your website or at events, but you can then discreetly offer a 'friends and family' or 'VIP' discount code. You can choose to offer the code to people who register for your newsletter or attend a trunk show, but this must be done privately through conversation or email, so that it is not public knowledge. The code can offer anything between 5 – 40%, which can be used at the check-out, and this can incentivise the customer to purchase straight away. The customer will also feel that they have a great offer and feel valued, but publicly no one will ever know that you offer discounts.

Here is an example to show you the benefit of this strategy using the shirt example.

- The shirt costs £10 and to wholesale you would receive £20.00.

- Using the direct to consumer strategy you have listed your shirt at the retail price of £72.00 (if you are VAT registered and have to add 20% VAT), so a greatly increased margin.

- If you then offer your customer a VIP discount code of 40% off at check out, you would still be selling the shirt at £57.60. This is double what you would have received from a wholesale order.

Add value rather than cut prices

Although I have advised offering a discreet 'VIP' or 'friends and family' discount code, I do not recommend generally discounting or having sales. Discounting and sales de-value your brand and can make it difficult to ever sell anything at full price. The high street is full of brands struggling to survive despite their cheap product and constant discounting and sales. Fast fashion has become all about a bare knuckle, knock down discount frenzy, and that is not the battle you want to be joining.

Many designers come to me with concerns about their product being too expensive. It is always likely that a start-up brand's prices will be high, as they are buying their fabrics and manufacturing in small quantities, which increases the end price of the product. There is little you can do about this if you have done your best in keeping your costs down. It is too risky to start cutting your profit margin, or worse still selling at cost price, as this will lead to certain failure of your brand.

If brands say to me that people have said their prices are too expensive, I advise them that they haven't explained the value enough. If you have created exclusivity and scarcity through limited edition collections, explained the value of your brand and what makes your product different and unique, then the customer shouldn't query the price. Then it is the case that they can't afford it rather than the product is priced too highly. You can add value through the brand experience, the packaging, unique designs and exclusive product.

My advice therefore is to set your prices by using the industry method to get it to recommended retail price and then look at how you can add value to make the customer appreciate the value in the piece.

Projecting your financial situation

Once you have started to work out your initial investment and your product prices, you need to start developing a system to project and manage your finances.

It can be very difficult to predict your start-up costs; therefore, many designers just don't bother. Failure to understand your finances and how your cash flow works can result in disaster for your business.

When you first start predicting figures for your financial plans it can feel like you are picking figures out of thin air. With detailed research, you will be able to estimate the more realistic figures that are essential for your planning.

Cash flow is the most basic level of accounting and is a way of predicting and recording the money coming in and out of your business. It is an essential tool to help you identify shortfalls between the amounts coming in and the money you need to run your business and pay for your services.

I advise all designers to develop a cash flow forecast before they start their business, to ensure they don't fall into the trap that so many start-brands do of running out of cash before the end of their first year.

The cash flow classes I run with fashion students looking to start their own businesses is always an eye opener for them, as they are always shocked at how much money they will need to set up and run their business. The end result is often that they need 10 or 20 times more than they had assumed. They realise that their business concepts and research needs a lot more work.

To manage your finances, you should consider the initial expenses you need to set up the business and then the on-going expenses you will have running the brand. Before you start work on your cash flow forecast you would need to do the research and gather the information to complete the plan.

Here are some examples of the numbers you need to find:

Initial expenses

- Incorporating your company. You can do this yourself online or you can pay an accountant to register the business for you.
- Initial legal fees for partnership agreements or trademarks.
- Research and travel costs to find suppliers and manufacturers or visiting trade shows.

Expenditure

The one-time costs for assets, items that will retain some value over time. Capital expenditure can include:

- Furniture.
- Computers.
- Shop fittings.
- Equipment such as sewing machines, steamers.

Expenses

These are items that do not retain value but are purchased to operate the business, such as:

- Office supplies.
- Advertising.
- Rent and utilities such as heat and light.
- Insurance.
- Staff salaries.
- Taxes.
- Marketing materials.
- Look book shoot costs including photographer, model etc.

In the next section I am going to talk you through the sections of the cash flow and what to include. You need to have all the research done so that you have exact figures to include and not use guesswork. There is no point in putting in certain numbers because they look better, you will just be conning yourself and will quickly get into trouble. You need the numbers to be accurate and realistic. You shouldn't try to balance the numbers in a cash flow forecast just to achieve a more favourable account. You need to be really honest!

Completing your cash flow forecast

A cash flow forecast is a crucial business tool, as it helps you identify times when you may have a shortfall in money, such as when you produce your collection and pay for it all before you make any sales. If you are not prepared for cash flow problems, then your business is likely to simply run out of money and subsequently fail. I have seen many brands over the years go out of business purely because they didn't manage their cash flow.

I have placed an example of a cash flow forecast below and there is a downloadable version on my website www.startyourownfashionlabel. com. This is just an example and you will have your own costs and services to pay, but hopefully this example will help you start the process. The example below only shows the first 4 months, but your plan needs to have 12 months and a predication total for year two and three.

Cash Flow Forecast					
	Pre-start	Month1	Month 2	Month 3	Month 4
INCOME					
Wholesale sales					
Retail sales					
On-line sales					
Loan					
Personal					
Investor					
TOTAL					
COST of SALE					
Fabric					
Trims					
Manufacturer					
Labour / salaries					
Packaging					
Sales Agent					
TOTAL					

EXPENSES					
Rent					
Utilities					
Staff Salaries					
Insurance					
Consultants					
Travel					
Website					
Telephone					
Office supplies					
Postage					
Advertising					
Marketing materials					
Photo shoots					
Events					
Loan repayments					
Tax					
Capital Purchases					
Contingency					
TOTAL					
Cash flow surplus or deficit -/+					

Income

The biggest errors I see on cash flow forecasts are the unrealistic sales predictions that brands make. It is great that you are optimistic about the sales you will make, but for the purposes of a cash flow forecast it is necessary to consider the worst-case scenario. What if you make little or no sales?

You should predict your sales based on the different channels you are selling through:

- Wholesale. How many stores do you think you will get into that year and how many pieces each store will buy from you?

- Online. How many sales will you make through your own e-commerce, online store?

- Retail. How many sales will you make through your own direct retail opportunities such a pop-up shops, events and trunk shows?

Remember, you can't sell more than you make! What I often see on a cash flow forecast is that the brand has made a set number of pieces, but in their sales predictions, they have sold more than they made.

Also, in the income section, you would list the money you are bringing into the business from your own personal savings, from a bank loan, government grant, or money from an investor. This is usually a lump sum that is listed in the pre-start stage or listed one-off in the month the money is released to the brand.

Cost of sales / direct costs

The cost of sales can also be known as direct costs and relates to the costs that you incur in designing and manufacturing the product that is for sale. The cost of sales includes the costs of direct materials, labour or factory, packaging and shipping. It can also include the commission charged by a sales agent if you have one. The cost of sales helps you measure your ability to design, source and manufacture goods at a reasonable cost and have a healthy profit margin. The cost of sales does not include indirect expenses such as office and marketing costs,

Expenses / indirect costs

Expenses are often referred to as indirect costs or the overheads of the business. In other words, they are the expenses that can't be assigned to the production of a particular product. The expenses include your rent, advertising, office supplies, accountancy services, and utilities. The expenses can be fixed costs such as the rent, which stays the same each month or an insurance bill, which you pay by monthly instalments. Other expenses will be variable such as electricity bills, which may fluctuate monthly or quarterly. Some of the expenses will occur every month such as rent, but other expenses will only occur occasionally such as creating marketing materials or a product campaign shoot.

Tips to improve your cash flow

It is necessary to check that you are taking every action you can to improve your cash flow and this is can be reliant on you negotiating better terms with both suppliers and customers. The more correctly you classify your direct and indirect costs, the more you will be able to determine your brands profitability and efficiency as well as identify potential areas for cost improvement. Here are a few tips to help you improve your cash flow:

Suppliers and Manufacturers

- Can you negotiate better terms from your suppliers, including better prices for your fabrics, manufacturing or extending the payment terms so that you have a longer period to pay for the goods?

Wholesaling

- If you wholesale, can you improve your payment terms? Can you ask the store for a deposit, or request payment in advance? If not, can you insist on payment on delivery, in 7 days or 30 days?

- Make sure you issue invoices to wholesale accounts promptly.

- Regularly chase outstanding payments and don't let payments slide. Block time in your diary to chase payments so that you don't forget.

- Consider including in your terms that you will exercise your rights to charge late payment penalties and charge interest on late payments.

- Can you offer a discount for prompt payments?

- Before agreeing to an order, credit check the company placing a wholesale order.

- Target new customers efficiently by focusing on one area/country at a time rather than a scattergun approach of trying lots of different international markets at the same time.

Improving Quality and Service

- Avoid having to make a refund on a sale by ensuring products are good quality.

- Deliver product on time to ensure it is accepted by wholesale accounts.

- For direct customers deliver as quickly as possible to compete with other brands.

General cost savings

- Don't buy or sit on surplus fabrics and stock. Find ways of selling any surplus to raise cash.

- Constantly look at cost savings across the company from office costs, staffing and services including banking and insurance.

- Monitor all costs monthly and don't let the accounts get out of hand.

- Can you lease equipment rather than buying it? Although it can be slightly more in the long term, for a small business the benefit of spreading the cost can be a great advantage on the cash flow.

Increase your prices!

Increasing prices can be scary for many brand owners as they worry that no one will buy their pieces. On the other hand, if you don't increase your prices so that you can cover your costs and make a profit, then there is a chance that you will go out of business anyway. You sometimes have to take the risk and look at how you add the value so that the customer will pay the increase.

Resources

Don't forget that on my website www.startyourownfashionlabel.com you can download loads of great resources to help you set up your business, including a Product Cost template, Cash Flow Forecast template and a Guide to Sponsorship.

Chapter 12 – Entrepreneurial Spirit

Setting up, running and growing your fashion label will be hard work. Every day there will be challenges to overcome, hours of work to put in, money to raise and spend, and a good deal of stress. Are you ready for it?

Designers and start-up business owners often ask me "What do I need to do to succeed?" They are looking for some kind of magic formula which will guarantee their success if they follow it. There is no set answer or formula for this! My one piece of advice to all start up businesses is, above all else "BE ENTREPRENEURIAL."

Most fashion designers tend to consider themselves designers rather then entrepreneurs, focusing on the creative side, rather than the business. To create a successful brand, you need to be entrepreneurial, looking at how you can stand out in the market, as well as how you can create an efficient business model that guarantees you success.

What does being entrepreneurial mean?

Being entrepreneurial isn't just about starting your own business. Being entrepreneurial is a mind-set, a way of thinking and acting. It is the art of critical questioning, innovation, meeting consumer needs and continuous improvement. It is about being constantly moving and seeking opportunities, being agile in your approach and never being complacent. An entrepreneur will also empower and motivate others, building genuine relationships for mutual benefit.

Here are some statements that I think address what it means to be an entrepreneur or entrepreneurial:

" If you are entrepreneurial then you will know your business and your industry inside and out."

" An entrepreneur will use their industry research and knowledge to identify opportunities or threats."

" An entrepreneur will build networks and share ideas freely, constantly looking for gaps in the market and new opportunities."

" An entrepreneur is constantly learning, seeking out new ideas, looking at future developments and being visionary in the development of their businesses."

" An entrepreneur recognises they don't have to have all the skills themselves, instead recruiting mentors, advisors and staff who can cover the areas they are on weak on."

" An entrepreneur has a constant hunger to find solutions to problems."

" An entrepreneur will take action; they are ready for battle and have the courage and the perseverance to deal with the many challenges they face."

" An entrepreneur can be flexible, balancing a strong vision with a willingness to change."

Do you recognise yourself in some, or all, of these statements? There are lots of online quizzes and personality tests for you to check your suitability to be an entrepreneur. Whilst these may be slightly entertaining, I don't advise you take them too seriously. Sometimes the findings will say that you are not suited to being an entrepreneur, but don't take this as a fact.

Whenever I have tried these personality tests, many advise that I am unsuitable to be an entrepreneur! As I have successfully created, grown and sold several businesses, I think the evidence proves that I am very much an entrepreneur. The tests can be useful in identifying some of your weaknesses. These tests did pick up some of the weaknesses that I have identified, and had to deal with through running my businesses. These weaknesses are:

- I hate doing numbers! I find accounts and finance boring and will avoid doing them at all costs. However I did force myself to do an accountancy course so that I can understand the accounts, but then found great accountants and book keepers to keep everything in order, on time and advise on cost saving.

- I am a starter, not a finisher. I love coming up with new ideas, concepts and challenges, but once I have successfully brought these to market, then I become bored with the day to day mundane tasks. I resolved this by having a great team who help me follow through the ideas, recruiting the finishers my businesses needed. I have also ensured that I develop agile businesses that have longevity and vision, so that the businesses don't become stagnant. This keeps me excited by what the business can do and achieve next.

Just because you have weaknesses doesn't mean you have to give up. Instead find ways to work around these, or find great people to work with you who can do the things you can't. Identifying your personal strengths and weaknesses is a good starting point for your entrepreneurial journey.

What are the characteristics of successful entrepreneurs?

Although there isn't a magic formula for success, there are some common characteristics that successful entrepreneurs share. I have picked out a few that I believe are essential if you are going to run your own fashion label.

Passion

If you aren't passionate about starting and growing your business then you need to get out now. Passion is what drives your business. Passion makes your brand unique to you. It is the reason behind your business, the 'why' you are doing it. Passion is what will drive you through the tough times and make the long hours, the hard work and the sacrifices worth it. Your passion is what excites your customer about your brand and product, without it your brand could be seen as bland and uninspiring.

Determination

You will need to be determined to succeed, overcoming obstacles and challenges. Your brand will take time to grow and success rarely happens over night. A lot of perceived 'overnight' successful businesses have in reality been working for years towards that moment when they are discovered.

Vision

For you to develop a business that grows and succeeds, you will need to have vision. You need to be looking to the future and developing a business that will adapt to and lead any changes. Start and grow a business that will be relevant in the future not just today.

Confidence and strong communication skills

You will need to be confident in your skills and your business ideas. You need to be able to communicate your ideas clearly, with passion and confidence, so that other people believe in you and your brand.

There is a fine line between confidence and arrogance and you will need to find the balance. There is no place for ego or arrogance in a successful business. There are already too many egotistical characters in the industry and ego can get in the way of success and put people off. Nor should you hide your light under a bushel, as you will need to inspire people to support your brand, therefore will have to find the balance.

You will need to develop strong written and oral communication skills to sell your business concept, vision and your products. Everything you say and write, even the shortest note, brief conversation or quick email tells the other person about your personality. Your words define you!

Communication needs to be managed efficiently. Answer emails promptly and present information in a concise, coherent format to show you are professional in your business dealings. You need to avoid vague or passive responses, as the most effective communication style for business is one that is assertive. Assertive communication is direct and respectful, keeping to the point and putting information across in a way that builds respect from the reader.

Flexibility

Successful businesses have to be flexible to adapt to changing circumstances and take advantage of new opportunities. A successful entrepreneur will be agile, constantly learning and adjusting to new ideas and demands. Being flexible or agile is a mind-set, it means you are capable of faster innovation, adapting to changing groups or occasions, and are prepared to take calculated risks. Many business advisors and consultants will quote being agile as being prepared to fail. They mean that the entrepreneur will learn from these experiences, overcome the challenges and see a failure as a learning experience.

Network

Networking is essential for every business owner. You need to invest time into building relationships and meeting people who will support your business, be your mentor or become your customer. The phrase on every successful entrepreneur's lips is that 'your network is your net worth'. In other words you are worth, or your value is, that of the people in your network. It is essential that business owners have a large, valuable network of contacts. The more engaged you are with your contacts, the more chance you will have of success in business. An important skill for any entrepreneur is to learn how to build, maintain and nurture their contact list to gain the biggest benefits from it.

Networking also helps you gain information and knowledge in a smart way. Networking is a form of research, where you can learn about industry trends, successful traits of business owners, and identify potential partners, investors or collaborators without having to spend a fortune on your own research. On a personal level, the benefit of networking is the added bonus of meeting and sharing ideas with like-minded professionals and high achievers, creating a mutual support and friendship group.

Growing and scaling your business

Having an initial great business idea is a wonderful start, but the idea on its own is not worth anything. You need the passion to create the business and the drive to execute your plan. You have to continue to develop your label and your ideas in order to take your business from start-up to successful brand.

You want your brand to be a huge success and you may be pushing hard to grow, but managing the growth of your business takes time, skills and knowledge and should not be rushed. If your business grows too quickly, then demand may suddenly exceed capacity, and you wont be able to deliver your orders. I have seen many brands suffer from 'death by success,' including these two examples:

- A brand that finished a Paris Fashion Week trade show with a full order book but no finance in place to manufacture the product. None of the retailers would pay deposits, and he couldn't find a bank that would provide him with a loan. He went bankrupt with a full order book.

- Another brand that had grown to a significant point but the investor suddenly pulled out. The brand had no contingency plan to pay the staff wages or manufacturers fees, so overnight went into administration.

Scaling a business is a very difficult balancing act and it takes a lot of skill, luck and support to get it right. How you scale your business will also depend on how you have financed your brand. If you don't have investment, which most don't, then the healthiest way to build your business is organically. This means growing your business slowly using the resources, skills and knowledge you have, and taking careful steps to grow, ensuring you have the capacity to deliver orders and manage your business.

Organic growth involves strategies such as:

- Having very clear objectives and goals to ensure you stay in control.

- Managing product development based on sales rather than creating new collections every season, particularly if the previous season didn't sell or receive interest.

- Taking the product you have already developed into new markets.

- Carefully managing the territories and markets you sell in, focusing on a particular country at a time rather than a scattergun approach of being international from the start.

- Slowly build an amazing team who will help drive the growth, not just be task driven. A great entrepreneur knows that they can't do it all. The best scenario is to create an entrepreneurial team of powerful people who will support, advise and take action to grow the business.

- Establish an entrepreneurial company culture where everyone can share ideas and concepts to the benefit of the brand.

As your business grows you will also need to create strategies to ensure the business stays agile, and doesn't become rigid in its approach or blinkered to opportunities that arise from a changing market. An agile business is one that is innovative, flexible and ready to adapt and respond to market changes and opportunities. To be an agile business you need to continue to research and network, be customer focussed and take time out to reflect on and evaluate your business processes.

Evaluation

When you are running your fashion label, it can be a daily slog to get everything done. There is always another challenge, another fire to fight, or another deadline that needs reaching. This means that many business owners forget or don't prioritise time to review their businesses. If you don't stop and evaluate your business, then how will you know if you are being successful? It is really important to measure what is and isn't working in your business, so that you don't keep doing the same thing over and over again if it doesn't work.

You need to have a plan when it comes to measuring your business success and schedule time to do it. You can measure various elements:

1. Look at your financial statements and review how much money is going in and out of your business.

2. Checking customer satisfaction by asking your customers for feedback or for ways to improve your product or range.

3. How many new customers you have attracted and how many sales are through customers making repeat orders.

4. When you have staff, then you will need to conduct performance reviews to look for areas of improvement and staff satisfaction.

5. A market review to compare your performance against competitors.

6. Assess your own expectations. Is the business going in the direction you want it to and are you happy with your progress?

As a start-up or small business, you are on a journey, and your business will always be a work in progress with no definitive finish line. You will have successes and failures along the way, but without time and a plan to evaluate, then you will not be able to measure your achievements.

Dealing with success

I see many designers and business owners who are so busy driving their businesses forward that they forget to take time out to celebrate their successes along the way. You may be obsessing about the future, but it is important to break that end goal down into smaller steps, and then celebrate each step as you achieve it.

You need to recognise everyday accomplishments and celebrate each small win, instead of rushing off to achieve the next goal. If you don't take time out to recognise and celebrate your achievements, then you will have a high probability of burn out. Celebrating your wins not only makes you feel great, it will also increase the positive attitude you need to face new challenges.

There will hopefully come a time with your fashion label when you think, "I've done it!" The brand is starting to become well known, the orders are flooding in, you have been featured in the top print fashion magazines and you are starting to be recognised. Amazing, well done! So what next? While it is important as I said to take out time to celebrate your achievements, you cannot stop there and not keep moving forward. Success can be short lived if you don't keep ahead of the competition, stay agile and continue to develop new skills. For a successful entrepreneur there is no end game, they just keep looking for new opportunities.

A final word of caution, whilst it is important to celebrate success, a successful entrepreneur won't let it go their heads. A successful entrepreneur understands the importance of humility and knows that arrogance doesn't gain the love and respect of others.

What if things don't go to plan?

You might not want to think about it, but things will go wrong. You will make mistakes along the way, because we all make mistakes. Making mistakes is how we learn. You will have to own up to and live with your mistakes and if you can't do that, then don't start a fashion label. Not all the bad things that happen will be your fault, or due to an error that you make. Sometimes bad things just happen. You will have to learn to live with these things too.

If something goes wrong, it doesn't mean you are a failure. Failure would come from not learning from your mistakes, or not taking action to fix problems or change and adapt your business accordingly. However, there are times when your great concept, your excellent product and your hard work aren't enough and things just don't work out. Success takes a lot of hard work and a lot of luck. Sometimes that luck just runs out. There are lots of reasons why start up fashion labels fail including a lack of focus, no clear planning, poor cash flow, loss of investment, no point of difference or poor understanding of the market.

It sounds bizarre, but prepare to fail. Everyone always talks about amazing success stories but there is very little talk about failure. This is a big mistake, and every entrepreneur and business start-up needs to change their mind-set towards failure, as there is a big chance that you might not succeed. There are a lot of risks in opening your own label and if you prepare for failure, then you are more likely to prepare contingency plans. You may develop plans that take into account certain problems that you may encounter, or have built a reserve of money to get you through the lean times. You will also need to prepare yourself emotionally for things going wrong. Dealing with things as they start to go wrong is where a true entrepreneur comes into action. An entrepreneur will take positive, brave steps to turn the business, they will be agile and respond quickly to make necessary changes.

When things go wrong, I have met many designers who take it personally and I often have to remind them that it is 'just business.' For your own mental health, you have to try and separate the business from yourself, look calmly at the situation and not respond in an emotional way to the problem. After all it is only fashion, it isn't life and death!

No matter how hard you try, unfortunately there may come a point when you have to accept that it's over. Dealing with this can be extremely difficult and you need to be prepared for a lot of strong emotions. Remember that you are not the first person to close a business or go bankrupt and you won't be the last. Just because your business did not work out this time, doesn't make you a failure in life. You should actually feel very proud of yourself, because you have done something that many people will never do and that is start your own fashion label. You should take pride in the fact that you were courageous enough to take the risk, pushed your ideas and put yourself out there in the world. That is an incredibly brave thing to do. It also may not be the end of the line. Many of today's most successful fashion entrepreneurs and businesses failed, sometimes more than once, before they succeeded. Brands including Chanel, Tommy Hilfiger, Christian Dior, Gucci, Calvin Klein and Michael Kors all filed for bankruptcy protection or had to shutter part of their businesses before rising to the success they are today. If your business does fail, these three things may help:

- **Take time to grieve.**

  When you have put your life and soul into your business, it can be a big shock when it has suddenly all gone. It could be that your business has struggled for a long time, so that once it closes it is actually a relief, like a weight has been lifted. Whether it is a shock or a relief, take time to rest and grieve. Just don't wallow in self-pity for too long.

  Reflect.

  You don't really know if something will work unless you try it. You took the risk, so now learn from the experience and reflect on what you would do again and what you would do differently.

- Get back out there.

  Hold your head high, as there is no reason to feel shame in trying something that didn't work. So pull up your super hero pants and go back out there, start networking again and conquer the world.

Final tips to help you through the challenges of being a fashion entrepreneur

FEELING OVERWHELMED?

Starting your own fashion label can be very overwhelming. You will be juggling a hundred different things at once and it can sometimes be very difficult to know what to do first or what is most important. The main way of dealing with overwhelm is to plan and be organised. Here are four tips to help you manage: -

1. Start by writing a list of everything you have to do. Put it all down on paper but don't worry about prioritising it, at this point you just need to write every task down.

2. Once you have written your list, take a few deep breathes and really concentrate on your breathing, this will help you feel calmer.

3. Go for a short walk outside. A five-minute walk in fresh air can have an amazing impact on feelings of being overwhelmed.

4. Come back from your walk and pick up your to-do list, but before you dive headlong into your list, select just one thing that you can easily accomplish today. Do this one task and then tick it off your list. Each small step completed helps raise your confidence and feelings of achievement, and you will soon find yourself flying through the rest of the tasks.

CELEBRATE YOUR ACHIEVEMENTS

Take a deep breathe. You are doing so much better than you think! Sometimes taking a deep breath isn't about coping with stress, but rather an opportunity for you to breathe deeply and reflect on all you have achieved. Entrepreneurs and business owners are often so busy fighting fires, chasing the next challenge or pushing the boundaries that they forget to take time to just reflect on what they have achieved, or how far they have come. If you don't take this time to reflect, then there is a tendency to feel that you have never succeeded. Every day as a business owner you achieve multiple things, sometimes only small things, but an achievement none the less.

Self-Care

Many self help books talk about work / life balance and I hear many business owners say they don't have time to do that. Perhaps we can talk about self-care instead, which is about making sure you don't burn out. Self-care doesn't mean you have to make a major life style change. It is about taking small steps to ensure you have time to rest and recuperate. If you take a little time out, you will also find that you have time to think and process what is happening in your business.

A few steps that you can take to improve your self-care are:

- o Before your day starts, give yourself time to be creative and be inspired. This could be a walk, a work out, or a time of quiet contemplation when you can consider your day ahead and what you want to achieve. It could be time out to reflect on your progress, as well as have time to find creative inspiration.

- o Find small ways throughout your day to take a step back for a few minutes to process what is happening. Take a step away from the desk, breathe in some fresh air, have a healthy cuppa or a chat with a colleague or fellow entrepreneur.

- o Healthy food and exercise can help you be in peak condition to run your business and deal with the stress, long hours and challenges of running a business.

- o Be in the moment. That means enjoy what you are doing. Remember in running your own fashion label you are living your dream! You wanted to run your own business, do things your way and achieve your own successes. So enjoy the ride!

Take action every day

Every day take action on at least one thing that will improve or grow your business. It can be very easy to get bogged down in the boring and minute detail of running your business day to day. An entrepreneur will make sure that every day they are taking another step towards their goals and objectives. A business grows by taking lots of small steps rather than waiting to take one massive leap forward. Start to take your small steps to a more successful brand today.

Stay focussed on your customer

In the process of growing your fashion label, don't get carried away creating and doing just what you love. You have to stay customer focussed. The most successful luxury brands put their customer and their customer's experience at the heart of everything they do. This is a good model to follow.

Best use of your time

If you are going to take action and grow your business, then you need to ensure that you are using your time effectively. As a start-up business you may have had to do everything yourself at the beginning, but as you start to grow, outsource all the tasks that could be done by other people. Focus your time and energy on the things that you do best and that have the greatest impact on the business growth. If you get too involved in the day-to-day detail, then you will not have the time and the headspace to improve your business, seek new opportunities or focus on growth.

Run a lean business

Starting and growing a fashion label takes more money then anyone imagines. Most start-up labels fail due to cash flow problems. You need to manage your money and run a lean business. There can be a misconception by start-up brands that they have to show-off or evidence success by having full catwalk shows, swish parties or a paid influencer following. My advice to every brand is don't spend money unless you have to and you certainly need to make sure you don't waste it. Running a lean business simply means minimising waste, getting the best return on investment on everything you spend and creating more value for your customers with fewer resources. To run a lean business, you need to be entrepreneurial and think outside the box, rather than just throw money at everything.

Investors don't solve all the problems

For start-up labels in the fashion industry getting outside investment is the exception, not the rule. I have read hundreds of business plans over the years with brands creating great concepts that were based on outside investment. These brands never came to market. Most start-up fashion labels now need to consider building their businesses slowly and organically. This is called bootstrapping your business, where you rely on your own savings and sales revenue to grow. The other side of investment is the change in dynamics of running your business. You will now have other people to answer to and they may have a different idea for the business than you. If you seek and attract investment, then it needs to be with someone who you can work with and trust, as your future will lay in their hands.

Let me leave you with a quote by Albert Schweitzer. This is a quote that I run my business by: "Success is not the key to happiness. Happiness is the key to success. If you love what you are doing, you will be successful."

Links and Resources

In this section I have included a list of links and resources to UK and international fashion industry organisations, which will prove useful when starting your fashion journey.

On my Start Your Own Fashion Label.com website, you will find lots of the resources I have mentioned in this book. The site is full of really easy to use guides and templates. On the site you can also book a one-to-one mentoring session with me, when you will have the opportunity to discuss all the elements of creating a successful label.

So head over to the site where you can use the unique discount code #Book10 to receive 10% off all orders.

www.startyourownfashionlabel.com

Sourcing, Fabrics, Manufacturing

Alibaba www.alibaba.com

Americas Apparel Producers' Network www.aapnetwork.net

Apparel Search www.apparelsearch.com

Apparel Sourcing Show www.apparelsourcingshow.com

Association of Suppliers to the British Clothing Industry www.asbci.co.uk

Common Objective www.commonobjective.co

Fabric Link www.fabriclink.com

Fabric Stock Exchange www.fabricstockexchange.com

Fashion SVP www.fashionsvp.com

Fashiondex www.fashiondex.com

Garment Contractors Association www.garmentcontractors.org

Global Organic Textile Standard www.global-standard.org

Let's Make It Here   www.letsmakeithere.org

Made in Britain www.madeingb.org

Make It British www.makeitbritish.co.uk

Makers Row www.makersrow.com

Premiere Vision Paris www.premierevision.com

Pure London Fair www.purelondon.com

Sustainable Apparel Coalition www.apparelcoalition.org

Texfusion www.texfusion.co.uk

Textile Exchange www.textileexchange.org

Textile Forum www.textileforum.org.uk

Texworld Paris www.texworld.messefrankfurt.com

The London Textile Fair www.thelondontextilefair.co.uk

The Sustainable Angle www.thesustainableangle.org

World Fair Trade Organisation www.wfto.com

Sustainable organisations

Clean Clothes Campaign www.cleanclothes.org

Common Objective www.commonobjective.co

Ecocert www.ecocert.com

Eco Textile News www.ecotextile.com

Ethical Trading Initiative www.ethicaltrade.org

Fashion Revolution www.fashionrevolution.org

Global Organic Textile Standard www.global-standard.org

Le Souk www.lesouk.co

Organic Trade Association www.ota.com

Sustainable Apparel Coalition www.apparelcoalition.org

Sustainable Fashion Alliance www.sustainablefashionalliance.com

Textile Exchange www.textileexchange.org

The Sustainable Angle www.thesustainableangle.org

World Fair Trade Organisation www.wfto.com

Fashion Week organisers, Trade Shows and Exhibitions

Berlin Fashion Week www.fashion-week-berlin.com

Capsule and Cabana https://cabanashow.com

CIFF, Copenhagen www.ciff.dk

Fashion East www.fashioneast.co.uk

Fashion Scout www.fashionscout.co.uk

Hong Kong Fashion Week www.hktdc.com

London Fashion Week www.londonfashionweek.co.uk

Make it British www.makeitbritish.co.uk

Micam, Milan shoes and accessories www.themicam.com

Moda UK www.moda-uk.co.uk

Modem on Line www.modemonline.com

Pitti Uomo www.pittimmagine.com

Pure www.purelondon.com

Scoop www.scoop-international.com

Sourcing at Magic www.ubmfashion.com

toFairs www.tofairs.com

Tranoi International www.tranoi.com

White Show Milan www.whiteshow.com

Who's Next www.whosnext-tradeshow.com

Pop-up shop organisers and platforms

Appear Here www.appearhere.co.uk

Lone Design Club www.lonedesignclub.com

Storefront www.thestorefront.com

We Are Pop Up www.wearepopup.com

Industry organisations and business support

British Fashion Council www.britishfashioncouncil.com

British Footwear Association www.britishfootwearassociation.co.uk

Camera National della Moda Italiana www.cameramoda.it

Centre for Fashion Enterprise www.fashion-enterprise.com

Centre for Sustainable Fashion www.sustainable-fashion.com

Common Objective www.commonobjective.co

Crafts Council, www.craftscouncil.org.uk

Department for International Trade www.great.gov.uk

Entrepreneurial Spark www.entrepreneurial-spark.com

Fairtrade Foundation www.fairtrade.org.uk

Fashion Group International www.fgi.org

Fashion Innovation Agency www.fialondon.com

Fashion Institute of Technology www.fitnyc.edu

Federation de la Haute Couture et de la Mode www.fhcm.paris

Great Business, UK www.greatbusiness.gov.uk/start/

Intellectual Property Office www.ipo.gov.uk

International Apparel Federation www.iafnet.com

London Fashion Week www.londonfashionweek.co.uk

New York Business Development Corporation www.nybdc.com

Paris Fashion Institute www.parisfashion.org

Small Business Administration www.sba.gov

Start Up Britain www.startupbritain.org

StartUps www.startups.co.uk

The Council of Fashion Designers Of America www.cfda.com

Trade tariff rates www.gov.uk/trade-tariff

UKFT the UK Fashion and Textile Association www.ukft.org

United States Fashion Industry Association www.usfashionindustry.com

United States Patent & Trademark Office www.uspto.gov

Finance and Crowd Funding

Crowd Funding

Crowd Cube www.crowdcube.com

Indiegogo www.indiegogo.com

Kickstarter www.kickstarter.com

Fund Raising

Angel List www.angel.co

Funding Circle www.fundingcircle.com

Seedrs www.seedrs.com

Start Up Loans www.startuploans.co.uk

Virgin Start Up Loans www.virginstartup.org

Accountancy systems and apps

Apptivo www.apptivo.com

Due www.due.com

Freshbooks www.freshbooks.com

Quickbooks www.quickbooks.com

Wave www.waveapps.com

Xero www.xero.com

Industry News Platforms

Business of Fashion www.businessoffashion.com

Diary Directory www.diarydirectory.com

Drapers www.drapersonline.com

Fashion Insight www.fashioninsight.co.uk

Fashion Monitor www.fashionmonitor.com

Fashion United www.fashionunited.uk

Fashionista www.fashionista.com

Positive Luxury www.positiveluxury.com

The Industry www.theindustry.fashion

Women's Wear Daily www.wwd.com

General professional services

Domain name, Website and E-commerce

123 reg www.123-reg.co.uk

Shopify e-commerce platform www.shopify.co.uk

Square Space www.squarespace.com

Whois www.whois.net

Wordpress www.wordpress.com

Photography and Models

I Heart Studios www.iheartstudios.com

Model Mayhem www.modelmayhem.com

Models.com www.models.com

Shutterstock www.shutterstock.com

U Shoot Studios www.ushootstudios.co.uk

Wolf & Badger Studios www.wolfandbadger.com/studios

Taking Payments

iZettel www.izettle.com

Paypal www.paypal.com

Stripe www.stripe.com

World Pay www.worldpay.com

Shared office and workspaces

Regus www.regus.co.uk

WeWork global offices www.wework.com

Flexi Offices www.flexioffices.co.uk

Workspace www.workspace.co.uk

Printed in Poland
by Amazon Fulfillment
Poland Sp. z o.o., Wrocław

49048714R00186